# GAYLENE'S TAKE

# GAYLENE'S TAKE

## Her Life in
## New Zealand
## Film

*Gaylene Preston*

TE HERENGA WAKA
UNIVERSITY PRESS

Te Herenga Waka University Press
Victoria University of Wellington
PO Box 600 Wellington
teherengawakapress.co.nz

A catalogue record is available from the
National Library of New Zealand.

ISBN 9781776920143

All photographs and illustrations are from the author's
personal collection unless otherwise indicated.

The photograph 'Napier Quake. Fire starts in Hastings St' by A.B. Hurst (1931)
is reproduced by kind permission of the Knowledge Bank, Hawke's Bay Digital
Archive Trust: knowledgebank.org.nz/still_image/hastings-street-napier-5/

Page 147: *The Politics of Housework* by Pat Mainardi was originally published
in 1969 by the Redstockings. Grateful thanks to Pat Mainardi and the New
England Free Press for granting permission to quote this excerpt.
The full text is available at: nefp.online/womens-liberation

An oral history and all of Gaylene Preston's films can be found at
the Dame Gaylene Preston Legacy Project, hosted by Ngā Taonga
Sound & Vision. www.ngataonga.org.nz

Printed in Singapore by Markono Print Media Pte Ltd

For Chelsie and Olive,
before I forget it all.

# Contents

## Part III

# *In Memoriam*

My mother has turned into a bird. She has nested in an airless room at the Rita Angus Retirement Village for weeks.

Her eyes light up when she sees me these days. Yesterday when I came, she was sitting with the others, looking under her cushion. 'There you are,' she said, beaming. 'I've been looking for you for ages.' She probably had. 'Did they let you come to this school after all, Gay?'

Today I make a cup of tea and we have something that vaguely resembles a conversation.

'How's tricks, old bean?'

'You have to talk to them, Gay. I think they're trying to kick me out.'

'No, Tui. You're allowed here. You're all paid up.'

'A whole new lot have arrived and I think that one over there is George.'

'Which George?'

Our family is full of Georges. There's Tui's father, George Macdonald, her father-in-law, George Preston, and she's always called my brother George, though his name is Edward.

'He hasn't seen me yet,' she says. 'Where's my money, Gay?' she whispers, and cries.

It's like her hard drive has fragmented. I suppose it has.

'What do you want for your birthday, Tui?'

'My funeral,' she replies firmly, in a rare flash of clarity.

Sometimes we watch the telly in her room with the en suite and the windows that look out onto a glassed-over atrium. It is never raining here. Always warm. The same every day.

She leans forward conspiratorially. 'How do they do it, Gay?'

'What?'

'Change my room every night. I go to sleep in one room and I wake up in another. They're cunning.'

Sometimes she is all laughs, happy to sing songs with me. 'Forever and ever, my heart will be true.'

Her essential steely backbone is now purely a personality imprint. Her back is crippled and bent into an appalling osteoporosis. Rusty bones, rusty brain. My mother.

Strangely, I quite like going to see her. She doesn't resist my embrace, and her sharp, judgemental crankiness has lost its bite. I hadn't realised just how much havoc senile dementia could wreak on a person. Before Tui became forgetful, she became incredibly emotionally erratic. She would suddenly fix me with a cold eye and say something nasty.

'Your father never loved you, you know. You were the one he didn't like.'

Out of nowhere, on a fine day, aimed to puncture the heart. If I get upset at these outbursts, she just tells me I have no sense of humour.

I have to admit I was a bit stretched in the humour department. I was living with you, my darling daughter, and I was trying to make my biggest and best film so far: *Perfect Strangers*. It was the first time I'd come up with a completely original work, a film out of my own head. Twisted, genre-bent – an expression of the psychology of the household, I suppose. At a time when Tui was sliding very, very slowly into a kind of twilight, I had a full bag of the thousands of details a feature film demands.

And you were fully wonderful, Chels. You battened down the

hatches and did your best not to cause extra strife, in that terribly intense fifteen-year-old way you had then. You were fiercely protective and came to all the premieres looking beautiful. My best ambassador.

Anyway, this book – if it becomes a book – is for you. I feel compelled to write it so that you can have an honest version straight from the armpit.

In 1916, when Tui was born, Europe was at war: 'the War to End All Wars'. She remembers when she saw her first car, first plane; when she heard her first radio broadcast. I remember the first man on the moon. Now we are going to Mars.

You were born into a global village. A place where tens of thousands of people die daily in poverty and illness yet are largely ignored by a media that prefers to report vacuous gossip. I don't really line myself up as part of that, but I am a part of this big human family currently overrunning this planet.

I fear, my darling, that my generation, born into this startling, mystical place of Aotearoa, has followed a short-sighted path. Your lot might be inclined to look back and wonder at how greedy and wasteful we were. To wonder why, in a country of only a few million people, we have any poverty at all. To consider why we didn't keep New Zealand GE-free, why we gave away our state-owned assets – and watched as those assets were stripped in the name of efficiency, forcing us to buy them back at a premium – and why we continue to marginalise those indigenous to this country who fill our jails and die too young.

Just know that these are questions we ask ourselves too – well, some of us, anyway.

The mind is strong but the flesh is weak, pitifully weak. It's in the Bible somewhere.

So here is a footprint that for a moment is firm in the sand. As I write, I think of the footprints on either side, and behind and ahead – less clear, fading. I think of Tui making her last stand against oblivion.

Kia kaha, Chelsie. Kia māia, kia manawanui.

# Part I

# 1

# Breath

Life is lived in moments. It's moments we remember. Like beads on a bracelet.

The moment you look into your newborn's eyes. 'Ah – of course. There you are.' Breath.

That moment I held my mother's hand as she lay dying, her bones were growing through her skin. Her closed eyes had retreated into their sockets. Her skull was emerging through her permed white hair. Her bird body made hardly any impression on the Ming-blue mohair rug, but she held my hand with a grip of iron. Her eyes were shut, her breaths shallow, hardly there. She had been like that for days. It was as though she was flitting along a fence line, looking for a hole to fly through, but then she would pull back and hold on even tighter.

Nothing moved. She breathed. I breathed.

I could hear distant clattering crockery down the corridor of Rita Angus Retirement Village where she lay. Staff laying tables for lunch. The air was oppressively still in this cubicle, with its window that looked out onto other windows exactly the same.

I believe that hearing is the last sense to leave us. I leaned down and smoothed Tui's baby-white hair from the pillow and whispered into her ear.

'Tui, you'll be able to dance again.'

Her eyelids flickered, she breathed faster, her grasp relaxed.

Twenty minutes later, she left us.

Weeks later, in a vision, I saw her clearly. A skinny girl silhouetted in bright light, her straight bobbed hair flying across her face, her bony arms thrown wide in abandoned joy. Dancing.

The herstory flows down through the mother. So I must begin with mine. She is very strong in me. I have to fight her off constantly, but she travels with me always. I am resisting writing this, because I have resisted her ever since I can remember. I have made films about her and featuring her. She is the strong character who shapes my opposition.

Tui was named after that dark metallic rainbow bird that swaggers and coughs through the New Zealand bush. But Tui didn't swagger and launch herself aggressively into the future like her namesake does. She was born to glide, to hold her family close, guarding against the violence that could erupt from nowhere. She grew up in two Depressions, her wings clipped. Her father was an alcoholic. She was full of secrets. Tui was the puzzle I was born to solve.

But I can't talk about Tui without beginning with her mother, Elsie, and a story she often told.

Elsie Patricia Janet Macdonald, née Cressey. They said the Cresseys grew like blackberries in Ahaura – the windswept little town near the faultline on the West Coast side of the Southern Alps, sheltering under the black mountains where Elsie's father grew up. Elsie's father was Edward, son of the Ahaura butcher Thomas Bennett Cressey, who seems to have sprung from nowhere. Some people in the family believe that Thomas arrived on a ship sailing in from England and changed his surname to that of the ship as he walked off the Lyttelton docks. In photographs, he is a little man wearing sharp knives. According to his children he had a sharp temper to match.

But, for the moment, we have my nan Elsie and her story.

Elsie told the story mainly when she was with her brother Ted. It was all about an incident down in the Ahaura graveyard, in the middle of the night, when she was seven and Ted was eight. According to Elsie, who always got a certain look in her eye when she told this story, she and Ted 'held the lights' while their father chiselled a biblical text off a gravestone that said *Children must obey their parents*. That's all Elsie would say.

'We held the lights while Dad chiselled the words off a grave, didn't we, Ted.'

He would nod, they'd both look into space for a moment with little satisfied smiles on their faces, then the conversation would move on. Sworn to secrecy, even after all those years.

It must have been as cold as charity down there in that cemetery with the concrete angels staring. A father, with his two little children, defacing a gravestone as the wet wind blew the clouds across the moon. I always imagined my great-grandfather, Edward, the man with the kind eyes in a tinted photograph in Nan's room, holding a mallet in his hand. He'd built the railways, so I was told. I had no trouble imagining him chiselling stone, but eradicating the text *Children must obey their parents*?

Years later, my aunty Irene – an impeccable family chronicler – told me she had found that gravestone right at the back of Ahaura Cemetery. The chisel marks were clearly evident. The gravestone was for one John Cressey. Irene found out that John had run away from home to be the butcher's boy at Black's Point, a few miles away. He had forsaken his father, but not his father's profession.

Later still, Helen Bollinger, an avid historian, was rummaging in the Black's Point Museum and found a pertinent document. There, among the yellowing news reports from gold mining days, was a coroner's report. It told of the lad who, carrying meat to the Globe Progress Mine at Reefton without a pack horse, was caught in a flash flood. His horse survived, but he was washed away. The drowning of John Cressey, butcher's boy at Black's Point, had led to a law change: it was now necessary for riders to have another horse to carry their load.

I imagine the day when his headstone was raised. Eight children lined up from youngest to eldest, with a cold wind blowing, all made to look at that warning carved into the unforgiving stone. This was

God's punishment. Paternal fear forged to live forever as a lesson to the others: 'Children, obey your parents in the Lord, for this is right.' Ephesians 6.1.

I imagine ten-year-old Edward, in 1885, making a silent vow to his dear older brother. He would wait until his father could no longer push him around, then he would come back.

'And so it came to pass,' as the Bible says. My great-grandfather Edward, with his two little children lighting his way, returned on a dark, dark night, and in the dark, dark cemetery, by the dark, dark angels, making sparks rise from his sharp chisel, he dug that terrible curse off and in the process freed the path for his own little ones, and whoever came to follow. He gave our Pākehā family a place to stand, a tūrangawaewae and a kaupapa. Permission to be disobedient and brave.

From that hastily chiselled groove do I spring. You need both of those things to make a film: disobedience and bravery, and a bit more. I am one of the lucky children, born much later, that Edward freed – officially.

Once, on my way to a film shoot with Alun Bollinger, we stopped at Ahaura Cemetery. We had gone tooling off from Black's Point in one of Alun's roaring Holdens, heading for Blackball to make a music video for a band I loved – Rick Bryant and the Neighbours. After the growling engine was turned off, and suffering from the inevitable petrol fumes that accompany a ride in a Bollinger car, we got out.

I am a bit spaced out. I can hear the damp. Everything drips. Cows appear and disappear through the low mist, lazily chewing their cud, watching us with preoccupied stares. We crash through thick blackberries, watched by green and black lichen-freckled angels, their limp hands lifted, imploring the world to do better.

There it is, right at the back, standing tall. A large concrete headstone, rounded at the top, with a border etched into the stone and two unmistakable hastily chiselled furrows at the base.

*Sacred to the memory of JOHN, the dearly beloved son of Thomas & Sarah Cressey who was drowned in the Inangahua River Reefton on Febr. 3rd 1885, aged 14 years*

I trace the chisel marks. This is a job done in a hurry, but after much thought. Two deep, uneven lines join up with the stonemason's official groove bordering the stone. This is no defacement. Aesthetics have been considered. A purposeful act. Of what? Anger? Love? Both?

Al and I pass a joint between us, pausing in this resting place of old Ahaura, among the gravestones animated by the mist and the unheavenly chorus of those gently farting cows. We take a few snaps and finally speed on to a riotous shoot at the Blackball Hilton, leaving the grave behind in the gloom.

# 2

# My First Film

Shaking with fear, as if he is looking down from an ice wall on Everest, Mr Thompson is stuck to the spot. The sheet he is wearing flaps in the wind, and his tiger mask hangs around his neck. There's a patch of wildflowers growing in the long grass just outside the walls of Fulbourn Psychiatric Hospital, and in the balmy Cambridge summer of 1972 I've taken a group of about fifteen long-stay institutionalised patients away from the clipped grounds inside the seven-hundred-bed county asylum to make our film *The Animals and The Lawnmower*.

It's not going as planned.

This is the Fulbourn Hospital Drama Group, and I am the arty, chirpy Kiwi who has turned up in their midst. It's all my idea. I have talked every single one of them into being here. They are wearing their 'costumes' and they carry the masks they have made in the art therapy room. A couple have enthusiastically put theirs on and now can't see properly. They stagger about, arms raised, as they hurtle headlong towards the railway line. The railway line I hadn't noticed when I'd decided that this field would be a great location to shoot a crucial part in our story. We only need one shot, but it has to be in long grass. At this moment, I have no idea whether there is a train due and when that might be, or even whether the line is in use at all. This railway line seems to be attracting them like a magnet. Olive, a rangy woman who has chosen to be a snake, with her papier-mâché snake's head perched on the top of her own, is energetically pursuing the chaplain, Bill, who has chosen to be a frog. Olive fancies him enormously.

'I sliiide along as long as I am . . . I sliiide along as long as I am . . .' she repeats in her smoker's voice, grinning widely, more and more energised as Bill hops away.

But snakes are faster than frogs, and she slithers quickly enough to catch him. He looks around for help. It's not going to come from me. I am trying to calm down Mr Thompson, who is gulping for air, shaking all over and clutching me for dear life. We are on the Hillary Step as far as he is concerned. His knees shake uncontrollably and he's in a cold sweat, hyperventilating. I try to steady his wobble and make eye contact. He's a big man. Once he is down, we will not get him up again.

'Breathe, Mr Thompson,' I say as calmly as I can. 'Breathe . . .'

As I look into his desperate eyes, I realise that our lives could not be more different, and that I have a bad habit of believing that everyone is the same. Mr Thompson has spent at least the last thirty years living in the same ward, every day a repetition of the last. And I have coerced him into leaving the hospital and coming out into a field where the ground is uneven, where the wildflowers moving in the wind have frightened him.

How could I have been so stupid? As the entire troupe head for various horizons, I realise that there aren't enough nursing staff with us. There's Suzanne – my friend from our Whole Earth Drama Group – who owns the 8mm camera we are using. She is a Cambridge Redstocking, part of our women's liberation group. An English aristocrat, she has led a sheltered life. She knows nothing of institutionalised patients and their fears. She is setting up the shot. Apart from Bill, the chaplain dressed as a frog, there is Felicity, the art therapist (I want her job), and a couple of Cambridge undergraduate friends from our drama group who have no experience of panic attacks but plenty of mind-altering drugs. That's got to come in handy in this situation, I think to myself as I hand Mr Thompson over to one of them.

What happens if a train comes through?

Felicity has had the same thought, and together we corral the little band into a safer spot, with Suzanne yelling instructions from behind the camera. Every time I run out of the shot so she can film them, someone follows me. Eventually, we abandon the whole enterprise.

'There will be something there,' Suzanne tells me as she packs up. 'But it won't be very good.'

The trip home takes even longer than it did to walk out the gates. Getting a few yards down the road feels like a marathon. We are nowhere near the stadium.

As we hold hands and shuffle our way back to the clipped lawns of the known world, we are late for tea. More anxiety. We speed up as the winsome toot of a train pierces the evening air. The what-ifs flood in, and I'm having a delayed panic attack of my own. I know who the lunatic is in this asylum.

Finally, we are safely on the concrete paths surrounded by familiar grey walls. Felicity, Bill and I retire to the back of the library, break into the librarian's filing cabinet and steal her sherry. Down the hatch.

I was twenty-three years old and without any paper qualifications, unlike my husband who had double degrees in law and literature. Now, he was doing a PhD at Gonville and Caius College. We were both fish out of water, and due to a banking error upon our arrival, our money had disappeared on a wire between the BNZ in New Zealand and Barclays in the UK. I got a waitressing job in a greasy spoon, where a big hairy chef wanted to kiss me all the time. I would wave my wedding ring at him, to no avail. I didn't have any friends to have a laugh with. I was miserable. One attempt to join a club – the Graduate Wives' Club – was a disaster. Everyone sat around sipping pink gins and listening to a slurring elderly luvvie talking about his glorious life in the West End. Not my bag, man.

But then I heard there were open auditions at the Cambridge University Amateur Dramatic Club. I knew that the ADC was famous – everything was famous in Cambridge. Go into any pub, and it's famous because some rumpty old writer threw up on the bar one night in 1910 then staggered off and wrote something brilliant. The ADC theatre had been the stomping ground of kazillions of well-known actors. Now that sounds more promising, I thought. There's a real community to be found when putting on a play. That's me. So I turn up one grey Saturday and join the line of hopefuls.

The auditorium is dark as a bored voice calls out from the void, 'Next . . .'

As I walk onto the stage I see a velvet-clad figure down there in the gloom, slumped in his seat, surrounded by a cluster of long-haired, similarly attired young men.

I arrive in the spotlight and realise that if I am to succeed I will have to put on my best English accent.

'Name.'

'Geelein Pruston.'

'Oh . . . you're an Australian.' His bored tone is now slightly annoyed. 'You'll be able to do an American accent.'

I'm outraged.

'I can – but not because of that. And anyway, I'm a New Zealander.'

'Thank you. Next . . .'

I was cast in *The Golden Screw*, a Tom Sankey work to be presented in an evening of three short plays. Our director, who actually was an Australian, wanted to make theatrical history – a fusion of Brecht and acid rock. Unfortunately, Wild Oats, a legendary local band he'd found to collaborate with on this great leap forward in theatrical audacity, did not share his vision. They refused to come to rehearsals. At the first (and only) performance, over-excited at being on an actual stage with an audience looking in the right direction, they ripped into unadulterated Hendrix guitar riffs and blasted us actors off the stage. Most of the crowd, who would have been very familiar with the real Jimi, headed to the bar to wait for us all to go away.

After our wrecked offering, we snuck into the auditorium to see the other plays on the programme. Our spirits were already down, falling even further as we watched the others make a decent fist of it – until the last play, by British playwright John Osborne. It was set in ancient Rome. The lead actor wore a toga and was tied to two cardboard pillars for his final soliloquy. Just as he reached full-throated conviction on the nature of existence and the pain of the human condition, he began slowly falling backwards, his hands still tied to the wobbly pillars.

His voice, at first low and dramatic, rose as he kept going, denying the inevitable until the very last moment when, with a scream, he landed with a thud, the columns crashing to the floor.

Silence. Very dramatic. He didn't move. The audience was confused. Was this the end? Time to clap? Scattered applause. The curtain was pulled, leaving his bare feet sticking out, before a face appeared asking if there was a doctor in the house.

We laughed until we cried. Nothing like someone else doing even worse than you to make everything just fine.

It was around this time, in 1969, that I saw an ad in the Cambridge newspaper for an assistant librarian at the local psychiatric hospital. Our money had arrived by then, but my husband and I were still pretty broke. Any respite from the groper at the greasy spoon was fine by me, so I found myself driving our Nash Metropolitan coupe into the vast grounds of Fulbourn Hospital.

The buildings loomed like Gothic Victorians turned to stone. Inside, the overheated fluorescent-lit corridors were polished and bare. Easy to get lost here. Who should I ask for directions? Not many people about. I could smell boiled cabbage. Must be lunchtime. I saw a stooped figure loitering. All bony elbows, fluttering nicotine-stained fingers, and a toothless grin. He giggled quietly to himself and led me down the wide shining corridors. He was a bit more helpful than I had come to expect from the British. He made a sudden turn, and there it was – the library.

A wall of high Victorian windows lit up a room full of books. Mysteries, romances, non-fiction, and clearly a Dewey Decimal system. I was out of my depth already. Do I lie, or do I not get the job?

The place was deserted. I called out, tentatively, 'Hello?'

Two voices, in unison: 'In here.'

The librarian, and the previous librarian, who it turned out was her friend, were in a room out the back.

'Welcome to the den of iniquity.'

I sat down in the cramped room stuffed with slightly risqué titles – these must be the 'restricted' books, I thought – and confessed that my paper qualifications extended to New Zealand University Entrance. I mentioned art school and my nine-month stint at Calvary Psychiatric Day Hospital, and my acting in university orientation theatre. At that, they almost clapped their hands. Could I produce the hospital Christmas play? Would I what? It sounded like fun. They were delighted. No Dewey Decimal system would stand in our way. Neither of them seemed to care about that.

The librarians were English countrywomen, both with a wry sense of humour. They would say, 'Oh, life in large lumps' if you asked them how they were, and, 'Apart from that, Mrs Lincoln, how was the play?' if they asked you how you were. Out came the sherry, and as I woozily followed them to the huge staff café for lunch, it seemed I had a job – and it would start the next day, with the first rehearsal of *Snow White and the Seven Dwarfs*. I was just what they were looking for. No more groping chefs, and it was warm.

If I hadn't come along, the librarian would have had to put on the Christmas play herself, and this terrified her. Her friend, the previous librarian, had inherited the job from the previous librarian, and on, back to the beginning of time. I was in the middle of a well-oiled machine. An institution within an institution. Many of the patients in the Fulbourn Hospital Drama Group had been at Fulbourn for years.

Only one of these long-stay patients spoke; the rest didn't need to. I came to understand that, if you have spent thirty or forty years in full-time care, there isn't really any point. Their part in the Christmas play was to shuffle around onstage, while patients from the acute

25

wards – mainly Cambridge housewives who had been labelled 'crazy' but who were clearly suffering from abuse, loneliness and exhausting poverty – read the script into microphones offstage. The actors formed a kind of tableau.

The whole thing was voluntary, and the staff who came along to help were am-dram enthusiasts who did it every year. I came to understand what a truly magnificent thing that was, in this sprawling institution where everything else was compulsory.

I threw myself into it, and got to know and love every one of them.

There was Jim Corby. No one could remember why he was in hospital, though this was true of most of the patients. He had lovely eyes and a gentle stoop in a solid frame, with big workingman's hands. When he spoke, it was in barely a whisper in the most glorious Fens accent I had ever heard. He would murmur 'Please' and 'Thank you', and that was about it. He used a private shorthand that was very hard to decipher. He played Snow White's father, the king. A kinder king you could not have wished for. He shuffled when he walked, holding out his arm for his queen to hold. She was less engaged and clumped about, scowling. But Jim didn't mind. He put on his crown, and with a secret smile shuffled the boards at Christmas time. The play was an enormous success.

A couple of years later, in 1971, we decided to do *Amahl and the Night Visitors*. Jim would be fine. Three kings in that play. Main parts. He would be a star. But no – Jim was quietly put out. His kind smile was gone, replaced by an expression of resigned sadness. Was it that he didn't like the other kings? Maybe he saw them as competition? No, not that. I soon realised that he liked being the king because he always had a queen. So, that Christmas, when the wise men came to the holy manger, at Fulbourn Hospital in Cambridge, there were three kings from the Orient, and a queen. Everyone was happy – especially Jim.

It's strange to think about it now. I never had a conversation with Jim Corby. But I have often wondered what happened to him, and all the other Jims of the world, after the men with clipboards from the National Health Service turned up and decided to downsize the hospital.

Mr Cooper was the talkative one. He had been a cook in the merchant navy. Always smoking, and when he sang, he did it lustily. Leaning back in a chair, legs crossed, rollie in hand, his glasses crooked on his nose, he would throw back his bald head and belt out an old song he must have remembered from growing up on the streets of Hackney.

*How can a guinea pig wag his tail if he hasn't got a tail to wag,*
*All other animals you will find,*
*Have got a little tail stuck on behind,*
*If they'd only put a tail on a guinea pig,*
*And finish off a decent job,*
*Veeeenah*
*Vaaah perrice of a guinea pig would go right up . . .*
*From a guinea up to fiiiirteee bob.*

I have no idea why Mr Cooper had been in hospital for so long either. I found him one day trying to light his fag from the butt end of his lit stub, but he kept falling asleep. He shook himself awake, and pushed his glasses up his nose.

'Why do I keep falling asleep all the time?' he asked me as he tried to light his smoke again.

'They're giving you too much Largactil, Mr Cooper. When they bring the little paper cups around, don't drink it all.'

But he was already sound asleep again, the smouldering butt fallen from his nicotine-stained fingers to the polished lino floor.

Fulbourn was huge. It provided food, shelter and full-time care for at least seven hundred souls, as well as outpatient clinics. By the time I arrived, in November 1969, it was an open-door hospital. There were three therapeutic communities, and an institutional process that believed in questioning traditional approaches to psychiatry. The place was run by a Cambridge-based board that backed a forward-thinking hospital superintendent named Dr David H. Clark. He was God. He said what went, whatever the task – from the treatment regimes throughout the place to the Christmas dinner menu. In many post-Victorian asylums, this power could be destructive. David Clark had arrived at Fulbourn in 1953, and he was hell-bent on levelling the hierarchical pyramid still found in hospitals today. After he returned from the war effort, having worked as a medical officer in Belsen, the British institutions were crowded with 'mentally ill' returned heroes. Something had to be done, and that something was group psychotherapy. The idea of group psychotherapy was that a psychiatrist would sit with twenty patients and encourage them to share their stories. In theory, with careful use of medication and by sharing their terrible pain and listening to one another, they could heal.

It was pretty much the golden age of the anti-psychiatry movement in Britain. David Clark's theory was that the hospital itself could become an effective healing tool. He was no radical, throwing aside all restraints. By gradually putting his theory into practice, the institution itself was geared for constant change. Progressive doctors from all over Europe were found on placements at Fulbourn during the years when I was there, 1969 to 1973, as I floated about the corridors poking my nose into everything from behind my book trolley.

Everyone used the library, from David Clark himself to the hospital cat. People would come in for a breather and a browse, and to have a yarn. I sat behind the desk wearing horn-rimmed spectacles, and though my grasp of the Dewey Decimal system did not improve, I was party to some great conversations. I learnt to talk to whomever turned up, from erudite psychiatrists to patients experiencing psychosis. Anyone who crossed the portals became a borrower at a county library that just happened to be embedded in a psychiatric institution. I kept my wits about me, because the world I had entered was like swimming in a Hieronymus Bosch painting rendered by Francis Bacon. But I was up for it.

However, on my trolley trips to the outer reaches of the hospital, I realised a disturbing thing. With the exception of the wood workshop and the gardening gangs, therapy at Fulbourn was all about talking. But here in Fulbourn, one third of the hospital population couldn't, didn't, talk.

But there was also the Occupational Therapy Department, which was almost exclusively devoted to something called industrial therapy. Every weekday, patients came to sit at long tables, where they would pack plastic wall plugs into paper bags. Thousands of them. The very people who often had difficulties with their fine motor control had to spend their days picking up tiny red and yellow objects and counting them into bags. It was tedious work for which they received prison wages. It was better than sitting on a ward in the day room staring into space, I supposed, and the morning teas in the workshop provided some community and respite, but I was never a fan. Industrial therapy. Seriously?

I knew that for people who don't talk, and who are institutionalised, non-verbal therapies offer a great deal. I knew this because of what I had learnt working as a psychiatric assistant for nine months at Calvary Psychiatric Day Hospital in Christchurch, after I'd left art school. Calvary was a small place full of spinning wheels and basket-making supplies. Run by two Australian nuns, the day hospital had two psychiatrists presiding – Jack Ballin, and a pure-born radical named David Livingstone. In 1968, Dr Livingstone was keen on taking patients off their medication and focusing instead on family therapy. As a completely unqualified assistant, my job occasionally involved a thing they called 'specialling'. That meant I had to watch only one patient all day – know where they were in the little cottage and keep an eye on how they were doing. I got to spend days in the company of people in various stages of psychosis. Whenever I could, I shoved paper and crayons in their direction. I learnt more in six months about 'Man in Search of Soul' than I ever could have reading Paul Klee in the art school library.

One lunchtime, reading a magazine, I saw that a Scottish

psychiatrist, R.D. Laing, was doing something similar. I pointed it out to one of the nuns, Sister Mary. 'Look, Sister – there's a Scottish psychiatrist doing what we are doing here.'

I remember that she looked at it with a certain tired interest. Just because it was in a magazine, and there was a big Valium pill on the cover, didn't mean it worked, in her opinion.

By the time I got to Fulbourn, there were no locked wards, but plenty of medicated, sedated patients. Fulbourn was already being eyed by government-sanctioned bean counters. A nationwide study was done to investigate long-stay patients. Why did they even exist? Ancient medical notes were sketchy. It was very expensive to keep these patients incarcerated. Women who had been sent away by their families rather than be allowed to have a baby out of wedlock were by now docile old ladies, holding their nearly forgotten grief to their chests along with the grubby stuffed toys that many carried with them always.

One old man was found to have been in hospital for years simply because he had no bones in his thumbs. A late child of elderly parents who had lived in a small village in the Fens, he was not particularly bright. After his mother died, he couldn't do up the buttons on his flies. Someone reported him for exposing himself outside a ladies' shop one afternoon, and he was duly arrested. Rather than see him go to trial, a kindly local policeman put him under the Mental Health Act and he was sent to languish in Fulbourn, where he settled into the hospital routine without complaint. All it would have taken for him to be released was for two psychiatrists to agree that he was fine. He never asked, nor caused enough trouble, to be noticed – and, thirty-five years later, he was still there. This was the kind of highly institutionalised patient the National Health Service was now intent on dumping.

A couple of enthusiastic men in suits arrive at the library with clipboards. They are doing a time and motion study of every department. The library is quiet, as usual. They look pleased – excited, even. Here is a hospital facility that can be downsized and outsourced easily. After a few puzzled words with the librarian, they are disappointed. The Fulbourn Hospital library services are funded by the County Library Service, which is outside their jurisdiction. They scuttle away to investigate Mr Burrows and his dear old woodwork men, who maintain all the furniture and fix broken door handles. The comradely bunch of men who worked with wood and all had their own cups were the first to go.

One of the most useful patients at Fulbourn Hospital was Stanley Harpington. Stanley was a dapper dresser, a true working-class English gentleman. I'd hear his clipped walk as he approached the library door, well-turned-out in Harris tweed and smartly ironed gabardine trousers tucked into his socks, his brown shoes shining. 'Good morning,' he would greet me, 'and how are we, m'duck?' He carried bicycle clips, and was all efficient, cheery business. He did his rounds every other day, visiting departments around the hospital to collect letters, patient notes and prescriptions, which would be sealed in manilla envelopes and carefully put in his sturdy leather satchel.

Singing hymns loudly (strictly Church of England), he would ride his bicycle the few miles into Cambridge, where he would make his deliveries and collect returns, such as X-rays from Addenbrooke's Hospital and book orders for us. You could see him in all weathers, his back ramrod straight, pedalling in his stately manner on the road to Cambridge, his briefcase in the basket in front. 'Oh God, our help in ages past . . .'

When the time and motion men submitted their findings in a big report on efficiency at the hospital, at the bottom of many departmental summaries was an asterisked note: *this excludes the work done by the patient Stanley Harpington.*

Well, of course, that made him a marked man. What say he fell off his bike? What say he read the strictly private medical notes in his possession? What say he lost them? I don't know what happened to him when the hospital was downsized and he, like many others, was 'outplaced' back into 'the community' in the 1980s. I like to think he went to a nice halfway house, with his bike safely stowed at the local vicarage. Unlikely, but not impossible.

*

After *Amahl and the Night Visitors*, I decided to keep the slot going. Both patients and staff had found the time on Tuesdays to come to the hall for rehearsals, so we started doing improvisations. A trailblazing therapist and performer named Sue Jennings was setting up a remedial drama group in London and a few of us started travelling to join her weekend workshops. When I'd first talked to David Clark about the virtues of non-verbal therapy, and drama therapy in particular, he said, 'Not in my hospital, you don't.' I guess if you flatten the pyramid so far that anything is possible, then the more extreme adventurers, be they assistant librarians or otherwise, might get away on you. But David Clark was thinking of primal therapy, a branch of therapy where people reenact disturbing experiences and express their rage and frustration and fear, usually by screaming.

With the chaplain Bill Lintott, a nurse or two, and a couple of terrific young psychiatrists, I began travelling to London for Sue's workshops. As our confidence grew, we invited her to come up to Fulbourn for a day of staff workshops. Gradually, drama therapy infiltrated most of the units in the hospital. A core group got together every now and then, and we would practise on ourselves. We started drama therapy groups in the wards we worked on. Being a free ranger meant I could shut the library for an hour or two, and off I would trot to one of the groups across the hospital. We had only one rule: anyone could come – patient, nurse, doctor, cleaner – but no one was allowed to watch. You were either on the bus or off the bus, to quote Ken Kesey.

At a staff meeting once a month, all the wards and departments got together to discuss matters of mutual interest. Along with the temperature of the boilers and how to save on the coal bill, our little group was able to agitate successfully for an art therapy department. A self-contained room was allocated, and they advertised for a trained art therapist. I really wanted the job, but lost out to Felicity, who had just completed a brand new course in art therapy at St Albans School of Art. Once I got over the ignominy, Felicity was roped in for the next adventure. After all our experimenting on ourselves, we were ready to do some actual drama therapy with the darlings of the Christmas play group.

The hall had been kept in great condition. Its high windows overlooked a well-maintained sprung floor – my mission was to help everyone make friends with this floor, but that was a long-term plan with these people who had not visited a floor in many years, except to pray. We organised chairs in a circle and turned off the fluorescent overhead lights.

In the low winter light, we huddle around my little tape recorder like people around a campfire. We pass the microphone round, everyone taking a turn. 'Say as little or as much as you like,' I instruct.

I begin, 'Once upon a time there was a country far away, where everybody was happy and the grass never needed cutting . . .'

I don't know why I said that. It just popped into my head. The microphone goes round, and by the time everyone has added as much or as little as they choose, it comes back to me. We have the story, all the way to 'and they all lived happily ever after'. Now we can improvise with a structure. Guess who the king is. Queens will rotate.

Every week, we do improvisations. Gradually, we get everyone off their chairs and onto the floor. Tentatively we begin drama games, which open these patients up to soft touching, and mirror movement, which helps them observe and connect to one another. Some have had no experience of any kind of soft touch for years and years. Now they are gently touching one another's faces with their eyes closed.

Slowly they stop shuffling, and start moving. They find noises they can make that belong to them. Unbidden they grow into creatures. And each creature they choose reflects their personality in some way – a personality that has been shrouded under a curtain of institutionalisation.

Over the next few months, the group began to speak more. Maude, one of Jim's queens, arrived at the library one day and wordlessly presented me with dog-eared exercise books full of handwriting in

33

pencil. She had barely spoken before, but she had been keeping a meticulous record of her life in the hospital. These were her diaries. Unfortunately, I was not alone when she presented them. I managed only a superficial glimpse before Ina, the librarian, whisked them off into that little den of hers at the back of the library. I tried to get them back for Maude, but where they went, nobody knew. I suspect they implicated staff members who were friends of Ina's, but I will never know.

Our opening up of institutional lives was causing trouble on the wards. Not everyone was so keen on our drama group. Shuffling around dressed as one of Snow White's dwarves was fine, but we were jiggling these folk out of their passivity, and the wards were having to deal with unpredictable behaviour. For example, Cyril wanted some tights. I took him down to the hospital shop and showed him the women's section. He paid for the largest pair and happily headed for home. That was when the shit hit the fan. A charge nurse came thundering down to the library to ask me what was going on with Cyril. I suggested that he might be feeling the cold. A withering look and an eye roll heavenwards was the exasperated response. I concluded that the real problems around the place were not the patients. Many staff at Fulbourn had good intentions, but they were institutionalised too.

Not in the drama group. We were de-institutionalising ourselves, and not a minute too soon. But I realised that I needed to protect these patients. What had I exposed them to? Was drama therapy merely fulfilling my own need to help, my own need to have a purpose, while causing these gentle souls to become 'troublemakers'? Was David Clark right? We weren't doing primal screaming or anything radical, but we were opening up very closed old wounds. Did we know what we were doing? Really?

In the future, when these hospitals were downsized and most of their patients outplaced to restlessly walk in circles in railway stations and sleep rough, the community they were all supposed to return to would not want them and would not be resourced to help. But, for the moment, there we were in the dusk of the hospital hall, sitting around a little tape recorder, passing round a microphone.

As the summer hit hot and 1972 headed towards Christmas, it dawned on me that the group thought they were getting ready to perform their story. We were doing drama therapy, but as far as the patients were concerned we were rehearsing for their play. They needed an audience.

Theatre institutionalises the drama. You learn your moves and repeat. But we wanted to keep it all fluid. That's what improvisation was about. My friend Suzanne's 8mm camera was good enough for me, even though I had never really contemplated making a film. At art school they had a course called Moving Image, but it was not part of the painting school and it was mainly men over in the design department doing abstract things with wind-up cameras and processing the film themselves. Far too technical for me. I had once been in a Canterbury University student review short film – my friend Shirley Grace and I put on school uniforms and biked around Hagley Park being naively suggestive – and it was fun, but I had no aspirations to get behind the camera.

Here in Cambridge a year later, I knew enough to know that a film was the solution. In filmmaking, the action never becomes institutionalised. You do every shot three or four times, and that's it. Move on to the next. The Whole Earth Drama Group in town had spent a year improvising around a play we would never perform: *MacRune's Guevara*. We would roll around, push one another over, pretend to be one another, test who was the most radical. Crazy.

I presented the idea of a film instead of a play for Christmas at the hospital meeting, and got a favourable response. A small allowance was sent our way from the entertainment fund, and with a promise to protect the privacy of those on screen, we set out making masks and sewing costumes. And that is how I found myself in the long grass in an English field, a stone's throw away from a seven-hundred-bed county asylum, holding a large, terrified man who knew he wasn't a tiger but who was certain that he was balancing on the edge of the abyss.

One day I came home to find a little pile of yellow film cans on our long dining room table. They sat beside a small mechanical thing that looked like a paper hole punch. Beside it was a note.

*Have eloped. Gone to Devon with Tony. Love, Suzanne.*

This was our film. Everything we had shot, the culmination of months of drama therapy, all contained in that pile of innocent-looking plastic. I was happy for Suzanne and Tony – all of the rolling around during the *MacRune's Guevara* rehearsals had clearly become an at-home thing – but this wasn't the deal. Suzanne was going to make the film. That's what the hospital had paid for, and now those little cans on the table were sitting in front of me, with no film to show.

I had no idea what to do. I didn't know that you could cut out the wobbly bits and glue the best bits together. I can't remember exactly how I worked it out. I explored the little editor that was left beside the film cans. This is standard 8mm, and fiddly. Everything is in miniature. You splice the film and scrape it and glue it together. Intricate and exacting. I had been accepted onto the only course in art therapy in Britain, at St Albans School of Art – I really did want Felicity's job – and I would be leaving Cambridge soon. I had to get them their film. No question. I had to.

And it had to have a soundtrack, and it had to be the story they'd made up. *The Animals and the Lawnmower.*

It's a much better film in my head than It is in reality. I had somehow laid hands on a lumbering, ex-BBC, hospital green reel-to-reel two-track tape recorder, and made a soundtrack using every voice that the patients had devised for their characters. I don't think I managed to fit in Mr Cooper's guinea pig song – the soundtrack is lost now.

When we gather one night in late September in the library, a sheet has been hung on the far wall, chairs laid out, and a big aluminium teapot full of stewed tea sits on a trolley with wine biscuits and glasses of cordial already poured and set out in lines. This is not a patient zone. Medical staff only. But tonight the place is packed with the Christmas play regulars. Even the hospital cat has turned up. Everyone has dressed in their best. It's a hospital premiere.

The tape recorder is twice as big as the standard 8mm home projector. I have to push GO on both machines at exactly the same moment. Sound and picture run separately; hope takes over after that. I can only cross my fingers that both will end more or less at the same time.

The little figures jump around, blurry but big on the screen.

They loved it. They wanted to see it again. Our actors became stars overnight. They walked taller after that.

Olive strode around the hospital, putting her face a little too close to other people's and asking, 'Have you seen m'film?' followed by a long, searching smile and a quiet cackle. 'Have you?'

A doctor said that he had picked up one of our actors hitchhiking on the road between Cambridge and Fulbourn. Once an influential lawyer, this patient had suffered a head injury in a bad road accident and his personality had changed. He became the bane of everyone's life, telling lies and stealing. But after seeing the film, the doctor said, 'I gave him a ride into town as I often do, but now I feel like I have a film star in the car.'

Our little 8mm shaky thing was forceful. In that hospital they had been like the furniture. Permanent fixtures, unseen. Now we saw that they were people, and more like the rest of us than we had ever thought. Such is the power of the close-up. *The Animals and the Lawnmower* became the hospital home movie.

Just before I left for St Albans School of Art, the hospital hosted the Royal College of Psychiatrists for the day. Along with erudite discussions on the finer points of psychotherapy, out came the sheet and up went the film.

After the film, the lights come up and all the psychiatrists blink.

Many of them really do look like those shrinks in the cartoons in the *New Yorker*: bald heads, horn-rimmed glasses, long-fingered hands folded over crossed legs. The questions begin.

'Don't you think you are encouraging these patients to regress into infantile fantasies?'

This is not what I had expected or even ever thought about. I suppose it relates to Cyril's tights, but not exactly.

'Yes . . . and what's wrong with infantile fantasies?' I ask.

Silence. Felicity is looking at me, her dark eyes wide with panic.

'And why is the word "infantile" always linked with fantasy?'

In the heat of the moment, it is the heart that speaks. Anyone who knows me will know that I can head into a rant at the twinkle of an eye. I blame Granny Cressey. She was the boss.

I return to the question. 'Yes, we are. Fantasy is an important part of human life. Imagination and storytelling is the cornerstone of humanity. Depriving these patients for years and years of positive imagining is the worst deprivation of institutional life. We all indulge in fantasy. Is how you got here today – tooling down the M1 from London in your red Ferrari – not an infantile fantasy?'

I have gone too far, and I grind to a halt. I become acutely aware of my status in this erudite room. The audience shifts in their seats with an indulgent titter. Then I see Dr David Clark sitting in the front row. He is beaming.

It was only three years after he warned me, sternly, 'Not in my hospital, you don't.' But after that Q&A, he wrote me the best reference one could ever have wished for.

'You are a born manipulator,' he said proudly.

I thanked him, and told him that after I got my art therapy qualification I was going to work in the wards of hospitals that were less progressive than Fulbourn. Shine a light where darkness fell, while I was young and enthusiastic.

'Don't do it,' he told me. 'You'll just get a flat head.'

He was right. But I had to find out the hard way.

Apart from David Clark's emphatic career advice, what I learnt during those years at Fulbourn I never forgot. With that funny little film, we had put drama therapy on the map in a way that we might never have done if instead we'd written a paper for the *British Journal of Occupational Therapy* or *Psychiatry Today*. This way, the hospital had a home movie that could be wheeled out for every dog fight. Creative therapies could be given a profile hitherto unthought of. I saw the power in it. I saw how the people in the film were now respected on their own terms.

This filmmaking thing was definitely my bag.

It wasn't until 2017 that I came back to Cambridge – to Jesus College, just down the road from Fulbourn.

I was with the former New Zealand prime minister Helen Clark, and we were there to screen a film I had made following her bid to become the first female Secretary-General of the United Nations. *My Year with Helen* is a feature documentary that embeds itself in UN institutional life to observe the tribes at work – diplomats, press, and civil society lobby groups – all in a strange dance as the diplomatic corps avoid telling journalists what they are up to, while lobbyists try to get the ear of the press and the press use every trick in the book to avoid them while quoting 'unofficial sources' to hint at what they think is really going on. The film exposes the strong glass ceiling that excludes even the most qualified women from global leadership. It renders a metaphor visible. As I sat with Helen at Jesus College for the spirited Q&A after our screening, I listened to those seriously qualified and influential political thinkers asking questions, and was reminded of that moment when we made the little 8mm film at Fulbourn Hospital. I was still up to the same tricks – still using film to focus the conversation for the consideration of people with the power to effect change. That experience had also shaped my ability to watch the tribes – the psychiatrists, the nurses, the cleaners, the patients. Bonding is the most important human urge. The need to belong. To have our gang. At the UN, it renders incredibly intelligent, good people blind.

\*

'To *My Year With Helen*!'

Under the chandeliers in the dining room at this 521-year-old college, a toast rang out. If life is lived in moments, then this was one. Our host, Julian Huppert, was sitting next to me at the table. Over dinner, I mentioned that I had not been back to Cambridge since I'd left in 1973.

'Oh, how long were you here?'

'Three years.'

'What college?'

'Fulbourn Hospital,' I said. 'It's not a college, it was a psychiatric hospital. It's probably closed by now. You wouldn't have heard of it.'

Then Julian told me, 'I am on the board that funds the inheritor.'

He invited me back to the Intellectual Forum at Jesus College in order to 'think and reflect'. How could I resist? In the early 1970s, when I was getting about in my yellow tights and Biba boots, I could not have entered those portals without prior signed permission. Who would have thought that it would be in the hallowed halls of that great male institution, made inclusive in the 1980s, that I would begin writing this book?

I also went to visit what is now the Cambridgeshire and Peterborough NHS Foundation Trust, and met the then-CEO, a woman named Anna Hills. The whole place now encompasses a huge community, with over four thousand patients each year, in a large and diverse mental health system. Their motto is PRIDE: Professionalism, Respect, Innovation, Dignity, Empowerment. Just words on a card, but you don't get that standard to fly without a lot of thinking and reflecting and imagining.

I am sure there are dark corners in their system now, as there were when I was there. With Anna Hills, the inheritor of David Clark's legacy, overlooking the old buildings now converted to offices, we talked about mental health, where pain and deprivation are extreme, and poverty provides the perfect Petri dish. Plus, there's an explosion of problems now with young people in terrible states turning up in A&E departments all over the Western world. But as we talked, I was moved to think that institutional cultures could move and change for the better. Once those good principles are there, they can proliferate, even long after buildings have been torn down. At the Cambridgeshire and Peterborough NHS Foundation Trust they have a thriving art therapy department.

More art, more art, more art, I say.

I wander around the closed Victorian stone buildings during a bank holiday. I peer through the library windows. No longer a library, it seems to have been turned into a media room. The railway line still runs through the field where I filmed that sequence. The grass is now mowed, and large stones mark graves of long-departed patients. They had been lying there unmarked and unacknowledged, unbeknown to us, but now their burial place is revealed. Blank stones, signifying lost lives. I am drawn to thinking about Sarah, my great-great-grandmother, and ponder the precipice that we stand on between 'mad' and 'sane', and the fateful collision of time and place.

The bus into Cambridge is waiting. I travel back, hardly recognising the city that has grown past these gates.

# 3

# Sarah and Elsie

Sarah was very little. Tiny feet, like a child's. I have a last that was used to mend her boots. It holds my front door open.

I only know Sarah from my aunty Irene's assiduous tracing of the Ridley women who sailed into Lyttelton on the *Cashmere*. Three of them did well; the other did not.

In 1855, when she was twenty-two, Sarah Brunning travelled from Gravesend in Kent with her widowed mother and two aunts to New Zealand. The colony was short of servants, so a call had been sent out for 'women of good character'. They signed on for an assisted fare to go on a great migration towards a better life. It took months, hunched in the gloom of the mid-decks of the *Cashmere*, through storms, cold and heat, to get to New Zealand – a country they could only have heard of as a phantom place. What on earth possessed them to do it? The developers who had staked out the city of Christchurch must have had tremendous gifts of the gab, to get the boats full. Or perhaps life was so constricted and difficult for those women that risking death was worth it. Maybe Sarah had no choice and had to go with her mother and her aunts, who seem to have been more resilient and strategic, especially when it came to marrying well. Still, she must have been brave, to go on that long journey around the Cape of Good Hope into the unknown.

Upon arrival, Sarah's mother and sisters skedaddled over the

Cashmere Hills to live in Christchurch, leaving young Sarah in a women's boarding house in Lyttelton. She visited them every Sunday. She might have found a scullery maid's job in one of the raucous boarding houses at the port, but on any account we know she would set out on the bridle track, sometimes through the snow, to go to church and eat a roast dinner with her mother and aunts afterwards. Up hill and down dale on the Cashmere Hills bridle track. Her mother married well – a man named Paul L'Auguilloued, who looked after the horses on colonial expeditions into north Westland, where explorers were taken to the mighty Kawatiri by local Māori. The river was renamed after Charles Buller, director of the New Zealand Company. Paul must have been important to these expeditions, because when he retired, suffering from consumption (TB, to us), he was given a stone house in Fendall Town (later Fendalton). Sarah's mother lived there until Paul died, leaving her the house and I imagine a horse or two.

Maybe it was at church one Sunday that Sarah met the dapper and charming Thomas Bennett Cressey, a butcher. They tied the knot in St Michael's Church – the forerunner of the first Christchurch Cathedral, built of sturdy wood. If Sarah was married in a pretty white dress, it was soon sewn into christening robes, as she would go on to have nine children. She and Thomas lived in a sod hut on leased land in south Ellesmere with no water or sanitation, and she was busy keeping the dirt floor clean, keeping his children alive, keeping the home warm against the southerlies. I can't imagine her laughing, but she must have sometimes. It is remotely possible that she was happy, but somehow I doubt it. Did she reckon herself a slave? I doubt that, too. This was a woman's lot and hardly ever questioned. Was Thomas a 'good provider'? No doubt.

It wasn't long before Thomas moved his family to Ahaura, where he had a large killing shed and could provide meat for the entire district. Was he a drinker? If not, he would have been an exception. Women in New Zealand managed to get the vote in 1893 partly because of the domestic destruction caused by their men drinking all the household money away. Just over half of the all-male parliament believed that women were more likely than men to vote for temperance, and after much campaigning and 32,000 women's signatures, both houses of parliament decided to give the vote to 'the fairer sex'.

But that would have brought no respite for Sarah, who didn't live to see the law change. Aged fifty, she was committed to Sunnyside Lunatic Asylum, arriving suffering from starvation and debilitating depression.

Notes from Sunny Side 1882.
This little woman was admitted 3rd June being then very low and emaciated, and continued to get weaker, and died on Saturday morning. She was in a very bad state.

When she died, she left her nine children and an unforgiving man.

I wonder about the last time she saw her social-climbing mother. What did her mother make of her situation? But we must not be too harsh about Sarah's mother. Why would you marry down? Women's rights were virtually non-existent and their husbands had control of all the money. Even if a woman was widowed, the property was automatically transferred to her eldest son once he turned twenty-one and was granted legal authority over her.

Two years after Sarah died, her son John was drowned in the Inangahua River and her husband's wrath was carved in stone down at Ahaura Cemetery. I like to think that had she still been alive, Sarah would not have agreed to that accusing text. Her son Edward certainly didn't.

Anyway, that's the sad tale of Sarah, the 'woman of good character', whose son Edward had kind eyes. It was Edward who made sure that a father's wrath could be eradicated and that cheeky girls – like his Elsie, and like us not yet born – could be rebels.

I'm grateful to him, and Uncle Ted, and my grandmother Elsie – who would never have dreamt how much rebel is required to get a film made.

*

Pākehā women often lose their names. Their stories, and the stories they told, come to us in fragments. I once asked my father, Ed, about his grandmother, Granny Butler. 'Don't know,' he said. 'Ask your mother.'

I protested: 'It's your grandmother we're talking about! What was her name?'

He looked at me a bit thoughtfully, and said, 'Granny . . . Mum said we had to let her win at cards.'

The only other thing he could remember was that she had one tooth in her head but could eat a steak. She spent her life on the goldfields, a world away from where she was born. A woman who, as I later found out, bore six live children in Canvastown and helped many more come into the world. And the only thing her grandson could remember was that she had one tooth in her head but could eat a steak. I think she may have terrified Ed.

Granny Butler had three children with Mr Butler before they married. A Preston cousin told me that she'd said her rather tardy wedding was because, when the priest was in the district, they were both too busy.

I know plenty about my maternal grandmother, my nan, Elsie. When I was a child, Elsie came to live with us.

She would sit too close to the fire, her legs mottled red, her ankles swollen over the tops of her old velvet slippers. She had a blind eye that was always rolled back into her head. If you got on that wrong side, she looked very angry. Fire and water. Her eye could summon up the dead. It had its own life, even though it was stuck there in her head. She got it from a stroke she'd had when she was 47. She got the stroke from too much housework. Her other eye was kind. Black as coal. She sat at our fireside embroidering – 'fancy work', she called it. My mother said it was good for her to use her hands. So she sat too close to the fire with the raw linen strung across her knees, embroidering the outlines of flowers in silky coloured cottons strewn about. If I behaved myself I was allowed to touch them.

Tablecloths for someone in the family. 'Cloths,' she called them.

'This one is going to Ida when it's finished,' she'd say, or, 'Mavis would like this.'

Then she would change her mind. 'This will suit your mother.'

Elsie's room in our little rehab house in Greymouth was meant to be our lounge, but it wasn't, because she'd had the stroke and, according to Tui, the doctor said she couldn't look after herself. So Nan looked after us. She peeled potatoes and dried the dishes and ate radishes with too much salt (bad for her blood pressure) and sang along with the radio. She loved Mario Lanza.

'He's a very clever man, Mario Lanza. He can sing a duet with himself,' she told me. Sure enough, when I listened carefully, he did. Fascinated, I found that if I whistled and sang at the same time I could get a tuneless duet going, but nothing remotely like Mario. I practised for a while but I didn't seem to be improving so I gave up. Years later when I learned about the technology of double voicing I was a bit disappointed on behalf of Nan and me.

Under a framed faded print of Jesus in her bedroom, she had a most mysterious instrument, all wood and old writing on the knobs. A pedal organ. The yellowing keys didn't work unless you pushed the pedals vigorously. Impossible to play if you are small, so I would implore Nan to play it. Placing her swollen feet onto the pedals, spreading her fingers over the keys, pulling stops for extra volume, she would lean forward and launch herself into a song. She sang in a high, sweet Edwardian voice, sliding the tune around. Because of the stroke, she couldn't get much steam up and the sound would flubber and flutter, rising and falling with her uneven pedalling. At certain moments her voice still triumphed over the waves.

'*Whaaat a frieend we have in Jeeesus, eraall our sins and griefs to bear.*'

She had a very personal relationship with Jesus. She knelt by her bed and whispered to him every night and morning and sometimes – if something bad had happened – during the day. Plenty bad had happened in Elsie's life, but she said most of her prayers for other people. When her daughter, my aunty, went into hospital and had a stillborn baby, it was only prayer that could get that dead mite up to heaven. I asked her what a stillborn baby looked like and she said it was like a beautiful rainbow parcel that was flown by two angels – one on either side – up to God. That God wasn't Jesus, though. He was the other one, on the wall of Nan's bedroom, the big God with the beard who sat on high with the sun shining out from behind his head. He was more like Nan's other eye – fiery and unpredictable. He could strike you down whenever he felt like it.

Once I was taken to the cemetery, I saw the angels. They were made of solid concrete, but I guessed it was through the power of prayer that they could spring to life and, amid fluttering feathers, fly to heaven up to the scary God, who would say, 'Thank you for the parcel.'

I preferred Jesus. He had a lamb and was also a fisher of men. He could gather them up in a net so they didn't drown. In the big framed picture above the pedal organ, he had all God's children, black, brown and yellow, sitting at his feet along with the sheep. Jesus was our friend. If you asked Elsie, she would put a word in to Jesus for things you wanted. Not for anything new, like a pair of patent leather shoes, or a bunny wool cardie with sparkles on like the girl over the road had; she was an 'only child' and had let me put on her cardie once, but then she'd got polio and they wouldn't let me go over there anymore. Nan wouldn't ask Jesus for a bunny wool cardie for me. She said that praying to Jesus was for something to happen, so we prayed for the polio to go away, and it did, and Ainsley Evandon just had to have a calliper on her leg for a while.

Nan and Jesus turned out to be quite a good pair. She would put in requests for me, like to be allowed to stay up to listen to Randy Stone on the radio, or to get a place in the elocution competitions. I knew that once I put my order in Nan would do the hard yards, kneeling at her bed in the morning and for ages at night. Often I went to sleep with the sound of her whispering, her s's whistling. Jesus and Nan were pretty much one hundred per cent reliable. You just had to remember to ask.

*

47

Before we leave my nan, I want to tell you what a sweet spirit she was, fast for a joke and a song. She was basically homeless when I bounced around on her knees as she embroidered, while sitting too close to the fire in our living room. Forced to live with her eldest daughter, and sometimes shipped off up the road with her battered little cardboard suitcase to stay with her other daughters for a few weeks, she was resolutely cheerful. She had brought up her five kids before there was any social welfare. My grandfather George was usually absent; when he was around he was fighting his alcoholism, and her as well. She hated asking for charity but was sometimes forced to, bringing up five kids on her own. She would put on her hat and coat and, giving her shame to Jesus, she would go to the Charities Board and throw herself on the kindness of strangers. But I never heard her complain. She may have saved that every night for Jesus to hear, but somehow I doubt it.

And she never stopped loving George, that errant husband of hers. After a seven-year separation, she managed to get divorced – only to take him back again. They couldn't marry in the Anglican Church where she cleaned every week. The Monsignor wrote a letter to the archbishop requesting a dispensation to be married at the altar, but no, it would have to be a registry office arrangement followed by a blessing in the church. It didn't last, anyway. But her loving him did. When Elsie lived with us, my grandfather occasionally turned up and Nan would fall for him all over again.

Tui would let him stay on. She would buy him new clothes from the Sally Army shop and give him a spot down the back garden where he could plant vegetables. Nana and George would have a few cuddles and laughs. But it wasn't long before I would find him down among the runner beans, crying. Tui would find bottles hidden about the place, and then one day he wouldn't be there anymore. George Macdonald, my ghostly living grandfather, the one I was supposed to be most like, the man with the wall eye like mine, the man who wrote poetry and was always, always forgiven.

When he died in the Octagon during a particularly cold Dunedin winter, he had already been buried before Tui was notified. She went down to collect his meagre belongings. A couple of creased photographs of his four-year-old son, who had died in childhood, and a worn journal that she brought home and burnt.

Meanwhile Elsie sat too close to the flames and whispered prayers to herself and ate too much salt with her radishes. Young curates of the Greymouth Anglican Church, the lost boys of Christianity, beat a path to our door, where they would talk to Nan about just about anything, and sip tea, and eat just one more slice of cake from Tui's tin, as Nan cooked her legs and sewed her wretched past into flowers.

# 4

# How I Discovered the Audience

I have been a terrible liar ever since I learnt to talk. I didn't realise I was doing it. I was keeping myself entertained. Telling fibs. Now they call me a storyteller. A kinder way to put it.

Once I could ride my trike, I was off visiting the neighbours. Ida Street in Greymouth was my hood. I would go next door to see Poppa McKechnie. He was a dear old man who mowed his lawns so often they were as soft as moss. I would find him in his garden and stay for a lolly. Mrs McKechnie was inside in her dressing gown, with her hair needing brushing. I never went in there. She would occasionally appear at the back door holding a lolly jar, the darkness of the kitchen behind her. Terrifying. She would call me, jar in hand, smiling like a wicked witch in a fairy tale. I'd want to run, but there was that lolly . . . I'd grab it, then scamper off to Poppa in the backyard. I loved hanging out with him in his garden. He knew the same songs as I did.

Next door to the McKechnies lived the Hardys – Merle and Duncan and their three kids, Lynn, Kay and Wayne. They were older than me and at school most of the time, so I hung out in Merle's kitchen. Her husband, Duncan, wrote poetry in his spare time. He'd even published a book: *Stray Thoughts*. My father, who without telling anyone in his family had left school when he was ten, viewed this singular nocturnal activity of Duncan's with deep suspicion. If Duncan hadn't smoked a pipe and worn a beret, Ed might have forgiven him the poetry. But Ed associated berets and pipes with poofters. His word. Poofters were people of the male persuasion who had reinvented themselves – unlike him, who went out of his way to be obstinately unconstructed. For Ed, being a poofter wasn't about being gay. Anyone who aspired to the upper class was a poofter. Accountants from Christchurch who rose in the ranks in the army during the war were poofters. Actually they were 'a pack of poofters', and though Duncan had been a conscientious objector during the war and therefore 'not one of those pack of poofters', he was still a poofter for the poetry and berets and the pipe.

Men have driven one another underground for centuries.

I was over at the Hardys' quite a bit. I stole my brother's leather bike toolkit and filled it with crayons, packed a colouring-in book, and off I would go, out the gate and down the road, timing my visit for Merle's morning baking. The Hardy house living room was very different from ours – not a lacy doily in sight over at the Hardys'. And though Merle's baking was a bit on the bran side, you knew where you were with Merle. She called a spoon a spatula. She had her own teeth, and ginger hair and freckles on her legs. You get to know the legs pretty well when you are little. 'Around our mothers' skirts' is really to do with their legs. I spent a lot of time under the kitchen table, drawing among the legs.

Merle did not tell lies. And she didn't tell stories either. When the women of the neighbourhood came over to our place for morning tea, she spoke about plain things. What she'd bought for dinner. How long to cook a pie. So did her friend Iris, who talked about her golf handicap. She and her husband Cyril came to live next door after Poppa McKechnie drove his car onto the railway line and the train came.

Famie Rochford from across the road, and my mother, Tui – they were the yarn spinners.

I know the underneath of the table well. There are pencil marks on the raw wood where the carpenter made the table so it could extend.

I like it down here among the legs, colouring in with my thin crayons in the dusky light. The husbands are at work. The women have been making beds, washing dishes, scrubbing their benches with sand soap, baking scones, hanging out the sheets. They arrive in our kitchen for a cuppa around ten. They like to talk about their 'hims'.

'He rode his bike into the garage last night completely plastered and forgot it hasn't got a floor anymore. He's on his back down there, bellowing like a big bull for me to come and pull him out of the blackberries. I say, "You can stay in there you silly bastard."' She laughs. 'Meek as a lamb this morning.'

That's Famie with the dancing dark eyes and the voice like velvet. She smokes tailor-mades and has brown legs as smooth and shiny as our piano. When she kicks off her shoes, her feet have calluses.

I love it under here because they have forgotten about me. I roll myself into a ball and kneel on my colouring-in book. The princess will have yellow hair . . .

'How's Cyril?'

That's my mother. She's asking Aunty Iris about my godfather. They are all called my aunties, though they aren't my real aunties. The men are all my not-real uncles, except for Cyril Neville, bookie of Greymouth. He is not called Uncle anything. He talks fast and loud, and my father thinks he's a big skite. That's because Cyril owns a horse that is going to race in the Melbourne Cup. Cyril collected money from all the neighbours and bet on his horse to win. When Dalray – a vastly underestimated horse – won the Melbourne Cup in 1952, Cyril took his cash from the tote in pillowcases. He won £63,000 cash on top of any prize money. They didn't live next door to us for long after that. When he came home from Melbourne, he gave my father enough money to buy a brand new Volkswagen van, resulting in him being ostracised down at the RSA for buying a German vehicle. Cyril bought me (his favourite godchild) a walkie-talkie doll and a mysteriously empty bulky dolls' wardrobe that I am sure was used to smuggle money and jewellery into the country. I'll never know. But for now, that hasn't happened yet, and Iris is stirring her tea at the table above me.

'I have no idea what Cyril is up to,' says Iris briskly. Unlike the others, she wears stockings in the morning and leather brogues on her feet. She has help in her house. She gets up after nine.

The others talk about the 'hims' because they rule their lives. The hims are important and frustrating, but each woman wants hers to be the best him, better than the others. My mother starts in on my father, Ed. He escaped from a prison camp during the war. They have just bought a fish 'n' chip shop.

'He came back to find that his father had given the fishing business to his brothers, the ones who hadn't gone away, leaving him working for wages. When we bought the shop, they told Ed he had to sign an agreement that he wouldn't sell raw fish in competition with them. He signed it, but on his last day at the factory when they had drinks and his brothers made speeches and presented him with the fountain pen, he told them, "You can keep your fountain pen."'

Then Tui looks down under the table and shoos me outside. 'Her ears were flapping.'

Indeed they were. I was constantly looking for clues. I needed to know why my mother was so unhappy and why my father wasn't. I needed to know why she told me, 'You will spend most of your life doing things you don't want to do, Gay.' Every word seemed to rattle my brain. 'You will always have to follow your husband. He will decide everything.' Well, that was easy; I just wouldn't have a husband. But spend your life doing things you didn't want to do? Why did I have to do that?

With the other kids at school and the women scrubbing benches, the radio was my friend. Music poured out of that mighty Columbus perched on its own shelf overlooking the sitting room. Nightingales sang, ghost riders rode and the sun in the morning came over the hill, filling the house with music. There was Housewives' Choice: 'Oh Johnny, oh Johnny, how you can love!' And a band that played 'The Chattanooga Choo Choo'. Radio serials presented by Grace Gibson

Productions gave us *Dr Paul*, with 'a story of adult love', and Aunt Daisy proclaimed every morning a good one. But for me, apart from *Listen with Mother*, it was the weekend request session that made me want to fly up to that big old valve radio and crawl inside to live. That was when they played *Sparky and the Talking Train* ('Help me, Sparky, help me, Sparky!') and Dr Seuss's *Gerald McBoing Boing*, about the lad who doesn't speak words but goes 'boing, boing' instead.

Another not-really-my-uncle, Uncle John, hosted the children's session on 3YZ, and once a week there was an episode of *Simon and the Gang*. This was my favourite. I waited for it all week, counting the days. They had madcap adventures, with a cliffhanger at the end of every episode. He was a silly galoot, that Simon.

Between episodes, I could at least fill my days visiting the neighbours. Mrs Bone and Jack lived next door at no. 12. I preferred Mrs Bone's pikelets recipe. Her place was a bran-free zone.

One morning I'm licking the bowl over in her kitchen, having timed my visit perfectly. Mrs Bone is doing the dishes, and the satisfying smell of cooling fresh pikelets is wafting around. Apropos of nothing much, I say, 'Simon came into the shop yesterday.'

This is the kind of thing my father says to Tui and Elsie when he comes home at night from the fish 'n' chip shop. He washes his hands before dinner and tells Tui who came into the shop that day. And Tui says, 'What did they say?' and Ed tells her all the news.

'Simon who?' asks Mrs Bone, vigorously scouring a pan.

'Simon, from *Simon and the Gang*.'

Mrs Bone puts the pan on the draining board and turns to give me her full attention. This is a welcome reaction. I'm not just prattling at the backs of people who have their hands in dishwater or who are sandpapering wood in the shed. This is total attention, a kind I am not used to.

'Did he? Simon from the children's session?'

'Yes.'

Mrs Bone pauses for a moment, and fixes me with a quizzical expression.

'What did he look like?'

No problem. I haven't actually met Simon, but I know exactly what he looks like. 'He's got blond hair and freckles and glasses and a two-wheeler.'

Mrs Bone opens the French doors between the kitchen and the sitting room, where old Jack sits in his big easy chair in the sun reading his newspaper.

'Jack – come and have a listen to this. Tell Jack.'

So I do. Old Jack Bone stands in the doorway holding the morning news, with the hole in his grey sock that has his gnarled big toe poking through. He has a funny little smile on his face that I find encouraging. I embellish.

'Well I never,' they both say, more or less in unison, then Mrs Bone serves the pikelets.

Perfect. I have found the thrill of the audience. And I'll never look back.

I loved telling fibs. Whoppers. It didn't occur to me till years later that Mrs Bone would've known I was making it up. As it happens, making stuff up has become my life's work. I've spent my adult life thinking about stories and their power.

Potent beings indeed are stories. A story is shaped by its audience. Stories can manipulate whole populations, especially the news, where current events become stories with beginnings, middles and ends, and at times feel like a soap opera.

Point of view is everything. We are all heroes in our own tales. Two children brought up in the same home can tell very different versions of their upbringings. For one it was a happy childhood; for the other it was purgatory. This isn't only about relationships, but is also about the way that memory is deeply coloured by emotional response and point of view. How a story is first told can easily become what we know as fact. The stories we tell ourselves – we call them our memories, but half the time we are really remembering how we chose to tell those stories in the first place.

If you are thinking that this is some kind of rider to my glossing over some things, in a way it is. This is my version, my story.

Making up stories is the heart of who I am – who we all are. It is a form of time travel. We tell ourselves stories to make sense of the past, to bind ourselves together in the telling and to dream of the future. From the moment my toes hit the floor in the morning until I turn out the light at night, part of my brain is ticking along, working out how to tell a story in a film I want to make. It's almost an affliction. If I haven't got a story rattling around in my head, I feel incomplete. Dreaming them up sustains me.

The best tales are illuminating. The worst tell lies as if they were truths. Either way, once a story is let loose it has a life of its own.

But they are all made up. That applies to all film genres – documentaries, dramas, news, commercials. Film is the medium most like lived experience, and the ability to manipulate an audience is boundless. Every single story manipulates emotional imagination. There's no other species on the planet that does this. And the stories we tell, and how we choose to tell them, define human existence.

One afternoon I was riding my trike between the Hardys' and Poppa's place when I fell off, skinning my knees and hands on the concrete. 'Roaring like a bull' as Tui called it, I headed for home, where I got sympathy and a licorice allsort. Tui tore up a sheet and wound my hands and knees in big white bandages, and told me I was a 'wounded soldier'. Feeling slightly better but with a strong need to garner sympathy from the wider district, I limped over to the Bones'. When Mrs Bone opened her kitchen door to me in big bandages, her reaction was perfect. 'What happened to you?'

'A big boy pushed me over.'

There it was. Out of my mouth. I could hardly say I fell off my trike, could I? My story now matched my being 'a wounded soldier'. And it worked. Her eyes widened in concern. She cracked open the orange cordial and opened her biscuit tin. I settled in to make up a few more details for another biscuit.

I returned home, well satisfied. As I came round the side of our house I heard Mrs Bone talking to Tui over the back fence. They were both bringing in the washing.

'Isn't that terrible. Who would push over a dear little girl?'

'Did she tell you that?'

'She told me a big boy pushed her over.'

Tui stopped and laughed. 'The only big boy out there was Poppa McKechnie, and he didn't push her over. No, she fell off her trike.'

I froze. Sprung. A much worse pain than my grazed knees. My mind was spinning, my stomach churning and my heart was thumping. Shame prickled my every pore. I could hardly go home now. I slunk back round the front, and made myself scarce for a while.

Did this curb my enthusiasm for lying? No. Making things up was so much more interesting than the same old, same old. I was the only kid I saw during the day in the school week. But the radio world was in colour, and I could turn on 'The Chattanooga Choo Choo' and go to the party. It was my escape from the endless housework my mother and Nan did all day. They were either peeling the spuds and getting a meal together or cleaning up after one. Monday was wash day, Tuesday was ironing day. Stripping every bed in the house to boil the sheets in the copper and get them on the long line, hoisted into the wind to dry, took all day. I liked to watch the ironing. I liked the way my mother could take a sunbeam skirt and make the pleats concertina. But the ironing was endless.

I was keeping an eye out for any possibility of escape. And by a stroke of luck, I found it.

My brother had trouble with his r's, and went to elocution lessons up in a big dark house, where he had to say funny things like 'Peter Piper picked a peck of pickled peppers'. His teacher sat on a dark green velvet couch with her legs crossed at the ankles while he stood before her to recite. He hated it. Along with those weird Peter Piper tongue-twisters, he had to memorise poems and recite them to his teacher every week. At home, he had to practise, and I was allowed to listen. I loved those practices. For one thing, I would get to lounge around in his room, where on the dressing table there was a crystal set. It made whistling noises from across the sea and crackly voices that came from a world away. He listened to Spike Milligan and Peter Sellers in *The Goon Show*, which to my young mind sounded like an adult version of *Simon and the Gang*. Try as I might, I couldn't understand them. My brother could do Eccles from *The Goon Show*. I didn't really understand Eccles either.

But I longed to recite in front of an audience too. I couldn't understand why my brother hated doing it. So when I went down to Sunday School, I started reciting poems. Sunday School could be pretty boring once we'd done 'Jesus Loves Me', and my entertaining everyone diverted us from long boring stories about lepers, whatever they were, and the Lamb of God, who was not even a lamb but a person. Janet Dunshea, the train driver's daughter who sang in the Holy Trinity choir, indulged my poetic interruptions. A poem about two drops of rain on a windowsill was my favourite. Janet Dunshea liked it too.

One crisp *Housewives Choice* morning, Tui called me into the hall, where she was talking on the big black phone that hung high on the wall in a walnut wooden box.

'Janet Dunshea says you know "Waiting at the Window"?'

I nodded, unsure if this was something I should be owning up to or not. The trouble with my lies was that I sometimes lost track.

'She wonders if you would like to recite it at the Sunday School concert?'

That sounded fine by me. I readily agreed. Tui continued with Janet.

'Well, she says she will, but she probably won't,' she said, and laughed.

I was outraged. Caught telling the truth, and she didn't believe me.

The day comes. Tui has me standing on the kitchen table to lengthen my best white dress, threading blue ribbon through a layer of lace. She's put my hair in curlers, which I hate, but I like the ribbon.

The week leading up to this day has been all arduous drilling. It doesn't matter how many times I say 'Waiting at the Window' for her, she makes me repeat it. That concert night, as the congregation gathers down at the church hall, my parents look magnificent. Tui is wearing an amazing blue frock with a sunbeam skirt that she has knitted with big round fine needles, and her white fur evening coat makes her skin shine. My father looks like Humphrey Bogart. I've never seen him with the church lot before.

I am on after the man who plays the saw and another who does bird whistles. 'If I were a blackbird, I'd whistle and sing . . .'

Janet introduces me. Then my mother and I walk up the aisle so she can lift me onto the stage. She perches on the edge, sitting along from my feet, looking up at me.

This doesn't feel right. No one else in the concert has had a person sitting on the stage beside them, so without a second thought I say, 'Oh no, Mummy, you can go back to your seat now, thank you. I can do it myself.'

My mother's face suddenly turns bright red and with a haughty raise of her shoulder she walks the walk of shame back into the middle of the hall and sits back down, from where she mouths the words at me. She will never know how close I come to stopping the recitation to make her stop that.

But the poem wins out, and for the moment I am on that stage, life seems all in the right order. Me – the great and glorious three-year-old me – at the centre, with only one thing to do. And then they clap. No joy or rage. Just pure pleasure.

The review in the Christmas church newsletter says: *The little tot Gaylene Preston stole the show with a spirited rendering of A.A. Milne before supper was served.*

This little town on the edge of the world was, according to some, a mid-century cultural desert, but I was raised by it to participate. It wasn't long before the radio people rang and in the 3YZ studio I was lifted by John Pike onto a table in front of a microphone nearly bigger than my head. It turned out that this was Uncle John, the children's session broadcaster, who I still didn't realise was also Simon and all of the other voices in *Simon and the Gang*. I recited 'Waiting at the Window', then 'Belinda the Cow' by Gloria Rawlinson. 'Belinda the cow was exceedingly vain, she hated the wind and was timid of rain, I'm sure I'll get freckles in this sunny place, and I'm certain that rain is not good for the face.'

I'd found a way out from under the table and had crawled into the radio.

\*

I'm sitting on the big brown couch. The sun is coming in and I can see the colours shining into the deep velvet crevasses. You could find colours in there from when the couch wasn't brown, from when it was purple and rusty yellow. My feet are sticking out in front of me and I settle myself back, sitting right up in order to concentrate. I'm listening to *Listen with Mother*. I listen to *Listen with Mother* every day. Not with Nan, who is still in bed in the mornings, and not with my mother, who doesn't sit down unless we have visitors.

The lady is singing and reading stories as usual. But today she says, 'Mothers, get a pen and paper while I sing this song. I'm going to tell you how you can make paints for your children.'

Painting. I have crayons and a colouring-in book, but the idea of painting is so incredible that I have to shimmy myself out of the couch and head out to find Tui.

The wash house is dark with only one little high window because the tongue and groove has never been painted. Tui is wearing a faded floral dress with the same colours that are in the seams of the couch. She's boiling the copper and stirring sheets. I pull at her skirt. She stops.

'The lady on the radio says you have to come now.'

Maybe Tui hasn't heard me properly, or maybe she is slightly annoyed that the lady on the radio is imposing herself on our home life. She looks down at me and I continue.

'It's for painting. You have to help me.'

She opens the tablet of blue that makes the sheets whiter than white, and begins to sprinkle it in.

'You listen for me,' she says.

Off I go, out of the wash house, over the veranda, through the kitchen, back into the living room, scruggling myself deep into the couch, bolt upright again to pay attention to the big old Columbus radio. Kate Harcourt finishes her song. You were supposed to be dancing but I'm not going to risk it. She tells us we can have an easel and paintbrushes, and how to make red, green and blue, and you can have a pinny made of an old plastic tablecloth if you like. That's all I need. Off I go, back to the wash house.

All I can see as I stand beside my mother is her legs, by the copper blue gas flame hissing, heating the water. I tell her quickly before I forget.

'You have red and blue and yellow and an easel and a plastic pinny.'

She hardly stops stirring, then her tired face appears through the steam, like a bedraggled God emerging through clouds.

'Too much mess,' is all she says before she disappears again.

The gas hisses and the steam clouds billow, and in my disappointment a crystal clear thought comes to me.

That's right for you, but it's not for me.

And therein lies the big struggle. My implacable resistance against this constricted world of women whom I loved. I was going to be different. I had the good sense to be born at a time when the whole country was for the kiddies, and I, along with thousands of others, was going to be educated out of hearth and home where my foremothers had ruled for centuries.

I carry them with me and honour them here.

# 5

# Go Outside and Play

Every now and then, my mother would turn to me and say something outrageous.

I was mucking around among the legs, 'helping' carry cups from the bench to the cupboard, when she said, 'How would you like a baby brother for your birthday?'

Somehow I knew I was supposed to be pleased about this. But I wasn't. I already had a brother. I wanted a Winkie bike. Winkie bikes were three-wheelers that looked like two-wheelers, with rubber tyres and spokes, not like my rusty old trike. They had a silver bell on the gleaming handlebars and a leather seat. I really wanted a Winkie bike, and now they were telling me I was getting a new baby brother and I was supposed to be pleased about it.

Disappointing.

I was packed off to my mother's beloved younger cousin, Aunty Dorothy, who was a dental nurse but had recently married so she'd had to give it up. Now she wanted a little girl like me. Over at Aunty Dorothy's I got much more attention than I ever got at home. Aunty Dorothy had an electric stove, so she didn't spend so much time stoking the coal range. She was keen on educational games but they exhausted me. I had a room of my own there, but it made me lonely. It took ages for Tui to get me that brother.

They arrive in Uncle George's taxi. My father is in the passenger seat, and I get in the back with Tui, who is nursing a small bundle. I'm allowed a peek. She pulls back the blanket and there is a scrunched-up little face with eyes tightly closed.

'This is Jan, your new sister.'

I am shocked. I'd got used to the brother idea. And she's got hair! I've never seen a baby with hair before. Hers goes straight up into a cone above her head.

My new sister. Janet Elsie. I am allowed to touch her but not hold her yet. When we get home, I see she behaves not like a real person. She kicks her legs around, and when she cries she runs the house. She's like an alien peanut. She's mine but I can't play with her. What's the point of getting a new baby for your birthday when you can't play with it? I decide to make the best of things and get on my rusty, trusty old trike to go around the neighbourhood and tell them all about her, but really to see if anyone has remembered my birthday and has got me a present.

Our baby got really sick not long after. She changed colour. She went from pink to yellow to red with spots. The bedroom was filled with worry and camphor bags and poultices. The house became quiet. Nan made endless barley soup. I spent more time behind the couch. It's all very well to enjoy being forgotten in my secret places, but that baby sister was taking up everyone's time. Had she slept too long? Had she eaten enough? Nan was spending ages stirring at the stove, and Tui was in a daze, breastfeeding the baby, with the blinds drawn during the day. As she got better, and after she could sit up, Jan took to rocking. She would hum a repetitive tune and bang her back against her cot. As she got bigger, she could rock her cot across the room. I have to admit I was impressed.

It was just settling down at home, with Nan and Tui singing again, when I had to go to school. Out came the treadle Singer sewing machine and, pedalling madly, my mother made me a gym frock and a couple of winceyette blouses. 'My big girl!' she said, as I stood before her wearing my heavy-duty school uniform and my new school bag and a blazer that she was still paying off.

I toddled down to the corner with my big brother to get on the bus. As I remember it, there were two. One went to the Catholic school and the other to ours. At the bus stop the boys pushed one another around. There was a chant. 'Catholic dogs stink like frogs in their mother's bathing togs.' And: 'Proddy dogs stink like frogs . . .' Apparently I was a Proddy. I'd found out something I didn't know and I hadn't even got to school yet.

The first shock of my first day is that Grey Main School is not grey, but red brick. Set high on concrete foundations, the school building towers over the puddle-strewn asphalt playground. I climb up the big concrete steps and go through heavy wooden doors and find myself in a long corridor that seems to stretch to forever, full of gumboots thrown underneath coats hung on hooks. Big boys hurl themselves around. The noise is frightening. A bell rings. Edward hurries off to be somewhere else, leaving me in a crowded classroom, full of kids sitting on the mat. They all seem to know one another. The best plan is to do what they are doing, though no one is smiling very much. The teacher comes in and everyone sits up hyper-straight, arching their backs, arms folded, eyes looking skyward. The teacher greets us and everyone greets her in a sing-song but I don't know her name. She hands out strange old books with weird children in them.

I just want to head home to Nan, Jan and the radio.

Suddenly the back wall of the classroom folds back, revealing a whole other class full of kids. A piano rolls out – everything seems to be on wheels here – and a teacher sits at the piano and everyone does a thing called 'Farmer in the Dell'. It involves singing in a circle and choosing people to go in the middle until, finally, one special one is chosen and everyone else swings in and out and picks at their head, because they are the cheese.

I am horrified. I never want to be chosen as the cheese. It seems to me that the best thing to do is become invisible.

*

This turned out to be easy. There were always thirty-five to forty kids in my classes at primary school, and the boys dominated. They pushed one another over while the girls sat quietly, sharpening their pencils, and were nasty to one another occasionally. The baby boom of 1947 had hit the education system like a tsunami. The child-based, play-based progressive primary school system was fuller than full. We sang every folk song known to man, except the Māori ones. We played recorders, banged drums and folk danced to Africa, singing 'Kum Ba Yah' and 'Hold 'em down, you Wazi warrior'.

Mrs Morrisy was my teacher. She wore full skirts and smelt good. I liked having a bit of a yarn with her before school in the mornings. She had a little glass vase of fresh flowers she brought in every day to put on her desk and a pottery mug with her pencils in. She had an engagement ring made of diamonds and put her pen down to listen. When I was spinning her yarns, I may have exaggerated a thing or two. I liked to think my fibs were getting more subtle, but one day Tui said to me, 'Don't tell Mrs Morrisy our family business.' I don't know what it was I'd said, but I was now getting into trouble for telling the truth. Life was becoming a minefield.

I would walk home for lunch once I was in primer four. Sometimes I went down to the fish 'n' chip shop and my father would give me sixpence-worth of chips. He had a big machine that rumbled the potatoes together so they came out peeled. He would put a peeled potato on a plate between two flat metal clamps and pull a big lever. The spud pushed down into a metal grill to fall beneath, into a bowl miraculously transformed into fat, raw chips. Sixpence-worth gave me golden crisp hot chips wrapped in a newsprint packet and smothered in tomato sauce. I ate them slowly on my way back to school. In this way, I managed to minimise playground time. The playground was full of big kids playing bullrush and basketball and skipping. Frightening things happened in the shelter sheds. I stayed on the edges with two other girls, and played 'fairies'.

When a big paintbrush was thrust into my chubby hand, I finally found out what the lady on the radio had been talking about.

With newsprint strung over a painting easel, I could slosh out big dripping paintings.

The paint flowed from the loaded brush, and a line transformed the paper. It was a magic power. Pure pleasure. I never got over it.

After school, I would head home to boss Jan around. She had trouble jumping, so I took great delight in asking her to, and when she couldn't, I'd roll around on the floor laughing at her until Nan told me to stop.

I started learning the piano and kept going up to elocution lessons. Since my Sunday School outing, I was in demand. I became one of the regulars, alongside the man who could whistle like a blackbird and Janet Dunshea, the train driver's daughter who could sing operetta. (I think she was my agent.) I would change into a pretty dress that Tui had made me, and I would be picked up by someone's father or grandfather and taken to halls where, after the concert, supper from the Edmonds Cook Book was served. The cream sponges were my favourite. Once she was old enough, Jan joined in. We entered the competitions, which were held every school holiday. Teeming with kids, their mothers and teachers – all mainly women, dropped off by their hubbies – we would recite, Jan in the under-sixes, me in the under-tens, then run over the road to watch the dancing. I really wanted to learn tap dancing, but Tui said she didn't want to make the costumes. So I played the piano and elocuted.

Nan was my number one fan. 'Play us a tune, Gay.' As I played, she would wipe her hands on her pinny and sit down to rest her swollen ankles for a minute.

A word about tap dancing. I have had a few moments in my adult life when tap dancing would have come in handy. For example, when I was presenting an award for Best Actress, live on national TV, when the video feed went down. I was left onstage for interminable minutes. I had no idea what to do and just stood there doing nothing on the telly.

*

I haven't told you much about the Preston side of the family.

I had to put my father's childhood together like a jigsaw puzzle. It was like he thought I knew it all already. He said he'd spent weekdays down the Cobden Beach in Greymouth, bodysurfing with other boys.

'What about after that?'

'Oh, we'd go down the abattoirs.'

'What for?'

'They'd give us entrails.'

'Entrails?'

'Sheep's hearts, brains, lambs livers. Take 'em home for Mum to cook.'

So that's how he got away with not going to school. At school, he said, he'd get beaten up by the Marist brothers, who he referred to as 'those bullying bastards'.

The Prestons are a big Catholic brood. My father's mother had eleven children – her last three pregnancies were all twins. In Bluff, the Prestons had a fishing boat that fished Foveaux Strait, and every year the mayor of Invercargill awarded a big silver trophy to the boat that could deliver the first oysters of the season to the mayoral desk. Preston Fisheries won it so often that they were presented with the trophy to keep. It has graced a Preston family mantelpiece ever since.

My father was ten when they all left Bluff to set up a fisheries business in Mawhera (Greymouth). A concrete factory building with their name on the front still stands at the Blaketown docks.

My father used to tell us a story that he left Bluff a boy and arrived in Greymouth a man. I knew it was a long way, but not that long, surely. I now know that going to the coast would not have been a mission for the faint-hearted, especially with a big family. It is still not easy to get to the West Coast. Those mountains down the spine of Te Wai Pounamu stand like sentinels protecting the thin coastal strip that runs almost the entire length of the island. The passes are few and high. There was no tunnel at Otira in 1922, so travellers had to take a Cobb & Co. coach over the steepest part of Arthur's Pass.

Mid journey, a wheel went over the side. The horses stopped. The coachman climbed down, threw open the door, and told women and children to stay put and the men to get out and push. Sitting by his mother with his twin sister, ten-year-old Ed stayed put as instructed. The coachman pointed at him.

'You. Out.'

He did, and helped to push the coach. That's the way he told the story of how he became a man. He loved a sly, wry tale, my father did.

Ed gave himself permission to wag school ever after. It was a big family, and his attendance at school would have been the least of their problems. In Greymouth, he went next door to live with the Gilmour girls. If he spent most of his time under their feet with his twin sister Aileen and her friends, his busy mother was the last to mind. 'Go outside and play' was the mantra for all of us. Now, going outside to play is considered child neglect.

Because he never really learnt to write fluently, people thought my father was dumb, which I think he found relaxing. No doubt he had a much better time than his brothers, who remained under the stern eye of their father, old George Preston, and the Catholic clergy. His sisters looked after him, and Ed knew how to keep them entertained. His eldest sister, Mag, played the piano for the movies. He would get in free by carrying her sheet music. In this way he saw most of the silents more than once. He taught himself a line of deadpan pratfalls that always made people laugh. Years later, when I saw the Buster Keaton movie *The General*, I couldn't believe how many of my father's gags Buster Keaton could do. Whenever his sisters came to stay with us in Ida Street, they were always laughing.

My grandmother, Gran Preston, Bridget née Butler, was a mild woman who didn't go looking for trouble. I never knew her much, because the Protestant/Catholic divide dominated the family. When Ed married Tui, he 'turned'. That was what they called someone who'd left the Catholic church for another religion. At the wedding in the Holy Trinity Church in Greymouth, his side of the church was empty. His mother and sisters came to the reception, his brothers not at all. The Pope forbade their attendance, supposedly. This is my mother's version. But he had never 'turned'. He was staunchly non-aligned. My father had given up religion at seven – one day he was an altar boy and the next an agnostic – and he stayed to his own path without argument. Middle children can get away with that. I'm a middle child of a middle child. Keep the home crowd diverted, and quietly do your own thing.

I am sure Ed's ability to stay relaxed even in dire circumstances contributed to his escape from an Italian prison camp during that war they didn't like to talk about. He spent 1942 and 1943 in Italy incarcerated with other allied soldiers, while my mother went slightly crazy at home. When she received the telegram that he was Missing Believed Killed, her fragile psyche could not cope. She found it easier to think he was dead. By the time she got the telegram to say he was alive, she had moved on and found solace in the arms of a very good dancer. When Ed came home, having escaped into Switzerland for a year, she returned to the marital bed, but barely forgave him for having left home in the first place.

No wonder the war was such a secret time in our house.

Whenever Ed told us anything about his years in camp, the tales were always entertaining. There was one mime he did that would have us all in stitches. It involved him trying to sew a button on his flies with cotton that was far too long and that made the needle dangerous. He could make that gag last for ages. Us kids rolled around helpless with laughter while he maintained a deadpan, slightly hurt, quizzical expression. When I saw the exact thing in a classic Italian film, I realised he must have learnt that act from one of his Italian guards in the prison camp.

Later, I recorded some of his tales. I'll leave it to him to tell you one of them.

'We didn't get on with the Italian officers, but the enlisted men, they were just like us. Giorgio was one of the guards. He was a funny little bugger. He used to come over to our hut all the time to learn English. And I remember one time we were asking him, "What did you do in civvy street, Giorgio? What did you do?" He had a horse and cart with fruit and vegetables, and he was telling us this story about how his horse bolted on him one day and the horse took off. The cart went arse overhead and spilled his stuff all over the street and people were coming out from everywhere and stealing his fruit and vegetables.

'And to tell the story, he gave me his rifle to hold. So he's telling the story – "People stealing fruit everywhere" – and then he finishes the story and looks up and I have his rifle and I point it at him. I said, "Stick 'em up George, c'mon, stick 'em up."

'"Oh no, no, no." He was really upset. So I said, "I wouldn't hurt you, Giorgio," and gave it back to him. But I shouldn't have done that. It gave him a hell of a fright.

'After that, he couldn't do enough for us.'

When Ed escaped, he seemed to have plenty of lire, so I think his ability to trade and get on with people he liked may have saved him.

The Norcassa fish 'n' chip shop was over the road from the railway station. When the guards came in during oyster season, Ed would give them a baker's dozen. Thirteen Bluff oysters for the price of twelve. He may not have been educated, but my father was smart, and those extra oysters occasionally paid off. When our family travelled on the chuffer that went through the big mountains between Greymouth and Christchurch, we would sometimes hear the guards whisper as they passed, 'I haven't seen yous.' Then they'd carry on up the train clipping the tickets.

Going to Christchurch was our big adventure. We had households of cousins over there. Catholic cousins who lived in big cold houses and had asthma. It was in the family. Mart was the brother Ed loved. Tui got on with his wife, Inky, so Jan and I would go with her to stay at Avonside Drive, across the road from the Avon River. We learnt to genuflect and say proper grace, and I found a friend in my cousin Marlene who knew how to get under the house in order to dodge the endless dishes. When Marlene told me I was the best non-Catholic she knew, my heart swelled with pride.

Living in Greymouth, it seemed as though everything important happened in Christchurch – and that's where my eye specialist was, Dr Lindsay Burns. When I was seven, I had to go into Calvary Hospital for an eye operation. I had a turned eye that had been operated on when I was a baby, and it had got worse. The second operation must have cost Tui and Ed a fortune. But I never heard a whisper of it. I think they went around the extended family and collected the money. So at the age of seven, carrying a little suitcase with my new crayons, colouring-in book and newly made pyjamas, Tui and I got on the brand new railcar to go through those black mountains to Calvary Hospital.

I don't remember the operation at all, but I had to stay in bed, very still, in an adult ward, for what felt like a year. Tui was staying with relatives a tram ride away, and I became miserable. With big bandages over my eye, I couldn't really see. Colouring in was a trial. The days were interminable and the food was terrible. Breakfast, served every morning on a wooden tray, was a glass of milk I didn't drink and porridge I just pushed around on my plate.

Tui visited in the afternoons and the evenings for one hour. But one night, my beautiful mother did not arrive. Everyone else had visitors. I watched the ward entrance. Five minutes before everyone had to leave, the bell was rung. I was quietly sobbing when she finally walked in, and upon seeing her I amplified my sobs. Everyone turned to look at us. Instead of throwing her arms around me, she was annoyed. She wasn't that late, and told me firmly, 'Stop that grizzling right now.' Staying with relatives and managing on her own while I was in hospital was taking its toll on us both.

Tui was the one who always coped. She was ever watchful – the carer not just for our family and Nan but for everyone in the extended family. Whatever was wrong, she would fix it. Our house was sometimes blessed with cousins whose mothers needed a break, or who needed asthma treatment they couldn't get where they lived, or who needed a place to stay while their mother was in hospital.

But that day when she was late, the nuns must have noticed my misery. The next morning, after my untouched breakfast was cleared, a young nun swept in carrying a tray. She placed it on the white linen bedspread in front of me. Upon it sat a white dinner plate covered with an aluminium dome. With a flourish she pulled off the lid and, there before me – a perfectly poached egg on toast.

You don't forget things like that. I remain well-disposed to the nuns in blue and white.

In the way life has of unfurling unpredictably, in the 1960s, straight out of art school, I got a job at Calvary Hospital with the Little Company of Mary. Those big-boned Australian nuns ran a psychiatric day hospital in a little cottage sheltered by a big chestnut tree. I became an assistant – my first proper job.

After Tui's unsympathetic reaction at visiting hour, I toughened up. 'Maturing' is what they called it. Complaining was whinging, crying was blubbing and not to be tolerated. Even young children like me were trained out of it.

I think now that Edwardian working-class habits, combined with terrible communal grief generated by the Great War, instilled a very stoic strand in Pākehā behaviour. By the mid-1950s it was well ingrained. Sobbing was only allowed for middle-class women with hankies to cry into.

But my growing habit of not complaining was nearly the end of me.

On the morning of Easter Thursday, the pain in my side was gnawing. Tui had left early to join Ed in the shop. Nan was left in charge. When I told her about the pain in my side, she thought I was giving her the runaround. I was going to school and that was that.

During that day, I wandered around in a blur as the pain got worse. After school, I walked to my piano lesson, every step a knife in my side. The concrete steps up to Mrs Best's house seemed insurmountable. I began to crawl, and fell at her front door. Most alarmed, she called my father to come and get me.

Easter Thursday was late night, so Ed came in the van and left me with Nan before heading back to the shop, where the queues were growing. Nan made me a hot water bottle and a cup of tea that I immediately threw up. I crawled into my bed and wrapped myself around the hot water bottle, trying to find a comfortable place to lie, when the excruciating pain suddenly stopped. Such relief. I sank into my thumping headache, and closed my eyes.

I am shaken awake to see very worried adults gathered above me. Tui and Ed have come home to find me unconscious. They have called our family doctor, who has come to our house in the middle of the night. He orders them to take me to hospital immediately. My appendix has burst. I don't remember much after that, except sudden new pain with every stride as my father carries me up a hospital corridor. His big warm arms are so strongly wrapped around me. I feel safe.

As I write this down, I realise that a family GP arriving in the middle of the night to attend to a child running a temperature is almost unimaginable now. This was a time when doctors did house calls, your GP knew the entire family, and much preventative medicine was practised over a cup of tea in the kitchen.

On that stormy Easter Thursday, it was Dr Barry Dallas who saved my life. In this small-town West Coast hospital, at two in the morning, a talented surgeon performed an emergency operation that in those days many did not survive.

Years later, in London, in what felt like another life, Dr Dallas's name came up during a dinner in Knightsbridge.

The father of the house seemed excited to meet me. 'New Zealand eh? What part?'

I was used to nobody in England knowing anything about New Zealand. Everyone would agree they wanted to go there without having the foggiest clue where it was. They generally believed it to be a small island somewhere in the middle of Sydney Harbour. To my surprise, he revealed that he had been a BBC radio reporter accompanying the royal tour of 1953–54.

'What town?' he asked.

'Greymouth. You wouldn't know it –'

Then came the story his family must have heard before, many times.

He told me that when climbing the Franz Josef Glacier with the Queen's entourage, someone wearing crampons had stood hard on his hand then twisted their foot to get it off.

'It looked like a bag of blood and bone,' he said. 'I thought, "I will never play the piano again." But a remarkable surgeon in Greymouth saved it. Barry Dallas. Do you know him?'

I certainly did. 'He saved my life when I was seven,' I said.

With that, he leapt up from the table to sit at the baby grand in his sitting room to play a showy-offy piece of Rachmaninoff, while the family rolled their eyes.

Dr Barry Dallas later became mayor of Greymouth and in the 1980s had a lot to do with getting the sea wall built that has mitigated the worst of the mighty Mawhera bursting its banks and flooding the quay. That's small-town New Zealand for you. Full of extremely clever people who just rolled up their sleeves and did things.

I spent three weeks in hospital, then had six weeks to recuperate at home. Bliss. I could listen to the morning serials again, where Dr Paul was still having trouble in the great story of adult love, and Simon and the Gang were going strong. I could go into my own little book world – *Winnie the Pooh*, *The Famous Five*, *Black Beauty*. I loved being in front of the fire at Ida Street. I could sing with Nan, draw, play the piano, boss Jan around and occasionally relax behind the couch with a chocolate box full of forbidden black-and-white mysteries. Every week or so, Tui would go to Miss Bryant's library to get a romance and a mystery. Jan and I could sometimes go with her – Jan to get a Noddy book, and me for endless Famous Fives. We could also order magazines from England. They would arrive in big bundles on a ship, and in this way I was brainwashed by the British Empire. I longed to have midnight feasts and japes in a dorm. As we grew up, my habit of ordering magazines from offshore never left me, and I joined the Beatles fan club to get Beatles mags and *Nova* magazine. Meanwhile, I think Tui read every Agatha Christie and Ngaio Marsh ever published.

Tui had matriculated when she was only thirteen. That was the exam that you sat after three years of high school. Having passed two years early, she had to leave school to work in a mattress factory stuffing kapok into covers. Her wages supported Elsie and the younger ones. Ed was the same; they'd both worked from their early teenage years.

Fortunately for me, their children were born at a better time. Thousands of us got catapulted into an educated middle class. Teachers were highly esteemed in our house, in stature only just beneath vicars. 'Don't come running home complaining to me about the teacher,' Tui would say. 'Your father and I are not interested.'

But when I returned to school after my weeks of recuperation, I was all at sea. This was standard one, and the kids had learnt all sorts of things that were a total puzzle. Like maths. I never managed to catch up. And they would line up and throw and catch a basketball. I never managed that one either. Tried. Failed. Couldn't. Now I know that I am monocular, which means my spatial cognition is faulty. I can't judge where any moving object, even if it is coming straight at me, actually is. No excuse for the maths.

Our teacher, Mr Hopkins, had a crew cut and wore a Ming-blue tie and brothel creepers. He would frown down on us through a window from the corridor as we lined up in the playground. He used this exaggerated frown to watch us suddenly snap to attention when we saw him.

Now I know that his frown was probably a pūkana. He would whip out his guitar and sing Māori songs like 'Me He Manu Rere' and 'Pokarekare Ana'. I had no idea what they meant, but I loved the lilt. Our classroom was dominated by a big model pā made of matchsticks.

I recently found out that Mr Hopkins was indeed Māori. He came from a whaling family, and in 1957 he would have been a trailblazer.

But outside the classroom, Māori people were invisible to us. Once, on an unusual trip up the coast gravel road, my father pointed out the pā. There was Arahura, nestled between the road and sea. The roofs were rusty. From above, the streets looked crooked. No lampposts. It looked like nowhere I had seen before. 'That's where the Māoris all live,' my father said, as we trundled past on our way home to Greymouth.

One morning Mr Hopkins was doling out our exercise books, which he had marked overnight. He sat at his desk and called out each name one by one. When he got to me, instead of calling out my name he waved my exercise book above his head and told me to take it to the headmaster. My heart went straight to my mouth.

The playground is deserted and windswept. With a quaking heart, I head over to the big school to sit outside Mr Rollinson's office. I have only ever seen Mr Rollinson striding around the playground with his head in the air. He is scarily remote. The lady behind the typewriter at the desk outside his office is busy, and Mr Rollinson is busy behind his closed door. He is a thin-haired version of the scary God on Nan's wall.

I cling to the bench in the corridor, as two jittery big boys share whispered bravado nearby.

Mr Rollinson emerges. He tells me to stay there while he takes the boys into his office. I hear him giving them the strap. They come out waving their hot red hands to cool them, tears bursting from their eyes. No more smirking. Now it's my turn.

Mr Rollinson sits behind his desk and asks me to hand over my now tightly rolled exercise book. He opens it and reads.

I look at my shoes. Black lace-ups. Scuffed. Not shiny patent leather with a strap, like Lynn Truman's.

At last, Mr Rollinson closes the pages and hands me my book back.

'Very good,' he says. He stands up, and without smiling shows me out.

Back in the playground, I gather myself.

Very good. VERY GOOD. I went through all that and all he can say is 'very good'? I am really annoyed. I don't dodge the puddles on my way back to our little prefab. I splash them high. Why have black lace-ups if you can't get them wet?

I continue to find school mysterious, and I don't go out of my way to find a gang. Group friendship eludes me. Who is best friends with who is an exhausting mystery. How to join the gang – that's one other thing I must have missed while I was away sick.

# 6

# Napier Capers

Wearing my new glasses, it feels to me like someone has turned the lights on. I can see.

I am a little blonde girl with skinny white legs. I wear shoes and socks and my first pair of glasses from my eye specialist in Christchurch. Out at Westshore where we swim, the water is lippy-lappy and warm. And it's sunny and bright along Marine Parade, with a skating rink and a soundshell where they run a holiday programme for us kids.

In Napier, the electric wires are underground, the buildings in town are brightly painted in pastel pink and blue, and the sea doesn't pound on the shore and rattle stones with a tiger roar. No more looming dark hills, no more streets strewn with powerlines, no more little colonial houses, no more blinding black light through the rain.

Tui had decided that the chances of my brother leaving school only to become a miner or a forester were very high in Greymouth, so with the money from the sale of the Norcassa fish 'n' chip shop, we sold up and moved from the West Coast to Napier in Hawke's Bay. Tui's sister and Ed's brother lived in Hastings. Hawke's Bay was the place where us kids could get what our parents were sure would be better opportunities.

We joined the great Pākehā migration north that had started in the 1950s and eventually saw the small South Island towns empty.

Tui told Ed that if he bought another fish 'n' chip shop it would be divorce, so they bought a milk run, and settled us into a house in McVay Street that came with the business.

So there we were. I joined Nelson Park School, housed in a much less imposing building than Grey Main. With no assembly hall, assemblies were held outside on the hot asphalt facing the front portico. We'd sit in lines to stare up at the headmaster, who stood under faux Greek columns sweating in his suit, his voice distorted by the whistling microphone as we were told important things I couldn't understand, or immediately forgot, or didn't hear anyway because my mind constantly wandered to the words painted above him: *In All Things Seek the Highest*. Along with the relentless heat and light, this phrase penetrated my little West Coast soul.

Even though we were encouraged to understand that no one was better than anyone else, somehow we knew we were supposed to win. The Pākehā psyche holds an internal faultline that accounts for the way we appear to be easy-going but are in fact driven extremists. One minute we're a country that is actually achieving socialism with a human face; next minute we have deregulated everything and become the leading neoliberal country in the world. When the pendulum swings here, it swings fast and wide. In 1958 I was growing up in a country where the gap between rich and poor had narrowed and New Zealand had relatively high wage rates. Now, that gap is so wide it is debilitating.

Nelson Park School had smaller classrooms than Grey Main, which I liked, but I still didn't fit in. My standard three class had had the same teacher since standard one. He was a sportsman and had trained the class to be a terrific softball team. He was an active teacher – good at throwing his wooden blackboard duster at people, and good at using the strap every day. The kids were physically confident and many didn't wear shoes, let alone socks. I continued my usual strategy of keeping my head down, and left them to their ball-throwing after school to go home to Nan to play the piano and play with Jan, who was now in primer two.

79

I collected her from her classroom every day and we would walk home. She thought I knew everything. I was never one to say 'I don't know' when asked a question; I would just make the answer up. It was not uncommon for this to turn out badly. One day we were walking home and she asked me what the yellow letters on the road, 'FP', meant. Without a blink I said, 'Oh, that's an uncle of ours, Frank. Frank Preston. He was quite famous round here so they write his initials on the road.'

When Jan told her friends at school and was ridiculed, I was sternly told to stop telling lies. But behind the scolding I could sense amusement. Even at six years old, it took Jan more than a day to forgive me. I didn't care, because by that stage I was full of myself. This was because of an unusual unfolding of events to do with my teacher.

I had only been there a week when I found myself up the front of the classroom in a line with my hand out, to get the strap. As usual I had no idea what I had done wrong, and along the row he came with his leather strap. *Thwack, thwack, thwack*. My blood was boiling. This teacher was no Mr Hopkins. This teacher was never going to be my friend. *Thwack, thwack,* as leather hit skin. I had been smacked before by Tui, but not often, and never when she was angry. Just a bit of a tap I never took particularly seriously. We were not a 'Wait till your father gets home' family. Once, after Ed came back from the war, Tui asked him to 'discipline' my brother. Ed took his wailing son into the bathroom, got his razor strop down from the hook, and turned to his by now screaming child. Putting his finger to his lips, Ed hit the bathtub with a loud wallop a couple of times. My brother stopped mid-wail. Then Ed signalled for him to resume.

It was their secret. When they came out from the bathroom, Tui was pale with shock. My father told her, 'Don't you ever ask me to do that again,' and she never did.

When I came home that Friday after the mass strapping at school, I didn't tell them at home. No point. The teacher was always right, and my parents were already worn to a frazzle, with Ed working every hour God gave him and Tui up ladders painting walls in the rundown house. I did tell Nan, who saw my being strapped as a badge of honour. I think she must have been strapped regularly as a girl. But it was different for me. Being on the receiving end of a leather strap swung at me by a big person had rocked my confidence. How was I going to survive until the Christmas holidays two months away?

The following Monday, I walked to school with a heavy heart. But when I got there, something was wrong. My classmates were gathered in groups. Some were crying.

Our teacher was not going to teach us anymore. This bulky, avuncular, noisy man, who threw chalk and trained his pupils to swing baseball bats so that the ball went all the way to the boundary – had died. A sudden gall bladder infection had killed him.

The class fell into a deep, lost sadness. He had been their teacher for almost a fifth of their lives. They loved him.

And all I thought was: 'Good.'

I did wonder if Nan had asked God to strike him down, but I knew that that was beyond even Nan's powers.

As the 1957 school year unfolded, and the grief-stricken kids in standard three at Nelson Park School were taught by a steady stream of relief teachers, I was the one child in the class who could concentrate. I could read and write well (thank you, Grey Main School), and my new glasses gave me a certain librarian authority. I could see the blackboard. I could finish my written work and help others to do theirs. My lack of maths was completely overlooked, because I could draw princesses and horses. I was still skinny and white with glasses, but overnight I'd become 'brainy'. At the end of the year, I was named Head Prefect. I wasn't invisible anymore. The teachers looked at me with approval. The sun shone down on me. And Napier in the Christmas holidays was just bliss.

The lethal earthquake of 1931 had flattened Napier. But it had also delivered up, along with a new gleaming ferro-concrete art deco town, a small army of community-minded folk. In the immediate aftermath of the earthquake, they had erected a tent town in McLean Park and concentrated on lifting morale. By 1957, they were silver-haired but still rolling their sleeves up, sweating in the heat and running kids' competitions galore down at the soundshell on Marine Parade. That's where Jan and I spent our entire school holidays.

Every year they ran a big talent quest in Napier, with the finals on New Year's Eve and a sizable cash prize. Māori bands came through from all over Hawke's Bay and blew us all away. Rock 'n' roll hit big. Every boy wanted to be Elvis, and every girl wanted to be Elvis's girlfriend. The Māori boys ruled the Parade in their rock 'n' roll duds and their slicked-back quiffs. Later, Jan sang folk songs in a little school group she formed, and one year I did a pretty weird version of Gerald McBoing Boing. (Bobby McFerrin, eat your heart out.) They also had a Best Legs competition. I won a guinea. Winner of Napier Best Legs Competition 1960. That's me. Only came second with Gerald.

In that move to Hawke's Bay, my brother had metamorphosed too. Edward turned into Ted, who owned an F-hole guitar. While we were setting up house, he had done his final fifth form year as a boarder at Greymouth High School with Samoan boys, and returned to McVay Street wearing lei and colourful shirts and playing the ukulele. He played the washboard in the Cool Four, a high-school band that practised at our place. Tui and Ed were too busy fixing up the kitchen to worry about the faded wallpaper in the front room. Ted and his mates painted every wall a different colour – bright blue, shocking pink, electric green, lemon yellow – and made it their band room. Jan and I would sneak in among the big boys to listen to them practising. Ted took to playing our piano like Jerry Lee Lewis. When he did 'Great Balls of Fire' we thought he was a genius. They had a tea chest bass at first and did a searing version of the Lonnie Donegan hit 'Rock Island Line'. Radio jock Cham the Man and engineer Rocky Duchet did a talent showcase that went out live from the local radio station on a Saturday night. When the Cool Four played on 3ZB, Jan and I were allowed to stay up late to listen, so we rocked around the radio at home. The *Lever Hit Parade* helmed by Selwyn Toogood was broadcast across the land, and I really did feel like life had turned the light on. Tammy was in love, and love letters were written in the sand . . .

Tui's sister Ida lived in Hastings with her husband, Vic, who was a well driller. The Prestons and the Boags spent plenty of time together, and my cousin Maxine and I became firm friends. She was younger but more responsible than me. Both middle girls, both with mothers who were hard on us. But Maxine thought I was spoilt, because the Preston girls didn't have to make their beds in the morning.

As we drove between Napier and Hastings, past the fertiliser plant with its bright lemon piles of superphosphate near the road, the car filled up with the smell of chemicals and we made jokes about how somebody farted. In the 1950s we had no idea of the environmental damage caused by superphosphates seeping into the groundwater. Maxine is now a long-standing Napier city councillor and deals with these issues, along with many others that were quietly simmering in the underbelly of our bright, white, lovely lives.

Though school was often profoundly confusing, at Nelson Park I hit my stride writing stories. I was Enid Blyton meets Randy Stone.

After listening to *Night Beat* on the radio – eyes wide open, sitting bolt upright in the dark when we were supposed to be asleep – I started writing strange police procedurals, like a little steam train. I would rush the formal part of an English lesson to get to the 'free writing'.

But the education system was under enormous stress. With the sheer number of babies born after the war, there just weren't enough trained teachers to go round. At the end of my standard four year, yet another relief teacher grabbed a story I had written in my exercise book and copied my bad spelling onto the blackboard. He called the class to attention and read out my colloquialisms. Bad grammar. Bad spelling. He encouraged the class to laugh at my turns of phrase. They didn't. They were just as mystified as I was.

At the time, I absorbed this public shaming without too much heartache. If the rest of the class had laughed, I might have felt differently. But it wasn't until thirty years later, when I began writing the story that became the film *Perfect Strangers*, that I realised I'd stopped writing my own made-up stories that day. Since then I had written only essays, applications and adaptations of other people's stories for film scripts. I'm still no good at grammar. I write as I speak. You may have noticed.

But in retrospect, I think that public putdown turned me in on myself. I became less resilient. I was a strung-out late developer, a young girl among other girls who were sprouting brave bosoms. Not me. And sometimes in Napier there were nasty jolty earthquakes, real sudden rattlers, that seemed to amplify my feelings of dislocation.

In our new Hawke's Bay life, Ed would get up at two in the morning to deliver milk to the Napier Public Hospital, then go back to the milk treatment station, unload the empties, load the truck again and deliver milk to the plutes who lived on Bluff Hill. He'd employed a string of milk boys, who he generally liked unless they stole the milk money. He'd get home by eight, eat breakfast, then drive out to Bay View to work in Robertson's Orchard. He did that year round, picking, spraying, pruning. The orchardists were two brothers, Alec and Doug, and our families became close friends.

Tui found a job in a hat factory, Harris Hats. After tea every night, she'd do the tokens, counting money into piles of pennies. Jan and I would count yellow milk tokens into little bags that we'd have stamped ED PRESTON MILK VENDOR.

It was a family affair. Tui kept the accounts. Things were saved up for. Ed bought her an electric sewing machine for her birthday, and she was joyous. Immediately she saved the child benefit she collected from the post office once a fortnight, bought yards of white net, and sewed and sewed and sewed. That was the beginning of the end of the naked windows in the front room, and sadly it was not long before the colourful walls surrendered to floral wallpaper.

I woke every school day to an ornate alarm clock playing a Viennese waltz. When it was wound up it would play really fast.

If I kept snoozing it would get slower and slower. Eventually it would stop, and blearily I'd head to the cold front room to practise my scales and arpeggios. Scales and arpeggios are a terrible way to learn any instrument. I saved up my pocket money and bought sheet music for 'Baby Elephant Walk' and 'Moon River'. Henry Mancini was my man. I'd seen the films these songs were in, but I needed the sheet music, because playing by ear was considered sinful. I had to read the sheet music, then memorise the piece. A laborious process, and not the best way to play the piano. So I never really learned to play the piano. I learned to 'work' the piano – at great expense, taught by the best piano teachers in the district. It was hard repetitive work.

Sadly, I was quite good at it. I wanted to play rock 'n' roll like my brother, but Tui had a fit at the very suggestion. I knew that giving up classical piano was out of the question. Over time, my illustrious Royal College of Music exam marks show a trend from distinctions to skin-of-the-teeth passes.

Ted left home for teacher's training college at Ardmore. The band boys all headed out to work in chemists or to sell paint. Life became depressingly suburban.

At Napier Intermediate, I hung out with Jim Vivieaere and his mate, who lived in a boys' home up on the hill. When Jim told me he was a Rarotongan prince, we giggled. I was transported by the possibility, but I didn't believe it for a minute and neither did he, really.

It turned out it was absolutely true. Jim was a Rarotongan prince. Once he graduated from art school he would become a trailblazing curator and facilitator of Pacific art, building a pathway from galleries in Tāmaki Makaurau to Rarotonga and beyond.

But back in form one, Jim and I were united by our mutual regard for one another's ability to draw. If you wanted a princess, I did it; if you wanted horses, Jim took over. We also shared a general sense of dislocation from the mainstream. We were disengaged.

Once a week, our class was marched from our little prefab, where our desks were crammed together in rows, to a spacious, high-ceilinged room in the old building. The art room. One day, we had a visitor.

The lesson is set, but I'm not doing it. I'm drawing a horse for someone. During art classes Jim and I are busier than usual, and I do Jim's overflow on the horse front. (He doesn't get asked to draw princesses.) Our teacher is more animated than usual, excited even. The art advisor has arrived. He is introduced to us – Mr Whiting. He's a good-looking Māori man who has a few laughs with our teacher then wanders about, looking over our shoulders with a genial sense of approval. Caught drawing horses, I try to hide them, but he doesn't seem to mind that I am off-task.

When the bell rings – something that always makes me jump, since the last cluster of earthquakes – Jim and I are asked to stay behind. Caught for the horses.

But no. We are told that for the next week, we don't need to go to school. We are to go to the basement of the museum for extra art.

Art. All day, every day. I can't believe it. No times tables or spelling tests, no sitting up with my arms folded, no being glared at. It's almost too good to be true.

The first day, I'm out of bed while the alarm clock is in full, fast 'Blue Danube', and my scales and arpeggios run in effortless ripples. By 8:15 I'm off on my bike to the museum, to find the whole building closed. I sit under a tree and wait. I look over at the new cathedral still being built. Napier is quiet.

I wonder what that hot day was like when the old brick cathedral fell down on the lady who couldn't be saved before the fire came.

That was the Napier earthquake story that was always told. A beam had fallen on a praying woman. She remained trapped inside the cathedral during the aftershocks and had to be given a lethal injection before fire engulfed the building. It was a terrible tale, shocking, overwhelming. The story hid as much as it revealed.

Eventually Jim arrives and we open a side door that takes us into the shadowy silence of the closed museum. Strange objects hover in the gloom. There's a mokomokai in there, along with Te Kooti's Bible.

It seems to me that these ancient exhibits have become untethered from their glass cases, and now spirit figures lounge in the shadows.

We follow the sound of voices coming from a staircase that leads to a basement which stretches the length of the building. The sun penetrates high windows at footpath level, where I can see busy feet walking outside. The sun illuminates a room full of unspeakable treasures. Shelves line the walls, crammed with every kind of paint and paper you could think of. Reams of creamy thick drawing paper, expensive paintbrushes still in their packets, tubes of paint, pencils, pastels – every art material of imported wonder sits before me. Clay is ready for action on a swanky pottery wheel alongside a sculpture armature with a head under construction.

I am in the Hawke's Bay Education Board art materials storeroom, which is also a studio for their art advisors. It looks like heaven. The week ahead stretches out like the beginning of the holidays.

At one end of a large high wooden table, a relaxed group of adults are having a smoke and a cup of Gregg's Instant. They introduce themselves. No Mr or Miss something-or-other, like our teachers at school. First names here. Our art room visitor's name is Cliff. Someone called Para is visiting today. A pottery woman in a tweed suit stubs out her cigarette and grabs her bag and is gone, not very interested in us. This I take as a good sign. They are heading out to schools around Hawke's Bay. As they leave, Cliff waves his hand around and tells us to make ourselves at home. We are left to do as we like in this magic kingdom. And you can boil the jug and drink instant coffee whenever you like.

In the basement I can work without bells interrupting, and my low-level anxiety finally settles, turning into delight. I have found my place. The art room. A life that is about getting up in the morning and actually doing what you like to do. Every day. And it was sitting here waiting for me all along.

Cliff Whiting and Para Matchitt were just two of the art advisors who came and went every day. They often did their own work after they returned from school visits. I noticed their love, care and attention for what they were doing. We all had to be kicked out when the museum closed at five. Without being able to articulate it at the time, I knew in my bones that I could just bide my time. I had found my escape.

I dusted my dressing table with less dread each day.

Talking about finding the art room can sound a bit trite. But art – drawing, writing, disappearing into a story – can feel like an escape into somewhere more interesting. I am sitting here, dear reader, as the rain pelts down outside, and my knees are cold, but I only become aware of that if I stop writing. It is a form of astral travel. I have never liked organised games but I have found a world of play. I'm absorbed in making something, in dreaming up problems and solving them. I have grown an internal world where I can please myself. As an adult my mantra became 'Make your play your work'. This of course contains a trap, because you never really feel like stopping, and social life can become an onerous duty. As Rita Angus said to Jacqueline Fahey, 'Gentility. So dangerous.' Artists are working all the time. It's challenging, it can drive them crazy, but they like it best.

Dusting my dressing table aside, I was pretty busy outside of the art room. Mona Walls, my music teacher, teamed me up with her son Peter, who was a brilliant piano player and around the same age as me. We were in hot demand that year, playing duets in local variety concerts. We did a mean, constantly accelerating Rondo alla Turca to some acclaim. I also took part in Miss Dykes' recital, held every year at the Napier Municipal Theatre.

If Helen Dykes had lived in LA she would have been famous. Shirley Temple was her template. Of considerable corseted girth, her ample bosom well strapped, her hair in a tight perm, she sat at a big upright German piano and plunked out songs from the stage and screen, singing loudly so that we didn't need to. Her studio was in a converted garage at the front of her brother's home but it could have been in West Hollywood as far as Miss Dykes was concerned.

The mothers of her talented youngsters were terrified into sewing very intricate costumes for the recital. We swung plastic umbrellas around in unison and smiled falsely, singing tunes from musicals we had never heard of, like 'Singin' in the Rain' and 'A, You're Adorable, B, You're So Beautiful'. Unlike all the other adults we knew, who still had all that was British embedded in their DNA, Miss Dykes was in thrall to American glitter and gloss. We were her fantasy kids' talent troupe, and no matter how bad our performances, she was ecstatic. Her Estée Lauder was even more pungent and her lipstick even brighter when, at Christmastime in an almost-packed Municipal Theatre, her recital was performed to adoring parents. On that magic night, they all forgot how annoying making the costumes had been.

Printed programmes noted every performer in every item. After his mother died, Peter Walls – by now the CEO of the New Zealand Symphony Orchestra – found among her papers a programme for Miss Dykes' Recital containing an italicised note, in much smaller font, stating that my piano performance was provided courtesy of my piano teacher, Mrs Mona Walls. (Peter wasn't mentioned.)

We loved it. Miss Dykes loved it. We were the children she'd never had.

One year she crammed Jan and me into her Morris Minor and, joining a small convoy of devoted mothers (not mine), we drove to Gisborne for the competitions. Along with us was a slightly strange, oddly childlike man who may have been someone's relative or friend. 'Don't worry about him, he's harmless,' Miss Dykes told us, and instructed us that if he did anything 'funny', to tell her immediately. I had no idea what she meant. Miss Dykes' positive certainty and relentless optimism must have protected us. Teddy was indeed harmless, a benign presence who laughed at all our jokes and had a little notebook he liked to write in. Off we went on an adventure, firmly rooted in the films of Busby Berkeley. The rain was the kind you sang in, even though the heater in the car didn't work and condensation on the windscreen was running down on the inside as the fragile windscreen wipers outside worked overtime.

Every Sunday, Miss Dykes would toot her horn and Jan and I would race out to cram into that little car to go down to 3ZB, the local radio station, to perform in radio plays. Neville Madden was our radio man. He was not like the glamorous Neville Chamberlain, 'Cham the Man', of radio talent quest fame. This Neville had a thin, clipped moustache and a sonorous BBC voice. He wore impeccably tailored tweed jackets and creased gaberdines. Carrying a clipboard in one hand and a constantly smoking cigarette in the other, he looked the perfect English version of a radio drama producer. Us kids were his cast. We'd practise for three Sundays, then the big day would come when we recorded. On those days, Neville Madden would run around between the glassed-in studio and the engineering booth, his tie loosening and dark pools of sweat gathering under his arms. Half-smoked cigarettes were rammed into the bellies of the heavy glass ashtrays that were scattered about as Neville lost his mind.

Occasionally Miss Dykes and he would get thin-lipped with one another on a recording day, but Miss Dykes later pointed out that Neville Madden had been in the war. Sometimes he'd slept only five hours a night. So he was to be forgiven.

In these endless Blytonesque adventures, I played everything from a gate to a crocodile and Janet, Joan or Mary to someone else's John. We performed in full runs with our script pages paperclipped to cardboard so they didn't rustle and spoil the sound. We tip-toed about, bathed in the red glow of the RECORD light, mouthing urgent instructions to one another.

Tui cared not a jot for children's radio plays. As far as she was concerned, I had to get my letters – Trinity College and Royal Schools examination qualifications – in order to fully achieve her ambition for me, which was to teach piano when I grew up and got married to that husband I was going to be following about. The word was that the most serious senior piano teacher in Napier was Miss Winifred McCarthy, so without any further discussion I had my last lesson with Mona Walls and began lessons with Miss McCarthy.

Miss McCarthy lived by herself in a big house on Shakespeare Road populated with porcelain antiques that had belonged to her parents and survived the earthquakes. Her dark front room was furnished with wine-brown-coloured sofas and a baby grand piano. She was the exact opposite to Miss Dykes. She sat on a chair to the side behind the piano stool, smoking Pall Malls, listening sadly to my attempts at Bach, pining for London where she had studied concert piano in her twenties at the Royal Academy of Music. Standing in the low sun as dust mites danced around her, remembering her life as a music student, she would tell me about the thrill of Covent Garden concerts where she sat in the cheap seats, and the Royal Opera House where she sat in the gods.

This I encouraged her to do. Johann Sebastian was not my favourite, and any time I could make her a cup of tea and encourage her to reminisce, my lesson could have less piano and more stories. It was here, dunking wine biscuits in milky tea as Miss McCarthy crossed her thin bandy legs, puffed on another Pall Mall tailor-made and leaned forward, that I learned more detail of the famous story of 'poor Dr Waterworth'. It was Dr Waterworth who had run down Shakespeare Road, just outside the window, to administer the lethal dose of morphine to a woman trapped under a beam in the cathedral. They hadn't been able to get her out. With the fire coming closer, the woman's son had run up the road and found Dr Waterworth. Poor Dr Waterworth, who had to administer a lethal injection just as the fire advanced towards them.

Even as I reached for another wine biscuit, I wondered, not for the first time, what was being hidden in this story. I wanted to find out more about that sunny morning in February 1931 when the whole place fell down.

Napier in the late 50s was a treasure trove of survivor stories. Earthquake survivors were everywhere and beginning to talk about it. When my father dropped me off outside St Mary's Home, where he had organised a holiday job for me, within minutes, with a starched cap perched on my head, wearing a crisp white uniform, I became 'Nurse Preston', in earthquake story heaven. As these elderly ladies had their backs washed and their poor swollen feet massaged, though they couldn't remember what had happened yesterday or even where they were today, they could tell me about that terrifying day when without warning the ground belched and sighed and the houses screamed as everything was thrown into the air in shuddering jolts that shook the place to smithereens.

It was easy to encourage these stories to flow. And every single one was surprising and I had heard none of them before.

Maybe I had become drawn to true stories after my fictional detective romps had been ridiculed in class. The more dramatic the better. And I didn't write the stories down. I remembered them in great detail.

The deputy headmistress of Napier Girls' High School told me she had found herself in charge of a group of girls who couldn't find their parents. 'We had to sleep outside on the ground up at the Botanical Gardens, where mothers had been evacuated from the hospital and were having babies on stretcher beds under the trees. Those girls grew up fast. But I had a boil on my bum that festered and grew. It was most uncomfortable, and I was too embarrassed to seek help, so it became badly infected. I ran a high fever, and nearly died of blood poisoning from an infected boil rather than actually in the earthquakes.'

Personal experience doesn't often feel particularly consequential but, simply told, it reveals a universe.

Another woman told me, 'The men came around wanting blankets. They said they would return them. I gave them my best woollen ones. They never gave them back. They said they would, but they didn't.' She sat there telling this story over and over in the dim day room. This was because I had rather too enthusiastically painted Santa and Rudolf and the sleigh all over their sunny windows for Christmas, leaving the ladies sitting in the gloom.

To me, these stories coloured the official one, which was all about the brave sailors of the *Veronica*, the ship that sailed to Napier to bring emergency supplies and young heroes to clean up the rubble amid the violent aftershocks. A grateful community still rang the *Veronica* bell at midnight on New Year's Eve. Heroes those sailors undoubtedly were, but it took me a half a lifetime to find out the true, ghastly, terrible thing of the most lethal earthquake in our history.

Thirty years after I sat in Miss McCarthy's shadowy lounge on Shakespeare Road, I made a film about the survivors.

\*

It was 1998 and the museum and art gallery were refurbishing their earthquake exhibition. Would I like to make a film that would play every hour in the basement? That basement, the very one where I had splashed about in the company of Jim Vivieaere, Cliff Whiting and Para Matchitt. I did not need to be asked twice.

Unlike the time when I was impersonating a nurse at St Mary's Home, these first-hand stories would be from survivors who were children at the time. The year 1931 was nearly seventy years ago by now, and the stories I was seeking were not fresh. They had been told over and over. It's like there is a tape recording stored in the brain of how a story is told, and it has been playing again and again, the story repeated rather than remembered. The tale gets polished and becomes a little too pat. This mechanism can be even more pronounced when the memory is of trauma.

In Napier, I wanted to find the people who had rarely been asked. Where in the official version were Māori experiences ever mentioned? I wanted to know. The books I found covered it in a sentence: our Māori were very good, they looked after themselves, or words to that effect. I knew where to start. Despite the woeful life expectancy statistics for Māori, I hoped we might find a kaumātua who had been a child in 1931 and might tell us something of their experience.

She comes to sit before the camera on the stage at the Century Theatre. Outside, the afternoon is balmy, but the theatre is cool and dim, with her seat carefully lit. Hana Cotter is a kaumātua of Ngāti Kahungunu and a leading campaigner in the local kōhanga reo movement. Her moko, a bright young woman with a caring heart, has brought her in. As Hana takes her seat and we prepare the lighting, she is quiet, possibly tired. I am excited. As I calm the butterflies in my stomach, I have no idea what her tale will be. We say a karakia.

Then I ask about her early life in Hastings growing up near Bridge Pā.

'Oh, we lived in a new house made of wood,' she says. 'We had very little in our home but we loved it because we thought we were rich. We had a floor. We had lino that was kept nice and shiny.'

From this moment, I know that her first-hand account is going to be exactly what I am after. She describes the earthquake arriving like a train crashing into their kitchen. Still in shock, she and her family gathered at the marae, where it was decided that two work crews, organised like shearing gangs, would go to help clear the rubble. One would go to Hastings and the other to Napier. Two girls went with each crew to make the cups of tea. 'We didn't realise what really it was like till we got here,' Hana says. 'Oh gosh, we thought it was the end of the world.'

The women got the cups of tea ready, but soon they began to help the men. 'You see them struggling with the bricks and that, well, you can't stand there and look. What do you do? You throw your coat off and get in there and start helping them with pulling some of the people that was, you know, captured underneath the bricks and that.'

I am listening intently. She slips in and out of the past and present tense. 'You couldn't look at what you see,' she says. 'We have to get a handkerchief and tie it in front of our nose, just our eyes, because some of them, the smell is coming up with the smoke and with the human flesh, I suppose, and all these . . . It was sad. We just couldn't turn away, it had to be done. Well, sometimes it takes about two or three of us to pull it out. And if it was too hard then we beckon to the boys to come and do it, but if us girls can do it, we went ahead and did it.'

The hair on the back of my neck is standing up and my body is fizzing. The spirits are walking, not for the first time in my experience of this museum.

'We didn't come through till the day after the earthquake. And others, I believe that were there, they took away those that . . . had breath in them, breath of life. But those that they couldn't, those are the ones that we tore out and put them onto the tray, and then they take them over to the cemetery and bury them there. When the tray was full, they take them over. It's sad, I tell you. It was sad. It really made us realise the importance of one another. When we went back, our kaumātua got us all together and we had to pray. You know they, they karakia-ed us – did what they could, they karakia-ed us and asked the blessings of the Lord to help us overcome whatever there is, and whatever we've been through.'

'Seek and ye shall find,' as Nan always said. Here is not only a first-hand account from the front line of the clean-up, but a story told from the point of view of the most unlikely person – a sixteen-year-old Māori teenager who threw her coat off to help her cousins pull bodies from hot bricks. Now there is an opportunity to enlarge the official version of this story.

Hana's account plays every hour in the exhibition, which has run for years. The audience cries with her.

But when I go looking through the black-and-white news footage, I can find no sign of any Māori work gangs, and certainly none of young Māori women helping pull bodies from the rubble. The visual archive is full of those brave sailors. Their white uniforms among local men in shirtsleeves – no Māori, no women. As with so many other official versions of history, their stories are left out.

Another astonishing tale is told by May Blair, the sister of one of those sailors. Her white-uniformed brother slipped away from the inner city to go home to check that his family was all right and to help his mother put up a tent in the backyard. He missed the boat back to the *Veronica* that night and was deemed Absent Without Leave. He panicked and went on the run, and was later dishonourably discharged. May says he never recovered from the shame of it.

And then came the fire. I find black-and-white photographs. There is the well-known image of a fireman walking away from a burning building, and there are more.

In the year after the quakes, the A.B. Hurst Studio sold little photo albums, mainly showing the city in the following days – Dr Moore's hospital on a lean, pretty girls standing in a crack nearly as deep as they were tall, the cathedral in ruins, cars teetering into fissures. In every album there was one image of the fire. Those photos were often mysterious. One photo showed a couple of boys standing beside their bikes, the air almost completely filled with white smoke. It revealed as much as it hid. I began collecting these photos.

When the 7.8 quake hit, the photographer Arthur Hurst was in his studio in a ferro-concrete building in Emerson Street. He grabbed his large-format camera, ran down the stairs, went into a chemist's shop through a broken window and filled his pockets with rolls of film stock. He may have gone back into his building to get his tripod. For the next couple of hours he recorded Napier mutating from a wrecked city into a huge firestorm. The first photo is of shocked people in their office clothes scurrying in blurs among wonky wooden buildings.

We see the fire start in Hastings Street, supposedly begun in a chemist's shop from a Bunsen burner. The fire brigade runs out of water because the reservoirs are cracked. A desperate bid to use sea water is made, but shingle clogs the hoses. Over the next few hours the fire takes hold and rampages through the city as rescuers stand by helplessly, finally forced to abandon their rescue efforts. The only building that stays straight and standing is the recently completed ferro-concrete State Advances Building. The last images are of completely deserted streets and a huge ball of fire rolling down Dickens Street, coming straight for the camera.

I had been right about the story Miss McCarthy had told me about the woman in the cathedral. Shocking though it is, that tale covers over the larger tragedy that was too big to be shared. It was hidden in plain view in the story of the woman in the cathedral.

The fire.

I knew about the fire, but hadn't made the connection. The terrible death toll was because there was no time to haul the trapped people out. Their deaths were from smoke inhalation.

I broke my own rule of filming only first-hand accounts, when Sally Sutherland, the granddaughter of Edith Barry, the woman who had been trapped, came in to be interviewed. We filmed the burnt coins that as a young child she had found in her grandmother's charred purse.

Towards the end of our time filming at the museum, I invited Arthur Hurst's daughter, Audrey McKelvie, to tell me her father's story.

Audrey was one of the mothers who had hovered in the background watching over us teenagers during the cultural blossoming of Napier in the 60s. Her son had a motorbike and had taken me on hair-raising rides around the St John's Cathedral car park after youth club on Friday nights – something both our mothers would have looked upon with considerable disapproval. We'd had no idea of the ground we stood on. We were the bright generation, raised in the light.

When Audrey arrived to be filmed, she brought with her 'Poppa's camera'. Here was another closely held tale, rich in detail and told with pride, recounted outside the family for the first time. Hers was the experience of a fifteen-year-old girl – one of those who grew up fast in the Napier Botanical Gardens – whose father, in a crisis, chose his camera over helping in the rubble, and paid the price.

Audrey spoke with sadness of the near-nervous breakdown he suffered after the quakes. People held negative opinions of a photographer who turned to his craft rather than join the rescue efforts. Hurst Studio was criticised by some for 'making money from disaster'. This is why a fire album was never put together. So I committed to laying hands on all eighteen images and putting them in order – not easy, because the negatives were burnt in a studio fire in the late 1960s. In ones and twos, with the museum's help and some foraging in various archives and family garages, I managed to put together about twelve prints, all in various stages of disrepair. It was not that hard to put them in order and bring that terrifying time to life. Sound effects and camera moves made a compelling sequence of that day when Napier exploded.

Sometimes, when I am back in Napier, I stand in that sunny art deco town I grew up in and can almost see a shadow of the wrecked, burnt town. All thanks to a local photographer with a brilliant eye and the presence of mind to face the blaze of the fire itself and later of searing public opinion.

Not only that, but thanks to their generously told personal recollections, the earthquake survivors' stories have been shared with thousands of visitors to the museum.

Collecting oral histories has grown from a childhood curiosity into a lifelong habit. I love it. I especially love finding images and adding sound effects and making films from fragments. If I can collect enough memories of one event, a story net emerges. It's like pulling fish from the sea. Stories intersect in unpredictable ways, revealing an event in three dimensions. A people's history.

And when I was making *Survivor Stories*, one of the subjects told me something else that was as surprising as it is inspiring. May Blair, the sister of the young sailor who went AWOL, was on her first day at technical college the day the earthquake hit. The big brick building fell down around her, killing a boy she knew. She was evacuated out of Napier with other earthquake refugees, and, to her everlasting shame, she never completed her education. Later, as a young mother on the school committee of Nelson Park School, it was May who suggested the motto that I had puzzled over during hot assemblies: *In All Things Seek the Highest.*

How ironic. All her life she had regretted that her education had so abruptly ended. That school motto must have encouraged many students to aim higher. I am just one of them.

# 7

# The Circus Is in Town

Back in the 60s, we were growing up in blithe amnesiac bliss. We had no idea of history. History was something that well-meaning educated white men told with enormous authority in books about the British and European wars of the days of yore. Nothing to do with me. I went to the new co-ed high school named after William Colenso. We were sent off to the library to find out all about him. The pages of the big book in the Napier Library, where Colenso's Māori 'mistress' featured, were well-thumbed. I felt sorry for Mrs Colenso, who in 1845 reportedly walked over rugged country from Waitangi to Gisborne to have her baby under the care of a fellow missionary.

On my first day, wearing my new school uniform, I parked my bike next to a girl who soon became my best friend. Kay McCormick's parents believed in talking to the teachers, and in this way they negotiated extra art for their daughter. Derek Olphert, the art teacher, was highly regarded and the main reason I had chosen Colenso High School in Mārewa. I went with Kay when she reported to the deputy head. A special schedule had been organised for her. Riding on her coattails, I got extra art too. Six hours a week squeezed from other subjects, including maths!

But this knowledge, I knew, had to be kept secret. Every time I answered the looming question 'What do you want to do when you grow up?' I seemed to get myself into deep water. When I was eleven,

I announced that I wanted to be a doctor. My admiration for doctors had never faded after my life was saved by one. Tui's reaction was immediate. She took me to the doctor.

'She wants to be a doctor, Dr Russell.'

I am sitting in Dr Russell's consulting rooms, looking at him over his big oak desk. Tui is hovering behind me. Dr Russell seems puzzled to see her distress. He wears a tweed jacket and has removed a wart from my foot.

'That is a fine ideal,' he tells me, as he looks over my shoulder at my mother.

'But we can't afford it, Doctor, and she'll just get married anyway.'

Dr Russell nods slowly as the penny drops. He gives me a long, kindly look.

'How's your maths, Gay?'

He must have known. He tells me that there is a lot of maths involved in training to become a doctor. So that is the end of that idea. Being a nurse or a teacher is much more acceptable for a girl. Owning up to wanting to be an artist was clearly not.

Our home didn't have anywhere to do art, except for the kitchen table after meals were cleared. And after Ted departed for training college, with the big front windows bedecked in two layers of frilled lace curtains, the cold front room where the piano stood had been transformed into the lounge. Floral Axminster carpet had invaded. It was for visitors only, and usually deserted, apart from Christmas time and during Ranfurly Shield games.

Behind our place was McLean Park, where all the representative rugby games were played. A shed down the yard at the back fence had been reinforced for us to stand on. From the roof, we could watch with binoculars for free. One sheet of the corrugated-iron fence had been cunningly turned into a gate so that, unseen by the throngs, we could keep an eye out from the shed roof and when the coast was clear, signal to those standing beneath us when to duck through without paying. We had a lot of friends when Hawke's Bay was winning.

On those occasions, after the game, there was beer and yarns to be had in the front room, but Tui would call me back.

'Don't go in there, Gay, it's men's talk.'

So I would help her in the kitchen, preparing sausage rolls and cups of tea. Not so interesting – although I have to admit that Tui's sausage roll recipe is pretty good. You can try it; it's printed at the back of this book.

Life could have inexplicable constrictions, but Jan and I managed to find plenty of holes in the social fabric. A bit like the back fence. We secretly auditioned for the Napier Operatic production of *The Music Man*. She scored the lead ingénue role, Amaryllis, while I managed to get a line or two in the chorus. Trouble. Not only a song in the show, but an immediate source of conflict at home. The front room filled up with serious people talking Tui into letting Jan, who was eleven, perform at night.

'Her school work could be affected,' Tui argued.

Finally, it was negotiated that Jan would play every alternate night and share the role with Yolande Gibson. (Both of them went on to be successful professional entertainers. The opera houses and municipal theatres of small towns delivered a lot of talent during the 50s and 60s.) And I loved that musical. The Napier leads were terrific and the am-dram adults had a whale of a time, falling in love with the wrong people and getting completely plastered at rowdy parties at classy houses on the hill. No one cared too much about me being there; it was one another they fancied. I remained aghast at my lack of bosom, but in retrospect, I think – coupled with my glasses – it kept me clear of marauding hands. I was a beanpole and was only rescued from obscurity once Twiggy came onto the scene a few years later.

At school I stuck to a little L-shape of the art room, away from the mainstream action, occasionally emerging to sing in the madrigal group and play the cello badly in the school orchestra. With Bill Mori and Alison Cavell, whose father had a monthly delivery of the *London Sunday Magazine* colour supplements, I devoured news of Swinging London. David Bailey and Jean Shrimpton were our heroes.

Any hint of gathered floral dresses had gone. Wearing black tights under a straight chequered skirt and affecting a certain bohemian air, I would sneak over to Nan's little palace to iron my hair.

Elsie had been given the all-clear to live independently. The disabilities from her stroke had gradually become manageable and she finally had a little pensioner flat of her own adjoining the school rugby fields. Photos of her eighteen grandchildren were everywhere, alongside the picture of Jesus. She was a slightly worried but eager participant in all of my escapades. She was what would now be called an 'enabler'. In the fourth form, when I got a bad report, I took it over to her to sign. 'Could do better', 'Only fair', and 'Careless' weren't going to give me an easy time at home. She sat down at her pale green Formica table, got out her little marbled fountain pen, and carefully signed 'Elsie Macdonald (grandmother)'.

Tui was the parent who was on my back, but I knew my father completely supported her. They were impossible to crack. If I badgered Ed to let me go out on a Friday night, he would ask, 'What does your mother say?' He wasn't physically there much, but he was totally available when he was, and he never missed dinner time. Tui said the way to a man's heart was through his stomach. She cooked him everything he loved, including tripe and sheep's hearts. He was like the father in the film *The Castle*.

After every meal: 'That was delicious Mum.'

He was our rock. Simple. Consistent. Uncritical, and always able to make Tui laugh, which calmed her down when she was worrying. Praise the goddess I didn't have two parents on my back. As long as I stuck to my scales and arpeggios in the front room each morning, life wasn't too taxing.

In 1964, near the end of my lower sixth-form year, I signed up to leave school and go to teacher's training college, following in my brother's footsteps. I had modified my growing up statement to a more acceptable goal of becoming a primary school teacher.

While I loved art, I was beginning to think that just because you enjoy something doesn't mean you are any good at it, and I had become convinced that being an artist was not something to which I could aspire. For School Cert, I had good marks in every subject except for art: 56%. Barely a pass. On the topic of 'rush hour', my painting of the rush from the train into the tearooms at Otira from the point of view of a New Zealand Railways cup had not impressed the examiners.

My 56% stood out alongside my 92% for geography and in the 80s for English. (Most people my age can tell you their School Cert marks. When I lived in London in the 70s, if I wanted to find out whether someone in the room was a Kiwi undercover, I would ask them what they got for School Cert. This question startled them but usually just after they'd blurted out the answer.)

I knew my geography mark was a complete fluke. In my last term of fifth form, I had been sure I could not pass School Certificate. I didn't know anyone in our family who had passed the first time. Actually I hardly knew anyone who had passed at all. I thought I was bound to fail in history and geography. I decided that I had left it too late to pay attention to the actual lessons, so I bought two little booklets in which past exam papers were published. I studied them with surgical precision. The geography exam had five topics. I decided they were unlikely to repeat any of them in a five-year period, and made a stab at what I thought would be asked in the current exam. I memorised maps of industrial activity in the Midlands, land use in Northland, and three others.

In the geography exam, I could not believe my luck. There they were. Industrial activity in the Midlands and land use in Northland. I regurgitated everything I had learnt and my mark was in the top hundred in the country. I felt a bit guilty when kids who really had paid attention looked at me with new respect. But this triumphant geography mark made my art mark look even more dismal.

I was promoted to the much more competitive A stream. I liked the B stream. The kids in the A stream had fathers who were accountants and lawyers on the City Council. When we went to school dances, their fathers dropped them off in swanky cars. Ed took me in the milk truck that delivered their milk every morning. No one was snobby, but I never felt that I fit.

One night after tea, when we were doing the dishes, Tui said, 'How would you like to come with me to see the Beatles tomorrow?'

I couldn't believe it. I had known about the Beatles even before 'I Wanna Hold Your Hand' came out, because I had a Liverpudlian pen pal who covered her letters in drawings of John, George, Paul and Ringo. Once I got with the programme, I joined the worldwide Beatles Fan Club and would get agitated if the post from England was late with our Beatles mags. Before the Beatles there were skiffle groups, and rock 'n' roll bands with singers fronting, and the Kingston Trio sang folk songs and played guitars, but here was a band of great singers who also played instruments and shook their heads, and their hair wasn't back-combed and the songs were theirs. They wore suits, and even the drummer sang. We all fell in love with them. We had Beatles tea towels and we wore Beatles boots. Our whole way of dressing changed. But we always felt behind the rest of the world. Everyone seemed to have their records before us.

One day, Ed bought a magnificent Philips television. Our sitting room was never the same again. We watched black-and-white American shows and *Coronation Street*, and Elsie Tanner became almost like part of the family. And on the few occasions when the lads from Liverpool appeared on our television, the entire neighbourhood crammed into our house to watch. All the adults agreed the Beatles were 'very clean', which must have been a universally held opinion, because they took the piss out of that in *A Hard Day's Night*.

In 1964, the big event of the year was that the Beatles were coming to New Zealand.

When those irreverent boys touched down, the place erupted. On the six o'clock news, we watched them arrive at Wellington Airport to be presented with huge tiki.

And now, after everyone had drunk their instant coffee served in black cups, and we were doing the dishes, here was my mother asking me if I wanted to go to see them! Would I what.

Jan was furious. At thirteen she was deemed too young to go. She was devastated, but I was too thrilled to care. Forty years later she presented me with some Beatles drinking glasses from Hamburg, and it was not until then that I knew I had been forgiven.

The night before the show, I didn't sleep. It was the most exciting thing I can remember. The next day Tui and I joined the teenage riff raff on the Newman's bus to take us to Wellington. I was the only one on the bus with my mother. A local news photographer arrived to take a picture of the Beatle maniacs, and Tui and I sat up the front smiling broadly. The photographer looked disappointed. I turned round. Even the most daring dudes had ducked behind the seats. They were truanting and didn't want to be identified. I don't think that photo of the empty bus was ever published.

The Wellington Town Hall seemed to levitate as excited teenagers hung off the balconies and everyone yelled and screamed. When the lights went down and a leather-clad, rather podgy Johnny Devlin slithered onto the stage to sing old-style rock 'n' roll, the crowd made their feelings known. Johnny wasn't exactly booed, but he had the hardest gig in Christendom. During the intermission a slightly agitated mood began to grow, and then, at last, there they were.

Brian Epstein's boys. Exactly like they were in the films and on TV. Their hair was longer, their suits were shining and they held their guitars high. When they shook their heads, that was it – the screaming around me drowned out the music, but who cared. I was George's girl forever. It was a great concert. I heard one song. I still have my Beatles fan mags, and I am still envious of friends of mine who snuck into the Hotel St George in Wellington and actually met a Beatle.

In my final term of sixth form, as I coasted to the end of my schooling, Bryan Dew arrived, fresh out of art school, to fill in for the term. He was a painter, not a dedicated teacher. He was just passing through really, and preparing for a local exhibition of his satirical, almost Hogarthian paintings of Kiwi suburban life. A christening, a wedding. He didn't paint many of these before he left New Zealand, but they are worth noting.

In my final year's report, gone is 'Tries hard' and 'Fair'. Instead, there it is – my first A, with the comment 'Talented'. When I thanked Mr Dew for it, he just said, 'Well, you are.'

This sent my head spinning.

'Do you think I could handle art school perhaps?'

'Of course' was all he said, and with that, I skipped home and threw our entire household into a spin. I announced I had decided to stay on at Colenso for another year to do Fine Arts Prelim in order to get into art school. I could flick my studentship for training college into a further three years of tertiary study, still bonded to be a teacher after graduation.

Over my mother's dead body. Tui did not want me going to art school. Implacably opposed. Not because she feared I would become an impoverished artist, but because she worried I would marry one. She was horrified at the way 'Poor Mrs Woollaston' had to live in a rundown house in Greymouth – without carpet or lace curtains, it was implied – while her painter husband, Toss, sold Rawleigh's products door-to-door to support his family and his art.

'Girls don't need to be clever,' Tui often said. No one on either side of the family had ever gone to university, let alone to study for three years at art school. This was off the planet.

Ed stayed out of it. I knew they loved me, and would welcome me staying in the nest for another year, but not so that I could then leave home and spend three years on a studentship to follow what was undoubtedly, to our little 'cultural desert', a dilettante profession.

At this point, something unexpected happened. I don't think it would happen now. It was pretty amazing it happened then. One by one, my teachers arrived at McVay Street to negotiate my future.

The first was Hilda Timms, my English teacher. She had taught our class to think critically using English literature: 'Do the ends justify the means? Write 500 words on the Roman plays of William Shakespeare.' In 1964, she had announced that she was going to Wellington to join the 'No Maoris, No Tour' anti-apartheid demonstrations. She dared the Education Board to sack her – they didn't – then returned and gleefully told us all about it. Several of her students went on to become political activists, including Blair Peach, who'd been one of Ed's milk boys, and who was tragically killed by London special forces during an anti-racist clash in Southall in 1979. But for now, Hilda Timms, to my amazement, was in the front room having a cup of tea with Tui, and I was shooed out.

Dianne Carr, in her white sports car, was the next to arrive. A recent returnee from that great mythological place, 'overseas', she exuded glamour and sophistication. She taught French and directed the school plays. She wanted to cast me as Eliza Doolittle in her next production of George Bernard Shaw's *Pygmalion*.

That did it. I pleaded. I would have agreed to anything.

Tui eventually folded. The deal was that I would not just be coasting along making my Fine Arts Prelim portfolio. I would study four subjects, including art and English, and sit my letters for the Trinity College piano exams. I agreed, although I was already far more interested in playing Henry Mancini than Handel. From that moment, Tui and Ed's cheeky girl was in the driver's seat.

That last year at Colenso was the making of me. Emboldened, I had an argument over my choice of subjects. I wanted to learn te reo Māori. But there were no classes for that at Colenso. I was told, 'It's a dead language. What do you want to study that for?'

'I want to know what the road signs mean,' I said.

They thought I was being provocative. Even this progressive school in the Napier suburbs didn't understand. They were wrong, and they do now, but I struggle to this day with rudimentary reo.

I studied biology in Jim McLay's class, where in 1965 he taught us about climate change and the dangers of superphosphates. I drew maps for the geography teacher. I based myself in the art room, using my locker in the prefects' room for discarded lunches, something that got me hauled over the coals in the office of the assistant headmistress,

Miss Kelt, for a discussion about my general untidiness and the state of my uniform in particular. I was a bad role model for the third formers, apparently. But, as one of the little band of senior art students led by Gary Hebley, I had acquired an inflated sense of entitlement, and Miss Kelt's stern words were like water off a duck's back.

Gary Hebley, another talented artist, arrived at the beginning of 1965. We took him under our wing and called him by his first name. My friend Alison Cavell ran the schedule.

'We are going out to Cape Kidnappers on Saturday to do some landscape drawing.'

'Oh yes. Who's driving?'

'You are.'

When we weren't taking up his spare time, Dianne Carr was. She had him painting sets for *Pygmalion* that would challenge any set design you might find on the West End, and she and Gary were falling for one another. Very discreetly, but totally.

Playing Eliza Doolittle in such a positive atmosphere was sheer bliss. The mothers (not mine) made costumes for Eliza based on those designed by Cecil Beaton for Audrey Hepburn in the film *My Fair Lady*. The *Hawke's Bay Photo News* turned up to photograph me in rather bad make-up for the cover.

I joined the St John's Cathedral Youth Club, which was populated mainly by girls from Napier Girls' High, who were more focused on serious romance than us Colenso kids were. I suffered several unfruitful crushes on boys who didn't seem to notice. On the other hand, I was disdainful of anyone who followed me around.

It was at the am-dram parties where I could really practise being grown up.

Amateur theatre had always been strong in Napier. In New Zealand in 1965 there was very little professional theatre, so it was the Little Theatre, built beside the railway line, where authentically local work was emerging. A former priest named Terry Doyle had left the Jesuits and written his own kitchen sink drama. I was cast in *The Season That Was Yesterday* and had my first sexual stirrings when kissing a rather married fellow thespian onstage. Much older than me, he was no Lothario and was more worried about his next line. I turned my sights elsewhere – to a Napier Boys' High boy who had a car and hardly knew I existed.

The railway line was right alongside the Little Theatre, and trains sometimes thundered past during plays. This was frustrating, because we would have to pause the scene, but during one performance it gave us an unlikely advantage. It was mid-season and we were just picking up speed during scene three at the beginning of the play, when someone fed in lines from the last scene. Someone else replied, and suddenly there we were, onstage, speeding along straight for the end. At this rate, it was going to be a very short show. We watched one another with horror as the lines kept coming, while racking our brains for how to get back to scene three. The haunting sound of the evening railcar offered a way back. We welcomed that rattling, squealing monster almost in tears. During the few seconds as the train thundered past, someone remembered a key line from the beginning, and with great relief, as the train headed for the station, we jumped back onto the right track. The audience seemed to know nothing of it. Plenty of beers out the back after that performance.

I was going to riotous Napier Repertory parties. Ted had returned from training college to start his first year of teaching at Te Awa Primary, where he taught every child in his class to play the ukulele. As a dashing young chap about town, he arrived at one of those lively parties to find his little sister propping up the home cocktail bar and nonchalantly sipping something exotic.

'What are you drinking?'

'A vodka and orange,' I replied casually.

I had horn-rimmed glasses by now and had what I hoped was a 'Mary' affect, à la Peter, Paul and Mary.

'No you're not,' he said, taking my drink off me. 'You need to be drinking beer.'

'But I don't like beer.'

'That's why you should drink it.'

Good advice, bro. Drinking what you don't particularly like has an upside and a downside. Upside – no hangovers. Downside – the next day, I am the one who can remember what everyone said.

Through all of this, the absolute constant family activity was going to the movies on a Saturday. Napier had three cinemas playing a single film for a fortnight. From 1957 to 1965, I would have seen nearly every film that toured the country. Both my parents loved the movies. Hollywood blockbusters, black-and-white English comedies, war films from both places. Ed would watch those and dismiss them as either 'Yankee blah' or 'Tommy rot'. He particularly disliked any film that was set in a prisoner-of-war camp. *The Great Escape* outraged him.

'They're all fanatics,' he declared, as we wandered out of the new Kerridge Odeon after a couple of hours of harrowing tunnel-digging. 'You just get put back in the war afterwards. Fanatics.'

He was still annoyed with a group of tunnel-diggers who, in secrecy, had dug their way out of the Italian prison camp he had been in. 'They were all rounded up within a day and we were put on half rations for a month. Selfish buggers.'

Apart from enjoying stories like the one about Giorgio, I wasn't particularly interested in my father's exploits during the war. He would drop stories into casual conversation, usually as a joke. He told me about how if you don't eat much, after a while your stomach shrinks and you don't get hungry. By the time I was interested in listening, many years later, he was dying.

None of the films I saw as a teenager reflected the country I lived in. But we didn't expect them to. The world of film was a place of sweating gladiators, a divided sea engulfing the Roman army so that the children of Israel could arrive at the Promised Land, Charlton Heston bringing news from God on stone tablets, Audrey Hepburn and Cary Grant wisecracking in European mountain resorts, Grace Kelly and Jimmy Stewart rescuing one another while falling in love. Their world was not ours. We paid our money; we were transported.

Occasionally Tui and I would go to the movies at night. We saw *Tiger Bay*, starring John Mills and his daughter Hayley. I wanted to be Hayley Mills. But I knew we didn't do that sort of thing where I lived.

Yul Brynner was my favourite. Jan caught me kissing his photo that I had pinned on my wall. I was getting over sharing my bedroom with this increasingly sharp little sister.

When the British New Wave hit, it was well-timed in my cultural evolution. I had gone off Hollywood but found a rich cinematic feast every Saturday in Napier, watching Dirk Bogarde and Sarah Miles in *The Servant*, Samantha Eggar and Terence Stamp in *The Collector* and David Warner in *Morgan – A Suitable Case for Treatment*. My film appreciation was broadening. When *Black Orpheus* screened, we lounged in the Africa Coffee Bar afterwards under the high black ceiling with string stretched across it to make it look modern. We discussed camera technique until nine o'clock at night, when they closed the place.

When it was time to leave home for Christchurch, I leapt on the railcar with my new/old cardboard suitcase, wearing a quite long miniskirt, my hair freshly ironed. I knew all the lyrics to 'The Times They Are a-Changin'', I had money in my purse that I'd earned working at Marsden's Bookshop all summer, and I felt like everything was possible. An artist not looking back. At last, I could sleep in and stop practising those damned arpeggios.

When I boarded the ferry, I walked straight into an all-night party. Guitars were out. The ship was crawling with suede-coated students. I drank too much, threw up, and had to go to bed before we'd even left Wellington Heads. I arrived in Christchurch worse for wear and was met by my future landlady, a well-educated mother in tweed and brogues.

As Mrs Bell drives me through Hagley Park in the early morning, I blearily look out the window. A white mist hangs between the silhouetted trunks of big black trees that stand strong against the light. I see an elephant slowly swinging its trunk as it wanders between the trees. Unhurried, magnificent.

Elephants, I think. What a nice idea to have elephants in a park. They don't have them in Napier.

Mrs Bell is telling me about the orientation play showing at the Council Chambers – *Exit the King.* Theatre of the absurd, starring Jan and Don Farr.

The circus is in town.

Although I haven't seen the movie yet, I have a 'I don't think we are in Kansas anymore' moment.

# 8

# Intersections

When I think about Christchurch, three very different times float in and out of my focus. School holidays spent sitting with Marlene and my other cousins in Avonside Drive. Lounging around at a bach in Governers Bay owned by Ed's friend Chib, drawing while Ed and Chib played chess. And joining the duffel-coated throngs who clogged the neo-Gothic stone varsity buildings, full of the protests and parties that shaped my young adulthood.

Many years later, I would stand in the red zone, filming *Hope and Wire*, my television drama made from hundreds of survivors' stories after the lethal earthquakes of 2010–11.

These times intersect in my mind, and sometimes collide, when I am in Christchurch.

At art school, I was aware that I was more sociable than almost everyone else. Too happy to be a good painter, I was told. Housed in rundown prefabs around a dilapidated homestead at Ilam, the art students, like their buildings, stood apart. Moved there from the centre stone portals where Rita and Doris et al. studied in the 1930s, the art school of 1966 was weirdly marooned, rather like the position that the visual arts inhabited in mid-century Kiwi culture. A beatnik, introverted, smoking, drinking student tradition was well established out at Ilam by the time I arrived. The artist took a back seat in society, and so did we.

The brave new exploration of abstracted landscape that so enlivened mid-century painting was being eclipsed by abstract expressionism, which was far too sophisticated for my suburban taste. Though figuratism was despised, we spent our days studying plaster casts of Michelangelo's David and drawing spheres, with two days a week for life drawing. I embarked on what became a three-year argument about pictorialism and narrative in modernist painting, but did not have the knowledge or resilience to win in what became a test of endurance.

I joined John Kim's drama group that Dickie Johnson was running, and spent Saturday mornings improvising without performing. I joined Drama Soc, wafted about in purple silks in Mervyn ('Proc') Thompson's production of *The Bacchae*, fell in and out of love with monotonous regularity – not with art students; I was partial to young men who owned cars – and joined the 'gels' who boarded at Helen Connon Hall. This set me apart from my art school classmates, most of whom wouldn't visit me there. They were either living in scungy flats with a revolving set of flatmates and fridges that don't work, or boarding with landladies who didn't let them out at night. The boys who were Christchurch natives formed a jug band, and we worshipped at their feet. Bill Hammond, Chris Grosz, Dobbyn. I held a candle for them that they never noticed. Much later, Bill would introduce me as someone who he went to art school with. I had to disagree. 'I went to art school, Bill. You only came in on a Friday.'

'Well I didn't need them to tell me how to paint.'

And indeed he didn't.

At Helen Connon Hall we lived as 'ladies' under the watchful eye of Betty O'Dowd, who ran the place with stern, benign indulgence. The hall provided three meals a day served on long tables at specific times. Miss the moment and you missed your dinner. Only four art students were accommodated at any given time. My earlier application, sent under Tui's supervision, had failed, but it became 'live' again when an Australian hippie draft dodger named Roger Donaldson cruised by, scooped up the most popular girl in the hostel and took her away from all that, thus creating a vacancy. Seeing as I wasn't allowed to go flatting, and I didn't want to board in strange households, this seemed a good option.

Helen Connon Hall was a three-storey brick building in the middle of town close to everywhere and suited me just fine. It was crammed with intelligent young women of great interest to the young men housed in similar circumstances at Rolleston House close by. In the middle of the upstairs hall, a small queue of women would sit by the phone, waiting for that crucial call for a Saturday night date.

I fell in with a crew of luminaries a year ahead of me. There was a revolving game of 500 going, and memorable sorties in the middle of the night to steal daffodils, armfuls of them, from Hagley Park. Once the Mamas and the Papas sang 'California Dreamin'', flower power really kicked in, even though drugs were still hard to find and the TV in the common room was black and white. On *Let's Go*, the half-hour for teenagers from the New Zealand Broadcasting Corporation's light entertainment department, the go-go dancers were clearly from the Hutt, and Pete Sinclair, despite his best efforts, was not cool. I painted dahlias on my friends' tights while they had them on, and was inclined to go to parties wearing just an op shop men's singlet and carrying a chrysanthemum. I always wore knickers though.

As I write this, I realise what a sense of wonder the world contained. I felt like I was on my own adventure. What other people were doing influenced us, but they were people we knew directly or people we'd heard about. You had to be resourceful. Nothing groovy fell into your lap, but you could find it if you were discerning.

The very cool, by definition, flowed from that mythical place: overseas. Despite my love of the jug band and the excellent amateur theatre, we still thought we were missing out. I came to think that the reason we spent our summers sitting on beaches staring out to sea was because we were pretty sure something was going on out there, and we desperately wanted to know what it was.

I have observed this yearning for elsewhere my entire lifetime.

It has shaped the great Kiwi cultural cringe. It has had us by the throat, to our own shame. No matter how hard we try, we always somehow agree that whatever is being done overseas is something we need to catch up with. Our artists only get to be fully acknowledged at home once they have found 'success' overseas. We dismantled a perfectly good, if slightly rickety, world-leading social welfare system and sold off our infrastructure, keenly embracing neoliberal theory straight out of Chicago Business School, because that was how they did it overseas, supposedly. The outcome of this form of privatisation is that, as I write this, many of our rivers and lakes are polluted, some of our beaches are unswimmable, we own very little of our own wealth and the gap between rich and poor is intractable. We have achieved fifth-generation poverty, particularly among Māori and Pacific peoples. That was all accomplished in the 1980s. Now we have a sizeable community that believes lies from America in the middle of a pandemic because they feel so disenfranchised.

In the 60s, when I was gadding about with the arty farties, the rivers sparkled without giardia, we danced to the Beach Boys, and Christchurch was a city of bicycles that all had bells.

I was surrounded by talent at art school. I desperately wanted to be good at something, but I really wasn't. I was a jack of all trades; I never shone, was never 'the one to watch'. But, unlike when I had lounged around happily at Colenso High School, here I felt affronted and undermined. Tui made me go home in the holidays, so I couldn't go to the student arts festivals. A feeling of missing out began to grow. In my third year, Tui caved, and I was allowed to leave Helen Connon Hall to go flatting with my best friend, Shirley Grace McGregor.

Shirley Grace was one of the most beautiful women ever to walk this earth. She was a brilliant photographer and painter, and we often found ourselves recovering from Saturday morning hangovers together in John Kim's actors' workshop. Shirley's impeccable vowels and incredible private school manners belied her true character as a deeply dependable wild child. She threw away her brown chequered skirts and brown brogues to troll the op shops for furs and Victorian lace. Flatting with the most beautiful young woman in the land had real advantages. At our well-populated parties I was surrounded by ardent young men with their eye on Shirl. This was not without its dangers – not for Shirl, but for the young men. Like all true artists, she liked to challenge people.

Once, we woke up on Saturday morning and decided to go to a party in Dunedin. This would be easy. Whenever we hitchhiked, we never had to put our thumb out for long. I had cut my hair into a short Twiggy style, and that day I was wearing a substantial wig and a Harvard sweatshirt. A Zephyr 10 driven by a middle-aged man pulled up. He leaned over and threw open the passenger door, grinning widely. Shirley got in the front and I climbed into the back, thinking I could snooze for the trip and leave the talking to Shirl. As she shut the passenger door, she introduced herself, threw her arm in my direction and, with a charming smile, said, 'This is Gaylene. She's an American.'

Without thinking I waved cheerfully and said, 'Hi!' in what I thought was an authentic Yankee greeting.

Big mistake. The driver had never met an American before and was fascinated. For the next couple of hours as he drove us to Timaru, in a conversation encouraged by my erstwhile friend in the front seat, I fielded his inquisitive questions in an accent that ranged from California to the deep South. I did not attempt the Bronx but I may have accidentally hit Brooklyn. I hadn't really met an American either, and I did not know what was going to come out of my mouth next. All for the entertainment of one Shirley Grace, who added extra degrees of difficulty if the conversation lulled. That was the thing. My competitive spirit, combined with my *Simon and the Gang* tendency, encouraged by Shirley's mischievous streak, meant that I always accepted her challenges and found myself up the creek big time. Infuriating.

When we finally got out of the car, I was on an adrenaline high after my two-hour improvisation. It occurred to me I could just pull off my wig: 'Fooled you. I come from Greymouth.'

But I was overcome by an unexpected burst of sense. He could have become outraged, and would have been forgiven for running us over.

Our mothers were constantly worrying about us and had no idea what we were actually up to. But they loved us. Mine sent down the funds to pay for my twenty-first birthday at the Sign of the Takahe, where we drank mulled wine around a big wooden table with the fire blazing. I was presented with a goldfish in a condom. When midnight came, Shirley announced that we should all watch me turn into a woman. At the final chime, when nothing happened, she ostentatiously presented me with silver-painted chest-expanders to help me develop an actual bosom.

We were friends for life. Through thick and thin.

After Shirley died, too young from breast cancer, I made a TV documentary that features her daughter Aimee reading from Shirley's diaries, intercut with Jan Bolwell dancing her own experience of a double mastectomy. Shirley left a legacy of brilliant work interrupted by punishing migraines and difficult relationships. I'd love her to be still around now to challenge me as I write this. She was a courageous, provocative thinker. She sits at my side occasionally. I'd like to jump in a car with her and go off on a Thelma and Louise jaunt. The spirit world doesn't send such good jokes, I find.

We had the occasional earthquake in Christchurch when I was at art school, but they weren't big crazy jolting things, like the ones that had freaked me out in Napier. When our flat in Christchurch elegantly shook during the Inangahua earthquake of 1968, I didn't even get out of bed.

The Christchurch that Shirley and I once galloped around has now almost completely disappeared. When the city threw itself as if in a mad tantrum into the air and then came crashing down, the psychic shockwaves travelled far further than the ripples that appeared in the earth.

*

At the time when I was stealing daffs with the card-players of Helen Connon Hall, just round the corner at another hostel there was a young man I'd later become great friends with. It always puzzled us that we didn't meet sooner.

It was not until 1979 that I met Graeme Tetley. I was researching a film at Naenae College, Lower Hutt, where he was working with a group of disaffected drama kids no one else knew what to do with. Talented teachers are magicians. Graeme had that special combination of talent and kindness, and a rare, cool-eyed social awareness. He had begun to embrace screenwriting, and over the following years we became firm friends, cooking up stories together.

Whenever he and I had a conversation, it was long and meandering. One day I was lounging around talking to Graeme on the phone, and it was only at the end of the conversation, when he described his breathtaking view across Lyttelton Harbour, that I realised he was not in Wellington.

It was February 2011, and he had just arrived to take up the post of artist in residence in the English department at Canterbury University, unpacking his life into a small cottage overlooking the harbour. His dream was to write a film that was set in Napier after the earthquakes. It would follow the amateur operatic society and the folk who had been performing blackface in the Frivs at an amateur theatre venue in Hastings. In the meantime, an unproduced TV series he had written was to be performed as a play by the Wanaka community at the Festival of Colour later that year.

After our call, I put the phone down, made a cup of tea and settled on the couch to read, and fell asleep. Some hours later I turned on the radio to hear that there had been an earthquake in Christchurch. I turned on the TV. The images were horrifying. I rang Graeme on his cellphone. No reply.

As the death toll rose and the devastating news of the smoking collapsed CTV Building invaded my sitting room, as dazed, shocked, bleeding people wandered about in the rubble of the wrecked CBD, Graeme was not answering his phone. It was not until after an

119

interminable sleepless night that my message app pinged.

'im ok' is all it said.

No punctuation. No caps. I knew he couldn't be.

Later that day, he rang me. Adrenaline high, having survived, he felt indestructible. He was driving around the peninsula to get back to Wellington as fast as he could, and now he was raving. He had watched Lyttelton disappear under a cloud of red dust. The power went off, the birds flew in a cacophony of reckless flight. He said he had never felt so alone.

A few years earlier, Graeme had written *Aftershock*, a telefeature that imagined a civil emergency when Wellington had the big one. Graeme told me that however much you think you know about a big shake, you know nothing.

He never felt remotely safe ever again. Six weeks later, after watching the tsunami at Fukushima unfold on his television, Graeme went to bed and suffered the heart attack that killed him.

I was told that after a severe earthquake, people's risk of cardiovascular events increases. There is a sharp rise in heart attacks. The wheelchair that sits in artist Peter Majendie's white chair memorial – in which 185 empty white chairs sit in an open space – is, to my mind, not just for those who were injured but for those like Graeme, who survived the immediate quakes but died later.

As the city lay in ruins, I was grieving, not only for the friend and colleague I had lost, but for the city that held so many memories. What could I do? I desperately wanted to contribute, but didn't know how.

Going down to make a first-hand documentary would only put more pressure on a city already stretched to the max. I felt uncomfortable with the idea. But I felt driven to make a record.

The trees are magnificent when I finally get to the broken city. It is as though they know that their very existence is under threat and they have thrown their branches wide in a burst of energetic seeding that leaves the natural world thriving as the people struggle. Neglected gardens around ruined houses have burst into magnificent colour with all kinds of blooms climbing up walls, along paths, into wrecked kitchens. The city is theirs, apart from the army guards lounging about in sentry boxes, bored but on duty, allowing no one in or out of the cordon that has been hastily strung around the still quaking inner city within hours of the main force.

Missing Graeme madly, I surround myself with all things Christchurch. Once more I fall upon the skills I have developed when making oral histories of the 1931 Napier earthquake. As Wellington fills up with earthquake refugees, I listen to every survivor story that comes my way. I have contacted everyone I know in Christchurch. A TV series is growing in my mind – a drama. Three character families are beginning to emerge, spanning class, age, race and district. This is how I can tell stories of the humanity and resilience, the greed and the loss. I include hundreds of accounts amalgamated into dramatised psychological collisions. News footage adds context, making a sweeping story of lives lived in the rocking ruins.

By the time necessary funding is found, two years have passed since the quakes of February 2011, and the garden city is still standing on shaking, rickety legs. The writer Dave Armstrong has stepped into Graeme's shoes to write with me to string it all together.

I arrive with producer Chris Hampson to shoot *Hope and Wire*. The title comes from a song written by Adam McGrath of the Lyttelton grunge folk band the Eastern, who sang in people's backyards in the aftermath.

The red zone is overrun by rats and rotting food in crooked buildings dominated by rumbling demolition trucks and mountains of cleared rubble. Empty shops stand as they were at that unimaginable moment. Two dust-encrusted coffee cups in a dirty café window speak of the terror, one overturned with a coffee spill now dry, the other upright with the crumbled remains of a biscuit still sitting on the saucer. A chair lies on the floor in the twilight of a place that is otherwise in order, except that the till is open and emptied and the wire cigarette packet holder on the wall is bare. A snapshot of a sunny Tuesday morning thrown into chaos. The heavily guarded and controlled inner city has been stripped of valuables.

When I was young, I would sometimes hear people referred to as 'having had a good war'. In 2013, the opportunists are having a good quake. Demolition companies are doing well, as is the government of the time, which has used every aspect of disaster economics to win another election.

To my surprise, I can find my way around quite easily using the trees as signposts. I remember the big chestnut on the corner of Bealey Ave and Colombo Street we sat underneath for sunny day group therapy sessions when I worked at Calvary Psychiatric Day Hospital in 1968. The big black macrocarpas of Hagley Park still stand tall against the light. The old house in Holmwood Road, where Shirley and I held court, is standing, but the Avonside Drive house of Preston cousins has been demolished.

Stripped bare, the city is like time peeled away. My memories feel dislocated. Battered bones of my hijinks of 1966 are lying about. It is easier to imagine this city when it was first built, when that great-great-grandmother I told you about, Sarah Cressey's mother, was living with her French husband in a new stone cottage in Fendall Town. I feel strangely at home.

We set up our cameras, basing ourselves at Templeton, outside the city boundary, where we can build replica slices of the ruined city so our actors stay safe.

The community is upset, on edge. Many think we have come to exploit their pain. Few are prepared to be our friends. The situation feels ready to blow at any moment. A film crew in the middle of town, meticulously recreating people's worst nightmare, is puzzling to some, deeply unsettling to most.

Filming in town was tricky, not just because of the obvious, like the small sudden shakes that could bring down masonry, but because of the endless paperwork. Using a location that was in the process of changing owners without warning was chaotic. A government agency, the Canterbury Earthquake Recovery Authority (CERA), was buying buildings and selling them to demolition companies. There was a striking contrast between what could be done in Napier in 1931 and what could be done in Christchurch in 2013. The incredibly complicated corporate ownership chains left the city in ruins for far too long, piling humanmade tragedy on top of the natural one.

We hunkered down in a lodge in Templeton hosted by a couple of Coasters, who kept us well stocked with whitebait. My trusty creative friends gave me the room with the ensuite while they all shared the tiny bathroom and queued for their shower in the morning. Someone knew that, while I am shooting, the bath is where I do my true creative problem-solving.

When we timed the scripts, they were too long. We tried to get an extra episode from the network, to no avail. Spending time and money shooting scenes that are not going to see the light of day is the worst thing. It impacts on the time available to shoot the scenes that will be in the picture, and limits resources in every way. Time is the enemy, so why shoot things you won't use? With only four weeks to go until the first day of shooting, I went to bed and cut the scripts by amalgamating and restructuring to get the timing closer. I wrote in between pre-production meetings and left the scripts at the end of the day for Chris Hampson to read overnight.

This complete script cutting was like a creative earthquake inside the production only weeks away from shooting. I was blessed to have tremendous expertise and experience around me in all departments. Otherwise they would not have been able to cope with the crazy circumstances. Nothing in this opus major was small. They rolled with the punches. Amalgamating second-layer characters was particularly taxing. Fortunately for me, my friend Christina Asher just happens to be one of the most talented casting agents in the world. Having cast the leads, she came down and cast hundreds of locals as the production swirled around us. Our cinematographer was Thom Burstyn. Thom shared his knowledge of the Japanese philosophy of wabi-sabi – beauty in the broken. (They have earthquakes too.) It was not unusual for me to receive an encouraging photograph from him late at night after a long day shooting.

When Dame Kate Harcourt came down to play Dot, Jonty's ninety-year-old mother, she took up the spare room at the lodge. Kate was the *Listen with Mother* lady on the radio who'd awoken my four-year-old aspirations to the artist's way. Life goes round if you live long enough. When Kate wasn't performing – which included doing stunts – she waited up for us with a nightcap as we staggered home after a hard day shooting in the sad, broken, liquefied-sand-filled dreams of the suburb ironically named Atlantis.

*Hope and Wire* is set among people who have to live outside. The social barriers between class and race have become fluid. I'd been inspired by a photo essay in the Christchurch *Press* by Iain McGregor, 'Camp Mother's Big Adventure', about a couple who were living under plastic outside their wrecked inner-city house, looking after whoever came their way. I never met the subjects, because I thought that they would think the characters were them specifically, and they are not. Rachel House and British actor Bernard Hill play Joycie and Len, who are the unlikely carers for people who travel through the yard of a wrecked old boarding house named Muntville. With everyone living outside, the people already there gain a different community: Dwayne, the hyperactive unfortunate abandoned boy, who Len calls 'hopeless'; and Monee, a young woman on the run with her dog, which has been trained to attack Asians by her white power boyfriend King, played by Kip Chapman. That story strand was based on the court case of a group who had been terrorising immigrants in the inner city; a Vietnamese man had been bitten badly. In the series, I made up that the wild child Monee is healed by the kindness of strangers living in the wreckage. In reality, she was sent to prison with the rest. Monee is played by my daughter Chelsie, Dwayne by Anton Tennet. All are hybrid characters.

Joel Tobeck plays their landlord, Greggo, who is so busy being one step ahead of his debtors that he never has any fun. Joel had great fun with that. Greggo lives in a different universe from his tenants and doesn't pay his dozer drivers. One of them, played by Jarod Rawiri, is living the dream with his wife, played by Miriama Ralph, with their two little kids in Atlantis. After the quakes, she can't stand the aftershocks and takes the kids to stay with her mother in Tāmaki Makaurau. Left on his own in a liquefaction-wrecked home, he descends into a violent depression and drives a bulldozer into Greggo's sitting room. These things happen. I didn't make up the events; I made up the characters. The Atlantis family are Māori. After the series screened on television, some people said there weren't any Māori living in Christchurch. Not long after, I was approached on a street in Christchurch by a man with a full moko, who planted himself in front of me and said, 'You're her, aren't you?'

'You mean Jane Campion. No, I'm the other one.'

'You made *Hope and Wire*?' he said.

'Guilty.'

He hugged me, and said, 'Thank you.'

The Fendalton couple – lawyer Jonty and his wife Ginny, played by Stephen Lovatt and Luanne Gordon – fight over their cracked swimming pool and their Bill Hammond painting, which she thought Jonty had insured but he hadn't. They deal with their teenage kids going wild and their marriage falling apart. But almost all the characters get redemption in *Hope and Wire*. It's a story. A story woven together from hundreds that were written, reported, overheard at the pub.

The actors always managed to turn up ready to make the script sing, finding pathos and humour amid the liquefaction dust.

The series ends in true Canterbury style, with a big party.

I can't think of Christchurch without a big party – one like the 1968 demolition party that was thrown by friends of ours, university lecturers, who were told to move because the landlord was going to pull the place down. They lived in a beautiful dilapidated villa in Riccarton. Before the planned demolition, people brought their screwdrivers to the house to 'rescue' lovely old mirrors and staircase railings, only for the neighbours to report them. When the police arrived, many highly regarded academic types jumped out what was left of the windows to avoid arrest. The landlord in question had been simply chucking the tenants out the fastest way he could. His story about pulling the house down was just that – a story. There are different motives behind the stories we tell.

When I was making *Hope and Wire*, I felt Graeme close. The young me, who had raced around those leaf-drenched streets, was nothing but memory now. This city had not seen change like this since colonial days. Those were the times I had imagined my grandmothers had lived through. The first settlers built St Michael's Church, the first cathedral, in kauri and matai to withstand earthquakes. In 2011 it did, unlike the stone church built later that did not.

We filmed at the cemetery where the Brunning sisters lie.

We screened a feature-length version to everyone we could find who had been extras and on the crew. The Riccarton cinema held over four hundred people, and at the end there was a standing ovation. We all cried together. Roger Sutton, the then-CEO of CERA, was among them. As he hugged me, he said, 'How did you do that?'

Of the many people involved with the Christchurch recovery, he was the one who knew the most and who had gone out of his way to clear the path for us, with his steadfast public relations manager, Linda Paterson, supporting us.

I was relieved, but not for long. A negative campaign had been flowing from disaffected local practitioners who saw our work as theft: we were coming to their city with much more money than they had. One review talked of 'a northern lens'. I hadn't experienced the earthquakes myself, so was considered an interloper. 'It's too soon!' came the loud cry from the south, as viewers in Auckland, who had by then forgotten the earthquakes, became emotionally involved again. But from my point of view, it was nearly too late. We filmed just one block ahead of the demolition crews as they cleared the city of all landmarks, making it truly flat, something not missed by local horticulturalists, who objected to the obliteration of the subtle topography of their city.

It will always be too soon for some people. How could it possibly not be? If you have lost your house, your livelihood, your neighbours, your family, how could watching a television drama based on real events feel anything other than exploitative?

But does that mean that in the larger space the silence descends? Like in Napier, when the earthquakes stayed in the private sphere, talked about around the hearth but not in public, with heartfelt stories of common experience staying by and large untold? I only heard about the Ahuriri taniwha in the 1990s. The story was told to me by a very old man, Hone Hōhepa, who had been told it by another very old man on the day of the quakes, when Hone was ten years old. This is a central story for Māori, who know it because they have an oral history tradition, whereas Pākehā need everything written down.

I believe that if the population at large had understood more about how the people of Napier and the government of the time reacted to the Hawke's Bay quakes, eighty years later maybe we would have dealt with the aftermath in Christchurch rather better.

Do we have to wait until people have died to explore heartbreaking social dislocation? This idea that you have to have been there, that you can only tell stories from direct personal experience, is not something I subscribe to. Stories from all kinds of points of view make our culture richer. Women telling stories about men, Māori telling stories about Pākehā. On and on. Many unforgettable women in literature were written by men. In 1968 Joni Mitchell wasn't even at that huge gathering at Woodstock. She watched it on TV. But it was she who wrote the iconic song 'Woodstock'. 'We are stardust,' she sings, and we thought we were.

# Part II

# 9

# A Nondescript Apartment Building

The Student Union doctor looks at me with a mixture of irritation and concern as he declares me nine weeks pregnant. He's wearing a white coat and looking grim. He washes his hands in the little basin in his consulting room and says, 'Don't worry, we can organise for you to go up to a farm in Taranaki to have it.'

I pull up my underwear. 'I'm not a cow. I won't be going to a farm,' I respond, to my own amazement.

He looks like I've just hit him on the head with a four-by-two. I was just another meekly compliant anxious student up until that moment.

I'm caught in a dire double standard. Nice girls don't have sex before marriage, nice girls therefore don't take any form of contraception, nice girls therefore get pregnant. In droves. The women who live openly with their boyfriends are looked upon with suspicion and considered 'fast', slutty. I live in one of the first countries to have the contraceptive pill, still largely untested by any population. It's us, Australia and Brazil. We are the guinea pigs. But since the pill is only available through GPs for married women, I'm not one of them.

My sudden outburst at the Student Union doctor was triggered by the recent experience of a friend of mine who, having found herself pregnant, tried every homegrown, housemaid's-tale method to lose the pregnancy. She drank gin and jumped off tables. That was supposed to do the trick. When it didn't, she took scalding-hot nettle baths. She went on a long horse trek across the mountains. But all she got was more healthily pregnant. In her last trimester, she was sent to a farm near Darfield. I went to see her one weekend. There she was, darling talented Bron, eight months pregnant, on her hands and knees, vigorously scrubbing the lino floor of a vast old farmhouse kitchen. She was housekeeping for a farmer and his wife who had five of their own with a sixth on the way. The farmer's wife was sick, so Bronwyn was cooking, cleaning and child-minding for all of them.

This treatment was meted out to 'unmarried mothers' as a kind of socially sanctioned punishment. Bron had no friends in the district and had agreed to give her baby up for adoption when it was born. She took on the whole thing with courage and a certain devil-may-care attitude that belied her desperation.

I was stunned by the situation. How could this be right? How could it be that women like us were being treated like outcasts from our own families? How could we be put out to pasture to have our babies, who would then be farmed out to adoptive parents who would give them a 'better life'?

When she arrived back at art school after the birth, Bron was a different person. Reckless, angry and brittle. Like many others, she never got over the loss of her baby. She spent most of the rest of her life looking for him, finding him, losing him again. In a final burst of defiance, she took her own life, which I know was a direct result of the trauma she'd experienced twenty years earlier.

Back in 1967, when I 'fell' – that was what they called it: you 'fell pregnant' – I could not have articulated how I felt. I could not have clearly seen the long march of women's loss of autonomy over their own bodies. But I knew in my bones that the farm option was not for me.

It wasn't that I thought I would be cast out from my family. It was tradition in our family to look after our own. We had a history of much younger sisters turning out to be daughters in the big extended

Edwardian family. I did not expect that going back home to tell my parents of my troubles was going to be a walk in the park – but I didn't believe that I would ever be cast out by them.

I wasn't so sure, however, that having an abortion would be viewed sympathetically. I was pretty sure that support for that idea would be absolutely out of the question. It would be forever devastating. I considered that their loss would be felt far more deeply than mine.

Tui went to church every Sunday. She would leave the meat and vegetables prepared, dress in her best coat and hat, and go to the little church down the road where the curate was liberal and the congregation were all friends of hers. My father would come home from his milk run, put on the meat and have the whole thing cooking along by the time Tui arrived home with Nan and often several great aunties for Sunday lunch. The church was Tui's mainstay, and the Bible says no to abortion. Apparently. I am not sure exactly where. This is the hard God who lived in Nan's bad eye.

I had given up religion myself, and didn't feel that a world bristling with nuclear missiles was a terrific place to be bringing in new humans. Even then, though I wouldn't have been able to express it, I felt it was up to a pregnant woman herself to decide whether she wanted to bring a child into the world or not.

But the very idea of an abortion was impossible to contemplate. It is a horrible word, redolent of blood and death. It had a smell to it, reeking of clandestine rooms with dirty money changing hands and police raids on dodgy doctors. Too many women of my mother's generation and before had died having back street abortions. Five quid for a clean knitting needle and a Russian roulette-style gamble on your life. Many years later, I tried to find out the statistics for deaths from septic abortion during World War Two, a time when my mother's generation were dying from love affairs with soldiers in the passionate heat of the coming and going of conflict. Although some deaths in public hospitals were recorded over that time, it's likely that many were either not recorded or were recorded as caused by peritonitis.

133

In 1967, I was not prepared to risk my life, but I was not prepared to have this child either.

The overwhelming reason I was so clear about that was that I knew this pregnancy was not going to be right for either the father or me. It wasn't anything to do with career choice or future dreams. It was to do with the relationship, which wasn't good. We had fallen in with one another and carried on a casually chummy, mutually enjoyable art school friendship that had become cosily sexual, but I knew that he was an alcoholic. When he drank, he got drunk and when he was drunk, he got morose and dark. Very dark. I had grown up in the shadow of the alcoholism that had shaped my grandmother's life and all her children's lives one way or another. I did not want to be tied to that particular well-worn tragedy. I didn't see it as taking a life. I felt the opposite. I felt that I would be saving a child from a difficult life with a father dealing with alcoholism.

I also felt that once you have a child with someone, you can never leave them. Wherever they are in the world, you will always be linked, whether you see them every day or don't even know their name. I could not face that prospect. But what was I to do? I knew I had to move fast. Every day I woke up and was still pregnant was another day for the foetus to grow. It had been the size of a grain of sand, now it was the size of a peanut. While there was still time, I wanted to deal with the situation calmly and fast. My pregnancy was a mistake, and going ahead and having the baby would be a mistake. Two wrongs don't make a right. It was as simple as that in my mind.

It wasn't only abortions that were illegal; so was homosexuality. In the Christchurch Amateur Dramatic Society, the sexual underground and the student body interacted. Lyttelton was a port full of illicit activities, particularly the buying and selling of drugs, and in Christchurch there was a chain by which abortion medication could be acquired. But it felt very risky to me. Taking a pill and waiting at home to miscarry had far too many dangers. What if I haemorrhaged? What if it didn't work? What damage was that going to do to the unborn child? Not an option. I had to get cracking and find a link that everyone had heard about, but nobody seemed to know how it worked.

When in trouble – and sure, was I in trouble – you are meant to talk about it. Let everyone know and put out a call for help. Impossible in a country where what you want to discuss is illegal. We made some very deft, discreet inquiries. I was ruthless. I didn't really give my boyfriend any room for his opinion.

Along the way, through a friendly gay lawyer, I acquired a phone number for a group of doctors in Sydney, Macquarie Street Specialists, who did safe medical abortions for a fee. A large one. They were breaking the law in their own country, but at the time surgical abortions were legally available under some circumstances in New South Wales. Women came from other states in Australia and from New Zealand to get the best option available.

I booked in and borrowed the money, we went halves on the operation and the plane fares, and off we went.

It was a warm and balmy Darlinghurst day. We walked up the street, searching for the right number on a nondescript brick-and-tile apartment building, and climbed the concrete steps to ring the doorbell. The metal door was covered by a grille that looked like an ornate fly screen but was in fact strong steel reinforcing, double-locked, over another equally sturdy door. Keeping people in or out, I wondered. The woman who appeared behind the screen looked us over with a jaundiced eye. A leathery-skinned bleached blonde with bright pink luminous lipstick, she had seen much in her years on this earth and not much of it had been pretty. She wore a starched white uniform and gold-plated bling around her neck, and her long painted fingernails sat on top of nicotine-stained fingers. Her voice was raspy as she rattled the locks with keys she carried on a chain around her waist. It was beginning to feel like a nasty fairy tale. The money was handed across. She counted it.

'Come in, dearie.'

My boyfriend was left to wander the tree-lined streets and come back in a couple of hours.

Inside, silent young women sat in various stages of preparation for surgery and recovery. One by one they looked up. Our eyes met. A baleful glance, then back to our own silent thoughts. There we sat, each on a single bed, in our floral surgical gowns. Our clothes and toilet bags were neatly organised at the foot of the bed. Our sanitary pads hung around our waists like tails, ready to be used after the operation. Someone was quietly crying. A young girl who looked no more than twelve sat like a statue with her worried mother beside her. The radio blared out all the latest hits. 'Hey there, Georgy Girl', and then, as it was my turn, 'Yummy yummy yummy, I've got love in my tummy' started joyfully playing.

In case of a police raid, the surgery was organised to become not a surgery in five minutes flat. This gave it a surreal floral motel aesthetic that felt vaguely *Brave New World*. The surgeon was a balding, kindly man in a hurry. I was eleven weeks pregnant, and the procedure was simple. All I felt was relief.

I didn't care what anyone else thought. I had no regrets. I didn't regard the confluence of cells inside my uterus as a living breathing being. I was so certain in my resolve that I did not have to grapple with the decision. I just knew I was doing the right thing.

It might have felt different had I not been so certain. No woman can approach a termination with glee. It's complicated, and I am sure that if I had gone ahead with the pregnancy, I would have loved the child – as many women I know subsequently did, when they had their 'illegitimate' (what a terrible word) children. But surely I had not been brought up to be a confident human person, in the twentieth century, to be treated as if I were a criminal for making the most important decision of my life.

This all happened over the August holidays. When I returned to art school, to my horror the rumour mill had elevated me to some kind of hero. I put my head down and walked the straight and narrow. I felt neither pride nor shame.

Many years later, an actress friend of mine came to stay in the house I live in now. She gleefully proclaimed the front room her 'conception room'. She had flatted in the house in the early 70s and conceived a child to her boyfriend, whose parents were adamant that her pregnancy be terminated. She was at the airport in Wellington when she was turned back and arrested, resulting in her eventually giving birth to her darling daughter.

She affixed a little memorial to the wall, and we acknowledged the moment of conception. That split second when a clock starts ticking and nothing is ever the same again, whatever the outcome.

A baby growing inside your body is the strangest thing. Wondrous and terrifying in equal measure. It was many years later, when my daughter bounced in, that I was lucky to enjoy every minute of being pregnant and every minute of giving birth. Every child a wanted child, I say. That's the least we owe ourselves as women, and as human beings.

After the abortion, I wanted to run away. I struggled on at art school. A new tutor from England arrived, full of theories about 'abstraction and the urban landscape'. I had no idea what an 'urban landscape' was. I couldn't relate.

I had been corresponding with my friend Andy Dennis all that year. Andy had sent me the Harvard sweatshirt I'd worn when I got into the car with Shirley on my long ride south as an American. Andy and I had an understanding that after he completed his postgrad year studying international law in Boston, he would return to my willing arms. He didn't. When his year was over and he graduated, rather than return, he went to pull pints in a London pub. Then, somehow, he heard about my abortion. I had never really contemplated how much gossip went on about it. Andy arrived back on his white charger and asked me to marry him.

It was the end of my final year at art school. In a kind of fog, I agreed. Andy had a scholarship to Cambridge University. *The* Cambridge University. The one with the punts on the river and the ancient stone buildings, May balls, the champagne teas at Grantchester. It was a long way away.

Andy was enthusiastic, and it seemed a really good option to escape, so as the dulcet strains of 'All Things Bright and Beautiful' played a little too fast, I galloped up the aisle at St Augustine's Church in Napier wearing a white babydoll maxi dress and a fashionable wig, with the groom and his groomsmen in morning dress carrying top hats. A Christchurch wedding in Napier. Tui's working-class Edwardian West Coast tendencies were not appeased.

Soon I would be out of there. I'd write home once a fortnight, call on birthdays and at Christmas, and the world would be my oyster.

# 10

# The Graduate Wife

I'm wearing three layers of clothing, a Christchurch op-shop fur coat made in 1940, long boots and thick woollen tights. Andy and I walk, hunched together like Bob and Suze Rotolo on the cover of Dylan's second album, through the snow.

We're going to the Gonville and Caius College graduate dining room to be served by polite working-class waiters in uniform. Up here, under the eaves of a very high three-hundred-year-old stone building, we eat at tables covered in white linen cloths. Not a word is spoken except an occasional whispered, 'Please pass the . . . thank you so much.' Beneath us, seated at long tables in the big dining hall, roughly one hundred undergraduates are noisily eating their inferior meal.

Every night, in the gloom, we eat with the same ten very contained, terribly clever young men. The postgraduate fellows are very pale and have unusually long fingers. They jump if I talk to them. When I try to find out anything about their studies, I end up silently nodding, understanding virtually nothing of the esoteric subjects they are writing about. They seem troubled, or perhaps they are just very shy. I am the only woman in the hall.

We've arrived in Cambridge just in time for a punishing winter. The wind blows straight from the Arctic with nothing in the way before it hits Cambridgeshire. The light is dull. Andy and I have been accommodated by the college in a semi-basement flat in Harvey Road. The windows at pavement level let in more draught than light. I sling up a painting easel right by the window, but I feel like I still can't see. The best thing about our dim flat is the enormous Aga that dominates the kitchen, with two ovens and big asbestos covers to keep the stovetop hot. We shovel cokettes in and the whole place stays warm.

I love cooking in this big belly of a coal range, but Andy has paid in advance for a term's worth of dinners, and they have to be eaten at the college. That is why we tramp across town to this old stone hall every night, where the porters make me sign in because I am not part of the college but a 'graduate wife'. Over the next term I remain a stranger, a graduate wife, invisibility guaranteed.

Cambridge is where everything is happening but you don't know where. The stone walls echo with secret goings-on. Along with being Mrs Dennis, I am not a graduate. It seems that Tui's future-telling for me has come true. I am condemned to following my husband about in the world while he does important things.

After the term is over, I have got to know no one.

Andy and I had only really ever lived together alone as man and wife, just the two of us, for about six weeks, when we lived in Holmwood Road in Christchurch in 1969. Then, without mentioning it to me, Andy found a cheaper deal over the road with some clever, disreputable friends of his, so that was that. But I didn't mind. I've always been more comfortable in shared living arrangements. After that, whenever I moved house with my first husband (I called him that from the beginning, thinking it would keep him on his toes; it didn't), we always set up a flat.

The Kiwi flat is a great institution. My generation galloped out of our secure, predictable nuclear families and set up communal living arrangements with like-minded friends, forming our own loose non-nuclear families. Hundreds of mouldering old houses were left in decaying central cities when the reputable fled for the suburbs. In those days, you could pay your rent, put money in the kitty for power and food, and you'd still have about half of your studentship as disposable income. We used this to go to parties, drink too much and cause trouble.

But these were also the days of trouble with a purpose. We protested at the drop of a hat. We marched to stop New Zealand doing anything that put it under the nuclear umbrella. We protested over exams. We put contraceptive vending machines into the Students' Association ladies' loos. That caused the biggest furore; Mr Muldoon, at that time the minister of finance, was dispatched down to the Canterbury campus to sort us out. It didn't work. We protested against apartheid in representative sporting teams. We fought for homosexual law reform. We turned over a car in Cathedral Square after a screening of Peter Watkins' *The War Game*, then raced back to the nearest flat to listen to reports of our exploits on the radio. We are a unique generation in refusing to fight in the Vietnam War. We sheltered young draft dodgers from Australia.

After that dreadful first winter in Cambridge, it didn't take that long for Andy and me to find our feet. Spring arrived. In 1970, Cambridge college life was rapidly changing and the young men's secret clubs were blossoming into radical protest groups. Ancient rules were being seriously bent, including the rule that undergraduates who chose not to live in the college must reside within a mile's radius of the town clock. As a postgraduate scholar, Andy could sign that the students under his roof had 'kept nights'. They sure did. The kids who came to live with us were radical misfits who were up to something other than living in college and getting a First. There was too much rock 'n' roll and social disruption to be had to make slinging on a suit and joining the establishment in any way interesting.

One windy rainy night around eleven, there is a knock at the door. It's Giles. His black hair is wet and tousled, his velvet jacket soaked, his eyes wide.

'Hey man, you got an axe?'

'Yes, Giles. But what do you want it for?' Andy is donning his responsible MA persona.

141

'We're going to burn the college down, man.'

'With an axe?'

'Yeah. We're gonna put glue in the locks.'

'With an axe?'

The children of the aristocracy are not very practical. We give him that good old Kiwi standby – a cup of tea and a lie down.

I was busy joining in too. If you don't know what you are doing and you have no purpose, then join in with others who do. And I was desperately lost while appearing not to be. Getting married had been a bridge too far.

I had realised it the day after the ceremony, when I woke up as 'Mrs Dennis'. The whole marriage thing, I knew then, was probably a mistake. There was something about all this Mrs and Mr couple hoo-ha that felt uncomfortable. I didn't know what it was, but it was like a stone in my shoe. You can feel lonely in a marriage, that's the worst thing. It wasn't Andy's fault. But we didn't really know one another in the way that people do if they have lived together for a year or two before they tie the knot.

In truth I got married to appease my parents, who would never have been happy for their daughter to be living with someone while unmarried. This was called living in sin, and nice girls did not do it. But I had compromised with my mother for the last time.

Feeling really weird wearing my new changed name, I tried to assume the role of good wife. I thought I would cook a few casseroles and become a 'lady painter', but Andy was having none of it. He didn't want me ironing his shirts either. Children were for much later, so I had married the right man as it happened. He was a single-minded non-conformist. I was too, really. We rubbed along all right, but we were friends rather than lovers.

Ever since I had hit existential angst at art school, I had grappled with my purpose in life. I badly wanted to contribute. I wanted to be good at something. To be an artist seemed an unattainable wild dream. How, and in what form, and what for? The desire to be an artist is a deep burning smouldering fire that, once lit, cannot be put out. It's a curse and a blessing, and it eats away at you if you do not serve. Fortunately, Andy's resistance to suburbia was the making of me.

But I was twenty-two. What was I going to do with my future? A misty tunnel stretched before me. According to my upbringing, I was supposed to be having children and cooking dinners, and according to my education I was meant to be forging a singular creative path.

When we got to Cambridge it was blindingly clear. I had followed my husband halfway round the world and I did not have a clue what I was doing. Not very clever. My mother's sage advice had got her through, but this was a new age, wasn't it? True, I couldn't get a mortgage without a male partner, and I couldn't get a legal abortion if I wanted one. I couldn't get the same pay as men for the same work, and if I got divorced, I couldn't claim a share in the family property unless 'fault' could be proved in court. But things were changing weren't they?

In 1967 it felt like the sun came out. We were flower power people. We were the Woodstock generation. We were going to change the world.

Well, not really. Free love? I thought that put more pressure on us women, not less. Open marriages? That was really the beatnik bohemian male triumphing. I felt marginalised as a young woman. If I couldn't rustle up a sexy look that got attention in the street, I felt like I had somehow disappeared. At the same time, I was feeling buttoned down. Life seemed full of contradictions.

Then it happened.

In my generation, everyone can remember where they were when they heard 'Jailhouse Rock' for the first time. When Elvis the Pelvis claimed our sitting room through the old Columbus radio, no longer were we a post-war generation. My brother put on his blue suede shoes and disappeared down to the milk bar to hang out around the jukebox. But, for me, the big life-changing moment was standing outside Waterstones bookshop in Cambridge and seeing the window full of only one book: *The Female Eunuch*.

There is a before and an after. Reading that book was the moment when my external and internal worlds collided. A bright light went on. Germaine Greer was not only owning up to being clever, but she wasn't talking quietly. She was yelling, in her undeniably Australian voice. 'Wake up, women, and here's why!' She challenged me. She told my nice girl to bugger off. What she was talking about was *relevant*. It wasn't polite. It was a cry of trailblazing rage that is still searing.

'Women don't understand how much men hate them,' for example.

I knew that the men close to me didn't hate me. They loved me, and the rest were relatively genial. But in the world at large, I felt all the time that I didn't fit. When I read *The Female Eunuch* it focused my internal lens. My fuzzy dissatisfaction became clearer and less comfortable, both at once. Now I had a philosophical framework to rethink everything. The lot. My own attitudes to my past, my childhood in Greymouth, my adolescence in Napier. I came to understand that how I felt about myself and the world around me was less to do with me personally, and more systemic to us all – men and women. Gender role definition. All God's children – we are not born equal at all. And I had internalised the problem. My brother was supposed to go to university and become someone terribly important, while I was supposed to marry someone dependable, put on a white cardy and teach music part-time. Neither of us did that, but it was hard to avoid that unconscious landscape. How women and men live together shapes us.

After reading Germaine Greer, I reassessed my art school days. I saw that even though women were by far the largest population in the painting department, their work was not taken seriously. 'It is a good zing you paint de small paintinks, Mrs Goldstein, zey fit more easily into the roobish tin.'

That was our Lithuanian painting teacher's considered remark to a mature student, piercing the quiet of our painting studio one Tuesday. We were serious about our work, and being told you were 'too happy to be a good painter', or that your best bet if you wanted to be a full-time artist was to marry a farmer, was hardly encouraging. It was implied that we weren't going to be any good because we were built to have babies. Once we did that – curtains on any other creative urges. That idea was so entrenched that Rita Angus wrote that she had reconciled herself with not having a family because it would wreck her art.

The nearest living role model for us, Doris Lusk, was referred to as 'dear old Doris'. She was as good a painter as any of them, but it was the men who ruled. They shaped art history too. When the pale images of 'New Zealand painting' were projected from our rumpty slide projector onto the painting department studio wall, the only mention of Rita Angus was that she was a Wellington portrait painter. It was implied that her one decent painting was of Betty Curnow, the poet Allen Curnow's wife. Discussion was all about the phallic cactus in the background.

Meanwhile, the landscape was astride with the greats – Colin McCahon, Toss Woollaston, Bill Sutton, Rudi Gopas – all terrific painters, and those last two were our painting tutors, but why the blind discrimination?

Once Germaine Greer's blunt tones resounded in my brain, I could see why I had been so uncomfortable at art school. And I could work out why I had not felt right in my marriage. Andy was no male chauvinist pig, but assumptions around married couples were extremely patriarchal. We lived with those every day – and now Mrs Dennis was going to have to radically question everything. That meant Andy would too.

The irony is that it was in Cambridge, running around the outskirts of the hallowed halls in this ancient bastion of male privilege, that I finally came of age.

One evening I found myself pacing outside a little house in a nondescript street smoking a nervous ciggie. I finally plucked up the courage to ring the doorbell. Entering that tiny front room and joining a meeting of the Cambridge Scarlet Women – sometimes called the Redstockings – I found a fearsomely intelligent bunch. And some of them were even more nervous than me.

The idea of going to an all-women's meeting in a little front room in someone's house filled me with dread. I had never been in a group of women discussing flower arranging, let alone one discussing personal politics. Were we all going to have to drink our menstrual blood? When I lived at Helen Connon Hall I had enjoyed the company of women, but we were focused outward – most of us on how to get, and keep, a boyfriend. This was different. Seriously challenging. Not a knitting circle. Or would we knit vulvas?

The rules of engagement were already established. A topic was suggested, and then everyone would speak one at a time, uninterrupted, going round the circle. I was used to rowdy debates in which the loudest voice (male) got the upper hand. But with this approach, even the shyest woman had a chance to speak, and what was discussed was personal and political at the same time. This was not an ideology you could read up on and then call yourself informed. How you lived day to day was the focus. Feminism. A simple idea of gender equity, focused on changing at least three thousand years of established Western social behaviours.

Easy. We'd have it done by lunchtime.

In retrospect we were taking for ourselves an analysis already espoused by the Suffragists, and adding to it. We were not only talking about women's rights, but every little thing relating to relationships and domestic life, as well as the big issues of childcare and autonomy over our own reproductive lives. New ways of thinking were being written down and appearing in pamphlets. None of this related to anything you could buy down at the newsagents. In those scurrilous rags it was all about women supposedly wrecking family life by working, and burning bras (and many who were there said that didn't happen; they were burning their stays, those gut-clenching elasticated corsets with suspenders that held stockings up). Scarlet Women dreamt of the day when Britain had a female prime minister (which did happen, but not with the results we'd hoped for). We analysed city planning for communal housing. We got down and dirty supporting the 'unsupported mothers' on social welfare, who still get a raw deal. And I read *The Politics of Housework*.

That was the moment for me, the moment when it all came home. This unassuming little pamphlet was written by Pat Mainardi and published by the New York Redstockings. *The Politics of Housework* is a treasured tiny sliver on my bookshelf. It still resonates today, especially this passage, in which Mainardi notes that many men

> are not accustomed to doing monotonous, repetitive work which never issues in any lasting, let alone important, achievement. This is why they would rather repair a cabinet than wash dishes. If human endeavors are like a pyramid with man's highest achievements at the top, then keeping oneself alive is at the bottom. Men have always had servants (us) to take care of this bottom stratum of life while they have confined their efforts to the rarefied upper regions. It is thus ironic when they ask of women – Where are your great painters, statesmen, etc.? Mme. Matisse ran a military shop so he could paint. Mrs. Martin Luther King kept his house and raised his babies.

I had always been in charge of the kitchen in whatever flat Andy and I occupied. I cooked for everyone. Once we were clear of that dreadful first term of obligated college dining, I'd sling a casserole in the big old Aga in the morning before dashing out to Fulbourn, and I'd serve it with greens at night. Not hard – but unfair, given that everyone else in the house was swanning about at the university library worrying about where to put the colon in a sentence. Things had to change. Up went a roster. And I didn't clean up.

Immediately, everything went pear-shaped. There was 'matter' in the sink, but I told myself off and trained myself out of cleaning up. You can't expect your spouse to clean up if you have already done it. Housework and childcare, if not shared, keep women down. As long as it is assumed that women are in charge of running the home, equity can hardly be achieved. I will know when we have hit equality. No woman will ever say again, 'I'm very lucky. My husband helps with the housework.'

Fancy having a whole planet where basically half the adult population isn't expected to cook for the family or clean up after them, and doesn't share equally in looking after little children. How did that become a thing? I suppose it's improving now, for privileged women in the West, but I am writing this in the 2020s, more than fifty years on from the second wave of feminism. Are we there yet? Most of the world's women are still carrying water. As I am writing this, the United States plunges towards restricting access to safe abortion once more.

The Cambridge Scarlet Women were producing a magazine they wanted to sell at the supermarket. It would bridge the gap between town and gown. It would put the correct slant on feminism without the gutter press going on about underwear and feminists hating mothers. I read it now and it is strangely quaint. This is a sign of progress.

They said I had to do the illustrations with cartoons and design the cover. I hadn't really done that before.

'You have to,' they said. 'There isn't anyone else.'

All those days I'd spent in Bill Sutton's life-drawing class had to be worth something. With a punishing deadline looming, I did it in the middle of the night after work, hunched under my anglepoise with *Nashville Skyline* on the deck.

The group hadn't decided on a title, so at some ungodly hour, with an eye on the print deadline, I took unilateral action and made one up: *Bloody Women!* I stole an etching of an angry farmer from an agrarian protest sometime in the nineteenth century, added a graphic of a Victorian housemaid from an issue of *Nova* magazine, and I stuck Germaine on the back, sitting confidently in the corner with a group of large naked women. I thought it was pretty cool. Provocative.

But, come the harsh light of day, the other Scarlets were not impressed.

'How do we sell that down at the supermarket!' my aristocratic academic sisters complained.

Unfortunately, they may have been right, because there was never a second edition. On the other hand, I had found a way to be useful, and my confidence was growing.

We weren't only thinking and talking, we were active – and some of our protests were a lot of fun. We could rock the boat around the Cambridge colleges without too much difficulty. Here is our report on a protest over women with prams being banned from the King's College grounds.

PRAMPAIGN. On Saturday, February 27th Scarlet Women and Women Are People had their first united action. They gathered outside St John's College to demonstrate against the absurd rule that no prams or pushchairs are allowed into the College grounds. At the sight of 40 women with about 20 children in their carriages, the St John's porter firmly bolted the main gates . . . If this action does not lead to capitulation, we shall escalate the campaign. The demands of the mass ranks of pram-pushing mothers must and will be met. We shall overcome!

A revolution it had to be, and a revolution it was. I felt empowered, not so much in a deeply personal sense – we never entirely get away from the things our mothers told us – but I never looked back. I was in demand, and there was plenty to be doing in Cambridge in 1971. I had a job that was not taxing, and the rest of my hours were filled with politics, rock 'n' roll and drawing.

In this magical time when everything seemed possible, I met Nick, an undergraduate brimming with talent at Trinity. We were in the Whole Earth Drama Group together – the group didn't last that long and we never performed after our ignominious outing at the ADC – but Nick and I became friends, and he was an accomplished cartoonist. So whenever I needed a hand, I'd go and find him to help me. With Andy, we started up Hot Grunt, a screen-printing company that made posters and T-shirts with political slogans. Some supported the anti-apartheid campaign to stop the British cricket team playing in South Africa: 'Balls to the MCC'. Dubček's 'Socialism with a human face' was another big seller, and we added William Blake to our catalogue with: 'The road of excess leads to the palace of wisdom'.

'No it doesn't,' a dentist once said, as he filled my mouth with hardware. 'What about alcoholics!'

But everything was taking off.

Our benefactor was a tall, pale, wispy, longhaired young man who loped around Cambridge doing a little light drug-dealing. His parents were well-known academics and he was on the run under their noses. He owned a shop called What's In a Name that stocked seriously classy, seriously low-priced boutique labels. He sold drugs out the back and held rock concerts out the front. His favourite indulgence was big posters for the concerts he promoted – the more psychedelic, the better. Nick and I designed the posters together, and Andy ran the nuts and bolts of the printing in a studio he'd found at his college. We pasted the posters up in the middle of the night while the town slept. We had a Mini Moke with open sides that was well-suited to this illegal activity. Every now and again we'd get caught by the police and taken down to the station. I was once nearly arrested for suggesting to an irritated policeman that he go and find some real criminals. Very unwise. There have been a few moments in my life when I know that if my skin were a different colour, the outcome would have been very different.

A steady stream of errant rock stars staggered through our house in altered states. Syd Barrett came round one day and stood close to the wall with his back to the room, watching the orange and white paisley wallpaper for a very long time. Everyone did their best to ignore this rearranged Pink Floyd legend in our sitting room. His eyes really were crazy diamonds. The dream was to get Twink from Pink Fairies together with Syd to launch a new band. They gave it a go, one fateful night, and played as the Last Minute Put Together Boogie Band. The gig of the century. The Corn Exchange was packed. You could get stoned just by breathing the air in there.

The band tuned up for a long time, then off they went. At last, Syd stepped forward for his highly anticipated guitar solo. For a few minutes his guitar soared, swooped, looped around – then he looked up and it suddenly stopped. It was like he was a puppet and someone had cut the string. He had seen the audience and thought a thousand thoughts. He plodded along for a few more bars, then that was that really. A sorry moment in rock history that I wish I hadn't witnessed.

Nick and I talked everything over with Andy. This was the age of expanded relationships. Together we decided I could have a husband and a lover living with me under the same roof. A lonely marriage became a rather full one. All I felt was deeply loved. Our little threesome suited me fine. Andy and Nick were good mates, and together we had adventures. Not sex. We kept that on a one-to-one basis. I think Andy agreed to this arrangement because it meant that the pressure of my constant questioning of everything was taken off him alone. He had someone else to talk to, and he didn't have a dissatisfied wife anymore. What's more, he was not immune to the occasional dalliance himself. Any residual guilt he may have felt was now assuaged. Living with one other person for the rest of your life was daft – or so we thought. Nick and I would go to the Tate, while Andy went to Lords with his mates. Perfect. Great while it lasted. But when the end of the year came, we all took off in different directions. You either do that, or you go into counselling for years. It's just too intense, ultimately.

I learnt a lot while gassing around Cambridge. I wonder just how that inner blossoming works. Would I have ever picked up a pen to draw a cartoon if the Scarlet Women hadn't made me? Would I have transferred that confidence out to the job at Fulbourn Hospital, where I started as an assistant librarian but ended up joining a trailblazing group that promoted art therapy and drama? Would I have made a funny little film that empowered the people who were in it as much as me? Who knows, but blossom I did.

I was becoming a liberated woman.

# 11

# Grendon

Blank concrete walls rise with no warning amid the lush green fields of Buckinghamshire. Outside the snug little village that gives it its name, HM Prison Grendon Underwood sits like a spaceship that's just arrived from a distant planet. And in a way it has. A Home Office experiment set up in 1960, it is a complete contradiction – a high-security jail run as a therapeutic community. Four wings of forty men, alongside two wings of adolescent violent offenders, all wearing their prison grey, living together and joining in group therapy every day.

To get to live here, you have to have either murdered or violently raped someone, or committed life-threatening arson. You need to be in the first half of a long sentence and have stopped saying you didn't do it, and you have to prove that you really, really want to be here. HM Prison Grendon Underwood: Pop. 240 prisoners (male), 40 prison officers (male), 4 psychiatrists (male), 4 psychologists (male), assorted social workers (male). And me. Well, there are other women who work here, but I've never met them. Life in the prison is very restricted. You can easily live a parallel life alongside God knows who.

As part of the art therapy course I talked my way onto at St Alban's School of Art in February 1974, I've been sent to Grendon Prison, seconded to the A wing, to do a pilot study in art therapy. I have just six weeks to prove that art therapy – open and non-interventional, almost the opposite to group psychotherapy – could be valuable here in the only HM prison therapeutic community in Britain. My main barriers are my youth and my gender.

I have a little bedroom in the overheated staff hostel that is huddled just outside the prison walls. It rains. It always rains. The men here are nice enough, but the hostel is one of those places where everyone keeps to themselves and there are little notices in the fridge. 'PLEASE DO NOT TOUCH – Graham's butter'. Amazing how many Grahams there are here at Grendon.

By the time I've endured ten hours of deathly silence in the hostel, where the windows don't open and you can hear someone fart three doors down, I'm screaming for something – anything – to relive the tedious dullness. So I go into the prison every morning with a certain sense of relief. At least there is a community here – a very unusual one, but one with plenty of talk.

It is here that I get into trouble every day. Not with the prisoners, who have plenty to gain by behaving well around me, but with the screws. The screws are like the charge nurses at Fulbourn Hospital – ordinary men who have answered the call to care for people in a controlled environment, only these guys are carers on steroids. The posters are all over the London tube, saying things like: *Join Her Majesty's Prison Service, Learn to Handle Men*. Prison officers are well paid and don't need tertiary education. They live in the villages around Grendon Underwood, attracted to the black-and-white rules to be found in HM prisons across Britain. But here at Grendon they find themselves in the ever-changing greys of therapeutic practice. No empiricals. What is right, wrong, good, bad – all up for discussion. Two worlds cohabit uneasily inside the prison walls. And that's just the staff.

I am viewed with suspicion.

'What are you doing walking around the prison looking like that?'

I'm wearing a jacket and a skirt. I'd thought I was demure.

'Flashing your legs around the wings, you'll get yourself raped, Missy.'

The next day I wear trousers with a long top down to my thighs.

That works for a few days, then: 'Why do you wear trousers all the time – you a lesbian or something?' The worst thing they can think of to call a woman is a lesbian.

Not for the first time, I keep my temper and my own counsel.

As the only young woman in the prison, I am treated like the Blessed Virgin and put on a pedestal whence I can do no harm. This is a very dangerous spot. Not only can you fall off without warning and become a slavered-over slut, it's almost impossible to be an effective therapist from way up here.

The head psychiatrist on A wing is a thin man with a harassed air and a turquoise pullover. I meet with him to report on how I think the art therapy can help. For example, if someone doesn't communicate well in talking therapy, then an individual, non-verbal approach might be more helpful. The head psychiatrist pays attention, in that non-committed way psychotherapists have, and mutters in a language I find oddly encased. This is not Fulbourn, with its youthful enthusiasts and anti-psychiatry crusaders.

The pilot study in art therapy involves working with four pre-selected men alongside their psychiatrist and psychologist. I have no idea how the men have been chosen, but I've asked that they be selected not for their art ability but for their need.

And so for two hours every weekday afternoon the men muck about with art materials. They make their pictures, and often I draw alongside them to keep them company. No pressure is put on them to talk about themselves or to analyse their work. I want to keep the time as open and non-judgemental as possible. After they make a picture or a sculpture, they can do what they like with it. At the end of our six weeks, one prisoner takes all of his artwork to burn. As he is a notorious arsonist, this is not considered particularly advisable or to reflect much progress. All his paintings are of burning buildings. But I have noticed that, as time went on, there were signs of a certain psychological shift – trees with leaves began to appear, and the fires in the buildings in his paintings got smaller. His psychologist agrees that the time spent scribbling has opened him up and he is now functioning better in the group, but actual progress? Hard to say.

Everything at Grendon was about how men functioned within the group. They attended big groups, small groups, every kind of group you could imagine, in order to do the hardest thing: face themselves. To face what had been done to them, and what they had done to others. It was not a soft option. They challenged and were challenged every day. Emotional disconnects are difficult to heal – and often terrifying, for anyone, anywhere. In the prison, the pressure to face up was relentless. It was a very brave individual who really took it on. All of the men were serving their sentence uninterrupted by the Mental Health Act. This meant that they'd get out the day their sentence finished, rather than when a committee of mental health experts agreed that they were no longer a danger to society. Poor bastards. I never met anyone there who wasn't a danger to themselves and others.

A childhood in an abusive family does lasting harm. Mix that with grinding poverty and a sense of life lived with no purpose, and a drug-fuelled gang offers great appeal to a young man. Join the army, join the prison service, join the local crims and fight one another.

You had to earn private space at Grendon. Having your own cell was a privilege, and guarded fiercely. Prisoners who caused trouble got 'ghosted' out. One day they were there, the next – gone. It always happened at night. Someone's gear would be removed from the dorm and then into the paddy wagon and then: 'Back to Wormwood Scrubs for you, buster.' Ghosted. The men learned the therapeutic lingo in an effort to stay in with the programme. During a heated exchange in a meeting, when some of them laughed at something, I heard someone say, 'I'm not being therapeutic, I'm being honest!'

During my first week, after tea, I sit in my first wing meeting. Forty grey-clad prisoners mill about and take seats in a big circle in the cafeteria. I'm impressed by the variety of looks that can be achieved with the same uniform. Some are dandies, others pumped-up thugs. No one appears to be paying me much heed, while keenly inspecting my person from a distance. I guess I'm doing the same to them.

This meeting is dealing with a big issue. Should Alf be ghosted? He's been caught in bed with a boy from one of the adolescent wings. The boy is sixteen years old. This is progress for Alf, his psychologist maintains. All his other relationships have been with boys under the age of consent.

There is a roar of derision from the men of A wing, and Jimmy from Glasgow stands up and lets Alf have it. 'Fuck fuck fuckety fuck. How come he can have it off with his toy boy and we can't have our wives in here?'

If you have never heard a Glaswegian swear, you have missed out on one of the most searing uses of the English language. But mainly Jimmy is saying 'cunt' in every sense. Cunty, cunting, cunted, and plain cunts flow from his mouth as one sentence. The other thirty-eight chime in wholeheartedly, and 'fucking cunting cunty cunt' rises like cigarette smoke above a party.

This is what I am thinking when Alf, the paedophile, directs his gaze to me. He is a slightly crumpled, stooped, pathetic character. He wears his prison-grey pullover over a meticulously ironed shirt buttoned at the collar and the cuffs fixed at his bony wrists. His shiny-kneed slacks have been tailored to a more fashionable flare. His hair is slightly lank. Everything about him is 'slightly', except his black piercing eyes, and at this moment of mayhem they fix on me. Up till now I have been ignored, a silent observer of this sad saga of male rage. Alf is outraged on my behalf.

'There's a lady present!' he yells over the baying crowd. Then he asks me straight out, 'What do you think of all this bad language?'

I know in an instant that I am on trial. If I say anything to indicate tolerance, I will be slutted for the rest of my time here – I will be used as their plaything, psychologically speaking, which could even extend to physical intimidation. But . . . if I take a punitively judgemental view, I'll be safely stuck up there with Mother Mary, wearing a halo and forever useless to the therapeutic programme I'm here to instigate. My mind is spinning.

They are all curious, waiting for me to reply. The longer the silence goes on, the harder it gets for me to speak. So I take a gulp and say what I am thinking. Thank you, Germaine.

'It's interesting that the most insulting thing you can call one another in here is the very thing you are claiming to miss the most.'

I can almost see the question marks sitting over their heads.

All dumbstruck. Even the most vociferous stops to think.

Slight amusement. Then there's a bit of a murmur of assent around the room, and the head psychiatrist in his blue pullover actually makes eye contact with me. Even the screws have to admit there's something to think about here.

Alf did get ghosted in the end. And life in the big group in A wing at HM Prison Grendon carried on amid tears, recriminations, tantrums and manipulations. 'Insight' was found, lost and recovered, and I got to do my six-week pilot study in 'art therapy in extreme institutions' with a certain amount of respect.

My time at Grendon was 'crisis development', as a friend of mine called it. Once everyone had got used to me and I had got used to them, I found I liked most of them. There's a weird disconnect between how people are day to day, and the terrible things they – we – do to one another, particularly to our nearest and dearest. Suffering is a human universal truth. We all know it and share it. When the layers are pulled away, it's only empathy for one another that counts.

At the time, I thought that my six weeks at Grendon when I was twenty-five was just an extremely interesting, hermetically sealed moment. A strange and intense time of being among rapists, murderers and paedophiles. But in fact it set me up for so much more, though I didn't know it yet. I found out that being the only woman in the room does not have to be scary. I'd thought it was unlikely to be of any real relevance to me, in my communal, gender-friendly, let's-talk-about-the-housework life at the time. But I was not to know that, in the next thirty years of my time on this earth, I would often be the only woman around the camera.

# 12

# Coming Home

The bath is hot and deep. A good long soak with lavender and patchouli oil soothes a troubled mind. It is Saturday afternoon and the sun is shining over the tops of the trees, sparkling up the water. In the moment I am telling you about – being in the bath – I am living in a beautiful communal house in Stockwell, with Nick, in 1975. The bath oil is concocted by Nick's Ukrainian mother, who, from her clinic in Knightsbridge, dispenses aromatherapy to Shirley Bassey, Michael Parkinson, most of the top brass at the BBC, and me. My being with Nick is her worst nightmare. An outspoken itinerant Kiwi is not the kind of person he was supposed to connect with at Cambridge.

When I am in the bath, my mind is free to wander in a way it doesn't otherwise. Thoughts pop up like visitors. I look like I'm staring at my feet by the taps, but I am not really seeing them. I am somewhere else entirely. Sideways thinking. Back to the womb. We all come from a lovely warm bath. Our bodies expand and lose their edges in the bath.

This particular bath sits on the middle floor of 17 Stockwell Park Crescent, once a boarding house, now a modern family home. A north London psychiatrist had it renovated for his family, but they refused to budge from the mouldering north London manor house they were renting. In London the river defines you, and his wife and

158

kids were firmly north Londoners. Our crescent is a tree-lined oasis surrounded by grubby housing estates and council flats down the road from a comprehensive school that has regular knife inspections. It is not uncommon to see a pall of black smoke rising above Stockwell and discover that another pile of tyres has been set alight.

'We're here too, you know, and you're all a bunch of WANKERS . . .'

Not really the place to bring up your posh, privately educated children.

Nick and I have moved in together. We have gas central heating, every room is newly painted – it's a palace. Each floor has two bedrooms and a bathroom in between. The ground floor has been extended, with a glass atrium and big sliding double-glazed doors opening out into the garden. This is the first teak and stainless-steel kitchen I have ever seen. Since leaving home, I have always lived in scungy old houses, with no particular aspirations to do otherwise, but when I heard my friends from Cambridge were setting up a communal house, I was in, boots and all. Our friend Stephen was completing his medical training at St Thomas' Hospital, and it was through his family connections that we were able to live there. I had met him during paste-up night for one of those endless Cambridge student rags we circulated.

The copy had been printed in long rolls, cut up and stuck together with 'cow gum'. I had drawn the cover – a broken wine glass with spilt wine – and written out the first sentences of the first article and laid it out diagonally in what I considered a dynamic aesthetic. This young medical student kept pulling it up and putting it on straight. I would then claim artistic freedom and make it crooked again. This became a long argument over a long night that went on and on. By the time the sun rose, we knew each other.

Some of my most enduring friendships with men have begun with an argument. If you can rage about the concepts without getting personal, then you've tested one another's mettle I suppose. I can't actually remember who won in the end.

The pamphlet we had put together was a collection of political essays focusing on the military junta ruling Greece. Greek academics had fled to Britain when their compatriots began to be disappeared and murdered. Some were sheltered in the colleges. Our pamphlet was to raise money for 'the Cambridge six' – the Cambridge students who had protested against the Greek tourism board holding a promotion, 'Greek Week', at the Garden House Hotel. Things turned nasty during the protest when the police waded in, making hundreds of arrests. Six young men among them got done over by the right-wing hanging judge, Melford Stevenson. One minute they were the pride and joy of their families, the next, they were doing time. Bang bang, Melford's silver hammer came down on their heads. They were never the same again. One year and one day in Wormwood Scrubs will do it. This is the recurring story of the 60s 'revolution'. The music and the style endure, but the establishment came down heavy on the politics.

By the time of the bath – that bath, the one that changed everything – Stockwell Park Crescent had filled with people who worked in the health sector. We were into personal politics and left-wing causes. I was pursuing my unsuccessful attempt at bringing art therapy and light to the back wards of Cell Barnes Subnormality Hospital, at St Albans. That was how it was known – a terrible punitive place where patients were locked away. Only God and those voiceless people know what went on in there.

Meanwhile, at home in south London, the politics of housework (my favourite) were discussed daily. We were trying to live with autonomy together. We had House Meetings. It was a relief from life at work, where nothing was up for discussion and any suggestion of how to improve things was viewed with suspicion and taken personally. Dr David Clark had been right. I was getting a flat head pushing against too many brick walls.

Stephen was setting up a radical general practice with one of our housemates, George Meredith. After they graduated, the two young doctors rented a little house in Lewisham, hung out their sign and opened their doors. They put a big black plastic bag in the entranceway and threw all the drug companies' bribes in there for anyone to rummage through. Piles of classy pens and leather-bound diaries. If you were registered with the practice, you became a shareholder, and there was an annual general meeting in which patients could have a say on how to improve patient services. A third doctor in this experiment specialised in women's health and she, with another member of our house, Maggie Mackenzie, focused on contraception, childbirth and women's well-being. Physiotherapy was a regular feature. The laying on of hands. This shouldn't be such a radical idea – but it is. How often, now, do you go to your time-poor GP, and they spend most of your appointment asking you questions while interfacing with their computer?

The Lewisham practice came to grief a few years later when a little-known group calling themselves the Maoist Tendency Doctors of South London joined the practice, stormed the annual meeting, and got enough votes to sack George and Stephen. Their radical experiment apparently wasn't radical enough. Such was the stupidity of the single-issue sectarianism that splintered the great leap forward of the 60s generation. George Meredith went to Goa, and ultimately became a leading disciple of Bhagwan Rajneesh. George became Devaraj, and later was nearly murdered when Bhagwan's right-hand woman, Sheela, had him poisoned, with an injection into his buttocks.

But that hadn't happened yet when I was lying in the bath at 17 Stockwell Park Crescent, letting all my worries wash away that lovely Sunday, as the sun got lower and lower.

I had nearly finished reading *Time Out*. This issue had a long article about Midge Mackenzie, who had just made a 16mm film featuring her disabled son. It was screening around London in cinemas. I was idly turning over not just the pages but the idea. Suddenly I thought, *I could do that*.

That thought went straight to my gut. My stomach churned and I found myself sitting up. If Midge Mackenzie could do it, then so could I. I too could make a film that could screen in a cinema near you. It was as if I had been hit by a thunderbolt – and in a way, I had. I didn't know that this outrageous idea would steer me back to my homeland, where the magnificent picture palaces were closing down to be demolished, and where the only movies that stirred folk from their La-Z-Boys on a Saturday were freighted in from Hollywood. But the hills were calling.

When my brother sent me Witi Ihimaera's book of short stories *Pounamu Pounamu*, that was it.

It took me a whole year to leave.

After my epiphany in the bath, I joined the London Women's Film Group, who had meetings on Earlham Street in Covent Garden. The West End was a dirty, exhaust-fume-belching, grumbling old place. My nose was always full of black coal-stained snot when I ventured into the building. I went through a battered front door and up a narrow hallway. The place had little rooms on every floor and the walls were covered in posters: 'Women Unite, Unite and Fight', and the four demands: '24-Hour Child Care. No Discrimination on Marital Status. Equal Pay for Equal Work. Abortion on Demand.' The raised fist of women's defiance was everywhere.

The LWFG met once a month after work, when everyone was absolutely exhausted. They did not welcome me with open arms. They had problems of their own. They were making a film in which women played men, and they were finding it problematic. Most of them were deeply frustrated artist activists pushing for women to get work in the British film industry. But to do that, you needed a union card. You could only get a union card if you had a job on a movie. You could only get a job on a movie if you had a union card.

How that pans out in practice is that a band of brothers choose mates to join their shooting teams in the camera department, art department, lighting, sound recording and so on. Men choose men. Much easier. No constraints on unbridled locker-room talk. That's partly why men like working in an all-male team. Lewd jokes. I worked with a grip once who called the DOP 'your D.O. penis'.

All the time. I direct close to the camera. It was like I wasn't there. Funnily enough we worked well together, this Aussie and me. But I wouldn't ever want to have a cup of tea with him. He'd arrived off the plane hardly able to stand. As he swayed before me at the luggage collection, he unburdened himself. 'Jeez, I'm so relieved. I thought you'd have hairy armpits.'

It's very hard for a woman to crack into the gang. The few who do tend to toe the line once they get there. This has changed since 1974, but not fast enough, and not across the board. You still tend to find women working together in the production office and in costume/ make-up, and men around the cameras.

If the prevailing culture is a bully culture, the lone woman tends to have to join in or ship out. In this competitive environment, becoming the biggest bully in the room is one well-worn way to get respect. It's either that or not lasting long, worn down by the endless bad jokes and the girlie pics in the grip truck. It's often said that women don't like competing. Poor things. It's all that nurturing their biology demands. Sounds quaint, but that idea prevailed for a very long time.

Women are not shrinking violets when it comes to ambition. But in the film production industry, a testosterone-driven work environment gets even more toxic the closer it gets to power and money. In my experience, the women who survive might not be all that likely to kindly offer a leg up to another woman. Having fought for legitimacy, they are inclined to protect their patch even more vociferously than men do. A woman who makes it into the patriarchy is not necessarily a feminist, as we know from Margaret Thatcher et al.

In 1974 the women who gathered in Earlham Street to discuss how the hell they were ever going to scale this colossus, to get feminist films made and distributed, were locked into a long conversation with one another. They were all writing books. My 8mm efforts, made as part of drama groups in the various institutions that I had been working in, were hardly central to their cause. And as well, I was beginning to question the burgeoning feminist orthodoxy swirling about.

\*

I arrive on Earlham Street one balmy Sunday afternoon. Street rubbish stench rises to greet me the minute I get out of the tube. Yet another rubbish strike. Used syringes decorate the drains. As I approach the London Women's Film Group headquarters, I see a mother outside with two young children hugging her skirts. She is crying. I open the door and beckon her in, assuming she's one of the bashed-up mothers who arrive there regularly, but she will not follow me in. When I ask her why, through sobs she tells me that she has been thrown out of a meeting because she has brought a 'man child' with her. I look at this 'man child'. He's grizzling, he's too hot, his nose is snotty, and he can be no more than four years old.

It's hard to believe her story, but I do. Our movement is fragmenting into passionate sectarian arguments. Lines are being drawn between the radical lesbian separatists – 'Fuck a man and you betray the cause' – and the faction who want wages for housework, and the rest. I look at this distraught woman and her miserable children on the footpath, and leave with her. We have a cup of tea in a nearby café and then I go home to Stockwell. That was the last time I set foot in that building on Earlham Street.

It wasn't the London Women's Film Group who threw her out, but chucking a woman out because she had her four-year-old son with her was not what we feminists were fighting for, I thought. And I hate fundamentalism of any kind, including feminist fundamentalism. I'm all for the debate, but let's get on with it.

I realise that I am very like my father in this regard. If I'm not in, I'm out. One minute he was an altar boy, and the next he had left the Catholic church, never to return. That was it.

None of this furthered my cause in 1975. I still wanted to get in with any group who were making films. I heard of an 8mm movement in London. Experimental art films. Derek Jarman was famously forging an entirely different innovation. But I was too shy to approach what appeared to be highly opinionated theatrical types. The one friend I'd made during my brief encounter with the London Women's Film

Group was Carola, who had connections to the 8mm crowd. She had a £50 grant from the British Arts Council to make a film, but she couldn't do it in the end. Rather than give the money back, she passed it on to me.

After walking away from the back wards at the so-called Subnormality Hospital, I'd got a job at Brixton College of Further Education. I used the money from Carola to make a film with a group of deaf students. Just as with the Fulbourn drama group, the class made up the story. Nick and I filmed it as a running, jumping and standing-still movie. It was how their minds worked. Brilliant sight gags.

By now it had become possible to put a sound stripe on the edge of the film, and 8mm projectors could be hooked up to speakers. This meant a soundtrack could be constructed. Though they couldn't hear themselves, the Brixton kids knew that in this film they were sometimes communicating verbally to the big hearing world.

The day dawned when Carola and I drove to South Bank to present this twelve-minute film to the Inner London Education Authority, who had unwittingly funded it. We set up the little projector and screened *Mojak Kojak Detective Daughters* to a velvet-coated (they all had them) Oxbridge-educated young man slumped in the gloom.

When the lights came up, he looked at the ceiling, and addressing no one in particular, spoke for several minutes. I gathered it was a critique of the film, but I couldn't recognise anything of *Mojak Kojak Detective Daughters* in what he was saying. Nothing. I had no idea what he was talking about at all. This was a shock.

I had studied *Abstraction and Empathy* by Wilhelm Worringer, I had read *The Mass Psychology of Fascism* by Wilhelm Reich. I had done the Wilhelms. I had got my head around some pretty hefty tomes – English translations from German are hard to read. But the language he was using was neither art history, psychology nor political theory. It was incomprehensible. He could have been speaking Swahili for all I knew. He carried on as we packed up our tiny projector and headed out of there. All I ever want anyone to say after they have watched any film of mine is, 'Love it. It's brilliant.'

When we got to the car, I asked Carola, 'But did he like it, do you think?'

Unperturbed, she thought he possibly may have. She subscribed to that notion.

I learnt later he had been using a theory of criticism called semiotics. Wikipedia will tell you semiotics is the study of meaning-making, processing signs, meaningful communication. To me, it is a way to keep the conversation about art as exclusive as possible. A terrible trend that has engulfed and clouded the language of cultural discourse in the visual arts for far too long, in my opinion. It has grown like a ghastly fungus infecting university departments all over the world. I am hoping it has gone away. This was a little 8mm film made with a group of profoundly deaf students at Brixton College of Further Education. They thought it was terrific. Especially when we screened it to the rest of the college. They held their heads up a little more and acquired a jaunty spring in their step after that. They didn't have to sit on their own in the college café anymore. They became cool overnight. I was seeing a trend here with these little films of mine.

That year there was an explosion of Australian film in London. I saw *Picnic at Hanging Rock* and thought: I could spend the next ten years chipping away at the edifice that is the British film industry, or I could head home and see if I can get in at the beginning of something. It was just a vague thought, though – an intuition I could not articulate.

Writing it down now makes it sound far more purposeful than it was. At the time, I felt it as strong waves of missing – I missed the hills, I missed the light, I missed the sea. Not the lippy-lappy pale grey imitation sea that the British wade in at the seaside, but the pounding Tasman that roars and rattles stones on the West Coast beaches.

I managed to get my part-time hours at Brixton College of Further Education to three consecutive days a week, which gave me four-day weekends. Disposable time with disposable income. I made myself a badge that said 'Einstein was a part-timer'. I made home movies with Nick and the housemates, *Creeps on the Crescent* being a popular drawcard to our parties, which we called 'arties'. I drew cartoons for left-wing groups, and every Monday I did art therapy on myself. I was fulfilled. Happy. But the urge to go home was gnawing at me.

Cartooning was done in a collective with Liz Mackie, well known for her clever, biting cartoons capturing the interior world of the working-class wild child. Liz became a great friend. Her stripy stovepipe trousers inspired me to wear similar ones, and I loved the all-night sessions we did with Nick, the three of us drawing side by side, Little Feat and Joan Armatrading on the turntable, complaining when our drawings went wonky. We'd swap and get someone else to draw the annoying bit. It reminded me of when Jim Vivieaere and I drew princesses and horses at Intermediate.

One group we cartooned for was a radical social worker collective who published the mag *CASE CON*. Our job was to gather the papers, try to make head or tail of them, and come up with cartoons to fill the holes in their layout. The dense Marxist-leaning analysis of what was wrong with the social welfare system was never that easy to brighten up. We did it with the aid of marijuana. (We had some lovely plants growing in the Stockwell Park Crescent atrium. Handy.) We worked until our eyes fell out, hit the deadline with minutes to spare, then drove across London at dawn to deliver the fruits to the Case Con Collective. They'd give us a bleary-eyed thank you, then we would head to the nearest greasy spoon to fill up on steak and eggs.

'They're cutting everything except the grass,' said two women sitting on a broken park bench, up to their knees in overgrown lawn outside council flats. That was about as funny as our cartoons got.

I walk up the stairs to 17 Stockwell Park Crescent carrying my Uher two-reel tape recorder, my shoulder bag slung round my neck. As my key turns in the lock, the door opens and the Stockwellians come thundering out.

'You're late!'

They throw my belongings into the hallway and blindfold me before steering me towards Stephen's car. My birthday is coming up and they've decided to take me on a 'magical mystery tour' after work, but I had no idea you could actually be late for that.

With a joint shoved my way and the others crammed into the back seat, I can hear the traffic getting heavier. There's a certain anxiety in the air. I decide to relax and go with it. The Stockwellians are driving us quite a long way. We go round roundabouts and over bridges. I'm starting to *really* enjoy the soundscape as traffic lights blip, horns howl and big wheels lumber past. A park is found, and I am deftly walked along a busy street and into a building. We are still late, apparently. I'm steered into a quiet cavernous interior. We stop. The blindfold is removed.

I am standing with my face almost touching two large black vinyl-covered double doors. I read, in bold white lettering, 'THIS. IS. NEW. ZEALAND.' I push the doors open into a theatre where the lights are fading. I can see perfectly, unlike the others who stumble around in the dark. I find my seat in the front row.

Three screens burst into life with a swooping helicopter shot that transports us over the magnificent mountains to a Sibelius orchestral soundtrack. I am flying with it. We soar with the music and we are transported to a country known only through brochures. Beautiful indeed. Tiny birds flutter, tūī cough, the bush gleams, politely smiling Pākehā with open faces stand in rooms eating terrible food, leaving piupiu-skirted Māori to swing the poi and do the haka.

Afterwards we go down the King's Road for a malted milkshake. This is my English friends' effort at curtailing my homesickness. They know that New Zealand is a place in the world. They know it has the best milkshakes. They have been puzzled at my delight upon sharing an important package of chocolate fish. Why go home when you can have it here, they are saying. But I am homesick. It has taken me by surprise. I don't want to be an expatriate. I want to go home. Seeing this three-screen masterwork from Hugh Macdonald and the National Film Unit has just made it worse.

168

It's going to be hard to leave. But I have become aware that – aside from this ground-breaking three-screen wonder, and a documentary by the National Film Unit about the pollution of New Zealand's waterways, which screened at the National Film Theatre – there is some larrikin filmmaking going on back home.

Shirley Grace is now married with a toddler daughter, and another on the way. She sends news of adventures on the Blerta bus – the Bruno Lawrence Electric Revelation Travelling Apparition. Following on from Ken Kesey's Merry Pranksters, Blerta is a group of musicians, filmmakers and actors tooling around country towns with their families, entertaining local kids during the day and doing drug-fuelled light shows during the night, then leaving town before the local authorities can catch up with them. That sounds like fun.

I leave Nick finishing his animation film to join me later, and I head out.


There's a corrugated iron shed at Wellington Airport. In December 1976 they call it the overseas terminal. When I land there after seven years away and thirty-six hours clattering around the world, the rain is so heavy on the roof that the passport men have given up asking questions. With my big old cardboard suitcase and $500, here I am.

Water streams up the windscreen of the baby Austin as Martin, my sister's boyfriend, drives me through the dark, Depression-era Mount Victoria tunnel to their flat in Kelburn. The rain is horizontal. You can't see a thing and it is even colder inside. We huddle around the sputtering open fire eating lamb chops, boiled potatoes and silverbeet as the cold wind blows carpet waves over the floorboards. What have I done?

My sister Jan is off touring with a theatre group called Red Mole, who are not unlike Whole Earth except they actually perform to audiences. Jan is Red Mole's musical director, and the group is the opening act for a rock 'n' roll band I have never heard of. When I go to the show at the Wellington Town Hall, the audience is mainly hippies in jeans. Red Mole's performance involves topless fire-eating

169

and masked stilt-walking, along with authentic mediaeval dancing. None of this has hit the English rock scene. Split Enz are dressed in harlequinesque costumes, wear make-up and have high hair. Ziggy Stardust meets Ubu theatre of the absurd. I think about our miserable failure fusing Brecht and acid rock at the ADC, and I worry for my sister – and the band.

The whole show is received with genial warmth by the completely stoned crowd, but I can't cope. I can't get my bearings culturally. Is this a rock concert or a theatre performance? It bears no resemblance to anything around the gig scene in Brixton. This is my home, but I don't know where I am. It's another planet, not just another country. As I watch Tim Finn leaping around the stage, the band look like aliens, but I'm feeling like a real one.

I make a mental note never to live in this godforsaken cold windy place. It's one week before Christmas, and I have barely ventured out of the draughty villa on Kelburn Parade. I wear my favourite woolly hat to bed, the one that was knitted for me by my Stockwellian friend Maggie Mackenzie. I pull it down over my head. I'm clinging to memories of my English home now. I'm missing my mates, the Kartoon Kollective, Nick, and the ideologically, surgically tuned arguments of the south London crowd. That little knitted beanie hat becomes my closest friend, but when I do venture outside, it is ripped from my head.

'Must remember never to live here,' I think as I hang on to a lamppost to stop myself being blown away by a southerly roaring up Featherston Street.

Jan is all business, and she's on my case.

'What do you want to do?'

I am pale and skinny and out of step. Everyone is constantly asking me that question. 'What do you want to do?' I can't answer. I'm doing it, aren't I?

I've come home, but I hardly know anyone anymore, including my own family. I have a 'plum in my mouth', and everyone's worried about me. My mother thinks I have come home to die.

# 13

# Pacific Adventures

Kilbirnie is on flat, reclaimed land between the airport and Lyall Bay. The freezing wind blows straight off the south coast from Antarctica.

'Colder than a mother-in-law's breath,' the taxi driver cheerily tells me as he deposits me outside an old converted pie factory across the road from the bus depot.

There isn't a soul about. Wellington in 1977 is empty. You could fire a gun down Courtenay Place on a Sunday at lunchtime and not hit anyone. I am wearing polka-dotted Ossie Clark trousers that I scored cheap from our main Hot Grunt client – who is currently calling himself 'Cliff Hanger' back in Cambridge – and have my portfolio of radical feminist cartoons under my arm. I'm here under Jan's beady eye. That sister of mine has continued with the hard question that I couldn't answer, and all she's got from me is that I'm done with working in institutions and am looking for a creative group to belong to.

'Oh, you should go out to Pacific Films then,' she told me.

She has composed music for *Hunting Horns*, a documentary television series with James McNeish, directed by Barry Barclay. She likes working with them out there in Kilbirnie. She knows nothing of my bath moment. She just wants me out from under her feet really, or at least paying rent, so there it is.

When I wander into Pacific Films that cold Tuesday afternoon, it feels like Walt Disney's garage around the time they made *Mickey Mouse*. A ragtag bunch of disconnected rooms, converted from their original use as a bakery into a film studio of sorts. The reception is a corridor with a woman sitting behind variegated glass answering a phone system that was antiquated even then.

I sit on an orange bench opposite her as people come and go – long-haired young men wearing bellbottoms and dark turtleneck sweaters, women looking purposeful. There's a good-humoured vibe to the place. I can hear people laughing somewhere in the bowels of the building.

I am shown over to 'the white house', across a small car park from the main building, and into John O'Shea's office.

Shepherdesses cavort across the greying wallpaper that harks to a time when this little bungalow was a suburban home with aspirations. The place is stacked full of books, overflowing filing cabinets, framed photographs that sit on top of more stacks, and in the middle of this paper cloud, oblivious to the chaos, sits the man himself. He's the boss. All of this is his. John is the man who made *Broken Barrier*, *Runaway* and *Don't Let It Get You*. He turns from his writing and beckons me to take the only free seat in the room as he absentmindedly flicks ash from his tie.

He's being polite. He's seeing me because he is grateful to Jan for her music. But there's no job here. Pacific Films has been the New Zealand Broadcasting Corporation's unofficial outpost documentary department since the NZBC was founded in 1960. They have made *Tangata Whenua – People of the Land*, Barry Barclay and Michael King's pioneering documentary series on Māori life and culture; they have made Tony Williams and Michael Heath's *The Day We Landed on the Most Perfect Planet in the Universe*, and many, many more. (All these films are in Ngā Taonga, the New Zealand Archive of Film, Television and Sound. You could spend your time less rewardingly than to pop in and watch them.)

The NZBC has recently been 'reformed', and with substantial funding from the Kirk Labour government, the only network in the country has gone in-house, bought gear and employed an army of young people to edit and direct local programmes. They are all now cosseted in a concrete tower at Avalon in Lower Hutt.

As he lights one smoke from another, John O'Shea tells me that Pacific Films is struggling. At this moment he is really annoyed because he has been referred to in an article in the local newspaper as a 'veteran filmmaker'.

He waves the offending newspaper at me angrily.

'Look at that!'

I do. I read the short article. Generally respectful.

'What's wrong with it?' I say, forgetting I am trying to get a job here.

'"Veteran". It makes you f-f-feel like a c-c-car.'

His stutter disarms me. But he doesn't mind me laughing.

I tell him about my 8mm home movies, and show him my portfolio of cartoons. In this little office crammed with past and future screen dreams, my work looks strident and a bit self-conscious. But John seems interested. He calls out to his son.

'Rory, come and look at this. A filmmaking sheila.'

Rory arrives and they both have a slightly amused secret society moment, but I don't feel put down. I feel noticed.

'She should go out to the women's unit at A-A-Avalon,' John suggests to Rory, who agrees, and disappears.

This is the first time I have heard of a women's unit at Avalon. But I have spent seven years working in institutions, including prisons. I tell John that I am over institutions, and will continue to look for something more creatively collaborative. I pack up my frayed portfolio and leave.

What I didn't know was that John O'Shea hated Avalon with a passion. He hated their tower, he hated their condescending attitude towards him, and he hated that he had to convince them of the worth of anything Pacific Films wanted to make in order to get the funds to make it. He especially despised their access to government money.

When we met, he was in locked horns with the powers that be at Avalon. He blamed them for the demise of his company, and when I turned down the option of even considering applying for work out there, I was in with John O'Shea.

A couple of months later, I was back in his office. It was still cold, with a hopeful one-bar heater glowing.

'You can come and be our a-a-art director,' he said.

It was a job he didn't really have and in a discipline I had absolutely no idea even existed.

'I have no idea what that is,' I told him, thinking he would enlighten me.

'Neither does anyone else. It's a s-s-secret profession. Nobody knows.'

'Well, you'd better put me on a month's trial, John. I only know about loony bins.'

'Perfect training.'

So I became Pacific Films' 'art director from London'. I had rainbows painted on the toes of my leather boots and had no idea whatsoever of what my job would entail, but I was a long way from chipping at the edifice trying to get a union card in London.

I'm about to start my first day at Pacific Films, one of the very few full-time independent film companies in the country. It's May, two weeks before my thirtieth birthday, and I'm standing at the top of the cable car on a beautiful crisp day overlooking this little city glistening in the sun. Anyone will tell you that you can't beat Wellington on a good day. It's a cliché because it's true. Up here in Kelburn, you really can smell the flowers. The light is startling. I can see across that glistening harbour all the way to the Akatarawa Range. Then something happens.

I realise I can't leave this place until I have made that feature film. The one I haven't ever owned up to wanting to make. The one that will screen in real cinemas, like the ones we used to go to every Saturday as a family in Napier. A movie. For the cinema. To go to on a Friday, down the main street. Because I can.

I remember that this is the reason why I came home to New Zealand. All is suddenly clear.

Immediately I bury the thought. I put it away deep into my pounding heart. Sudden insights are brief. Ignore them at your peril.

I arrive at work at nine o'clock. Nobody is there. I take refuge from the cold wind in the porch. A white Datsun arrives and a little man with a fistful of keys alights. He gives me a less than friendly once-over, lets me in, shows me to a seat in what I am to discover is the tearoom and turns on one bar of a two-bar heater. Briskly instructing me not to turn it on any further, he leaves. This is Eric Anderson, the Pacific Films accountant. I'm another hungry mouth to feed, and I don't think he approves.

Over the next hour people amble in. It's John who arrives last. He's late.

'Follow me,' he tells me vaguely, and strides off through studio doors into a subterranean warren of editing rooms and desks littered with works in progress.

He opens a door and I find myself standing right in front of a large screen. A few men in suits are seated facing the screen, and they turn to look with great expectation at me. At this point I wish I could disappear. John sees my plight and ushers me towards a young man wearing a brown corduroy jacket standing to one side. Using his considerable bulk to shield us from the expectant audience, John whispers, 'P-p-pretend you know one another.'

I am left vacantly nodding in what I hope might be a familiar fashion at a curly-headed, freckle-faced man about my own age. He lifts his head in recognition in what I now know as the 'coastie hello'. How do you pretend you know one another? Unfazed, Craig Walters effortlessly includes me.

I have entered the great Pacific Films conspiracy. There's them – the 'others', the 'clients', the 'outsiders' – and then there's us. The strange thing is that having been told to pretend we already knew one another, we do. For life. Never intimate friends, but always convivial.

175

And after that introduction we just keep on pretending. It works. Without really meaning to do it so efficiently, John has fast-tracked me into the shooting gang. All men. They call me Bruce to help me feel at home. Having a nickname certainly puts me among the greats. My newly acquired friend is Crunch, or 'Crunch the Lunch', because as production manager, one of his many tasks is dealing out the lunch money on location.

They shoot basically everything, large and small, that Pacific is making at the time, and at the moment they're making commercials and training films to pay the rent. Along with the nicknames, John encourages the team to show disdain for these vital commissions by giving them fake names. 'Piss Pour' is the in-house name for a training film commissioned by New Zealand Breweries. This is my first task as Pacific Films' 'new art director from London'. They had already filmed at a pub downtown called Chloe's Bar, but during the edit some erudite soul pointed out that the apostrophe was in the wrong place on the sign, so now it needs to be corrected and re-shot.

So on my first day I find myself with Crunch at the wine bar, assessing the job at hand. I am relieved to find that each letter is made of polystyrene. We find a ladder and I swap the letters. Rory and the camera assistant, Michael Hardcastle, arrive to set up the camera, match the lighting, and shoot a couple of slates. I've never seen a slate before. But I have, of course. It's the universally known symbol for film. The slate is held in front of the camera before each numbered take, with the clapperboard open. Once the camera is rolling, the board is clapped shut, making a sharp sound. Syncing up sound to picture is a well-worn technical road. No more pushing GO on a rickety little projector and a big hospital-sized tape recorder. I'm in the industry now.

Then off goes Crunch out to the National Film Unit lab in Miramar to get the negative processed.

Job done. I'm starting to realise that, though I don't know what I'm doing, help is probably going to be available.

I'm dying to see the completed film. It's the result of my first work as a professional art director. I assume that it will be all about making cocktails. I'm shocked to discover that, instead, 'Piss Pour' intricately demonstrates for complete idiots how to efficiently squirt beer from hoses into as many jugs as possible as fast as possible without spilling a drop of the brewery's precious product. Welcome home Gaylene.

After every completed job at Pacific, large or small, we'd go to the pub to acknowledge the effort.

Though the bars now closed at ten, the habit of the six o'clock swill was still alive and well. After the pub, everyone would gallop out, flagons under their arms like ready-to-fire cannons, and gather at the nearest large house for a party – rowdy affairs where everyone got paralytic drunk, yelled at one another and behaved badly under a pall of cigarette smoke. You had to look after yourself at these parties. You'd get felt up at the most unexpected moment by the most unexpected person. I usually managed to get myself in a spot with my back to a wall where I could see any drunken hoon approaching, and take defensive action. It was either this or stay home.

It was at a party that I found myself stuttering it out – my deeply buried desire to make a movie.

This night, I'm squeezed into the hallway of a house overlooking Oriental Bay, drinking beer out of a Marmite jar, and Barry Barclay is quizzing me.

When I first joined Pacific, he was away in Sri Lanka trying to make a film that never eventuated. The United Nations money had fallen over. Now Bazza is back and he's organising his next sortie from his office out the back of the white house. He and John have a great mutual respect and co-conspirator relationship. They will go on to make Bazza's trailblazers – *Ngāti* and *Te Rua* then, sadly, after years of successful collaboration, they'll fall out big time. But that hasn't happened yet. For the moment, Bazza has his intense dark eyes fixed on me.

'So what are you going to do?'

That question again.

'Well, John says if I do the art direction, the rest of the time I can join the other departments to see where I fit.'

'And where do you think that is?'

'Well . . . Rory said I can join the camera department for a day or two.'

I don't tell him I've joined the camera department for one day already. What a disaster. Rory sent me off to the van to lug gear too heavy for me to carry, and my clapperboard skills were about as good as my waitress brain was, when I had trouble remembering orders at the greasy spoon at Cambridge. Try as I might, I couldn't remember whether I had changed the take number or not. When the footage came back from the lab, the editors laughed because so many takes had two numbers.

Bazza persists. 'What do you want to do?'

Time to fess up. I know the answer, so why be so coy?

'Well . . . I think I could direct?'

The world doesn't stop. He doesn't fall over laughing, clutching his stomach and pointing his finger. *Wants to be a director! Ha ha!* But his response surprises me.

'How old are you?'

'Thirty.'

'You'd better get cracking then, you're old enough.'

An immediate challenge. I've outed myself at a party. Now I will have to do it, I think as I take a nervous gulp from the Marmite jar.

Pacific Films worked every hour God gave them. I was paid $90 a week. I could just manage to live on that. I bought a Honda 200 and I wore a leather jacket that Maggie Kelly had given me. She was a recent arrival from London too, working as an assistant editor down at the old pie factory. We became firm friends after John O'Shea introduced us when he was giving one of the frequent visitors to Pacific Films a guided tour.

'This is Gaylene and Margaret. Two o-o-old dropouts trying to drop back in again.'

The visitors looked bemused, John gave us a conspiratorial laugh,

Maggie and I looked at one another. Was that what we were doing? Probably. He'd done it again. Pulled the rug out and put us back on our feet in one easy motion.

Just off the reception area was the tearoom – a narrow beige room with wooden benches on four sides built into the wall around a knee-height wooden table. The centre of everything. Upon arrival in the morning, everyone grabbed a cup of well-stewed tea from the big aluminium teapot that was never empty. We sat in a configuration much like a London tube carriage, high windows above us. Sometimes the conversation was just about impossible to decipher.

'The Arri could be running slow, it's not maintaining sync.'

'24 or 25?'

'Could be the new Kodak neg – slipping in the gate.'

They might have been speaking a different language, but I loved it. Another raft of secrets to uncover.

John was the funniest when he was angriest. He had nicknames for all the NZBC television commissioners. He could describe the network as though it was the Kremlin during the worst of Stalin's gulags. John hated the hand that fed him. He was a proud man and considered that the bosses who were doing well out there were not exactly the sharpest knives in the drawer. He described one new appointment as 'the first time a r-rat has joined a sinking ship'. Sadly, wishful thinking – the sinking ship part.

It was Pacific Films that was slowly falling beneath the waves. For John, this company and the young people who worked for him were family. Maybe understandable, as he was brought up by his aunt and uncle after his mother died when John was only seven days old. His Irish Catholic ire would rise whenever anyone left the fold. He considered this to be desertion. In the pecking order, whoever had had the temerity to take their chances in the newly emerging independent commercials industry became second only to the Television Kommissioners. For those remaining, the upside was that if you constantly blamed someone who wasn't there, everyone else got off scot-free.

179

I had come from a marijuana-smoking inner city communal house in London to an entirely different environment. They preferred to drink alcohol with their joints, women were called sheilas, and we drank in the public bar. But with the men at Pacific, I always felt I was an equal. No lewd jokes when I was around. They just weren't like that. Plenty of laughs, though, and we liked the same music: New Orleans rock. They respected what I did know and taught me the rest.

My domain was the art room. There was a rumour that Harry Wong had painted it entirely black in the early 70s, when totally black rooms were popular psychedelics diversions. You could go in there, take LSD, crank up the stereo and trip out. Not something to include in the official history of Pacific Films, but the company had a history of creative innovation and invention so I never questioned the interior décor. Along with the art room, I inherited a darkroom, a couple of useful-looking long tables, a big wooden tripod and a Bolex for shooting animation. But before I could throw myself into graphics, I was sent off in the Pacific car to spot locations. The current commercials all involved interiors.

I enjoyed talking my way into houses to look at their lounges. Having been away as long as I had, I found the Kiwi aesthetic fascinating. No one at Pacific took too much notice of my sorties to the outer reaches of Lower Hutt, except one day when, over tea in the tearoom, I mentioned I was going to meet a well-known couple to look at their bathroom. Everyone suddenly expressed enormous enthusiasm to come along.

The woman looked surprised when I arrived in a van with four young men. We traipsed into her beautiful modernist house to look at a bathroom with a sunken bath and a breathtaking view of the harbour. Nothing remotely like what I knew we needed. No one was in any hurry to leave, though. This was the bathroom in which the mistress of the house was rumoured to regularly entertain Robert Muldoon. We looked at where he may have sat, overlooking the harbour, then headed off. Pacific thrived on outrageous rumours, particularly when they were about politicians.

The surprises kept coming. After the training film for New Zealand Breweries, my next job was to borrow a human skeleton for a sheep dip commercial to be shot in Dr Margaret Sparrow's surgery up a hundred concrete steps hugging the hill in Kelburn. As Crunch and I carried 'George' – a name the nurses had given the skeleton, over years of anatomy lessons at Wellington Hospital – not only was it windy, but the slippery path was tortuous. The commercial would show a sheep sitting in a dentist's chair in the surgery receiving an injection of hydatids medication, while George/Georgina was supposed to add authenticity by hanging crookedly from his or her armature in the background. I was not at all sure that using a real skeleton of an unknown, unnamed person in a sheep dip commercial in New Zealand was appropriate or ethical but I was assured that the agency had asked for it, and what the agency wanted was what the agency got.

This was the first time I'd seen five people around a camera. Operator, focus puller, clapper/loader, grip, gaffer. I know now that this is a tiny crew, but for me then, an absolute eye-opener. John O'Shea had known that the best place for me to have a ringside seat on this filmmaking thing was going to be from the point of view of the art department. I could learn something while making myself useful.

Sort of.

When it came to returning the priceless skeleton to the Wellington Hospital teaching school, the trip down from Margaret's surgery was even more difficult than the journey up. Laying this real bag of bones into the back of the Pacific Films Kingswood was a nightmare. The wires holding George together were old and had moved more in the last twenty-four hours than probably the last twenty-four years, and not everything remained connected. The anxious head nursing tutor was waiting for us in the hospital car park. Desperately trying to remember all those years in Bill Sutton's life drawing classes, I was left in the back of the Pacific Films station wagon, astride the skeleton, trying to wire the arms back up, as Crunch tried not to laugh and diverted the head nursing tutor on questions of health and safety.

I was in a cold sweat. As we gently pulled the human bones out of the back of the car, I noticed that the hands were hanging strangely. Too late now. I said a quiet prayer to George or Georgina, and we bid farewell. Back it went into the building to hang limply in a classroom corner, one hand looking decidedly wonky. Some situations, you just have to walk away and get out of there. We did our best to leave Margaret's surgery as we found it, but she probably wondered how to remove sticky gaffer tape from her ceiling and why lights were left without light bulbs.

Later I was to work as set-dresser for John Reid's feature film *Middle Age Spread*. During that shoot, under pressure to organise an easy access to the first shot of the day, we sawed the bottom off Ian and Josie Mune's bedroom door. Unsurprisingly it was never the same again. Sorry, Ian. Never let a film crew in your house (in your house). It's a song I made up.

# 14

# Lonely Planet

Rory called it 'the Trojan'. This 35mm big bastard projector was bolted to the floor and cut off from the theatre by a soundproof-ish wall with a small hole for the light to pass through. In the projection room it sounded like a traction engine. This particular day, about fifteen men in suits representing the New Zealand Dairy Board were gathered to watch the promotional film they had commissioned: *Cows, Computers and Customers*. A typical O'Shea title. The unofficial title of the breweries film didn't leave the building – but *Cows, Computers and Customers* was official.

I had struggled over Letraset titling to make the words work over the opening image – a wide-shot zoom-in of cows peacefully chewing cud in Taranaki, with the maunga tapu perfectly captured centre-screen – and I was there to check my work. The gathered suits waited expectantly. In this projection room where I had met Crunch, I was now a regular. The lights went down and the film began – but to my surprise, the mountain was neatly projecting into the corner of the room. The rest spread onto the walls. A weird wraparound. Cows wandered on green fields in front of the mountain, up to the corner and around the wall. The music plunked along.

'Cows, computers and customers,' said the confident narrator. Moving as one, the suits, who had been facing forward, turned to the side and kept obediently watching as though nothing unusual was happening. John whispered a loud expletive and strode out the back into the projection room, slamming the door behind him. I turned around in my seat to watch him through the glass silently gesticulating to the hapless projectionist. The film slowly wound down as the music dived down several octaves.

We sat there in darkness, swamped by silence. With a musical plink, the fluorescent lights flicked on. Still facing the corner, the Dairy Board fellows blinked at one another in the light, looking mildly perplexed. No one said anything. John's head appeared around the door.

'Has there been an e-earthquake recently?'

Everyone frowned and shook their heads. They didn't think so.

John exploded. 'Bloody Paul Maunder!' Then he disappeared again.

This made no sense to the suits. They had never heard of Paul Maunder.

I knew who Paul Maunder was. He had worked at the National Film Unit and had directed politically motivated plays at Circa Theatre. Paul had been using Pacific Films' facilities to make his feature film *Sons for the Return Home*. His producer and John had fallen out, and Paul was the blame du jour. Well, the blame du month actually. He wasn't there. Ipso facto, his fault.

How 'the Trojan' – roughly the size of a forklift – could be moved sideways like that is still something of a mystery. The Trojan was bolted to the floor in four places. Paul Maunder could not have been the culprit. Paul Maunder was slight and far too much of an aesthete to even think of such a thing. By this time, everyone in the screening theatre had turned to watch the drama unfolding in the projection room behind us.

Ivan, the Pacific Films handyman, arrived, and scratched his shiny bald head. Ivan was the reason I couldn't carry the camera gear. He made heart rimu wooden carry-cases for every new light camera that Pacific invested in. He wore thin red braces and always a neat string rhinestone cowboy tie and a white shirt stretched over his portly frame. He went to Texas every year with his boyfriend, who owned the only decent sound gear in the country. That was on permanent loan in the sound studio in the old pie factory. His boyfriend was rumoured to have lent his amps and speakers to the Rolling Stones when they came to Wellington in 1965. He interrupted the concert by striding onto the stage in the middle of 'Satisfaction' to yell at Mick Jagger, 'I don't care who you are – TURN IT DOWN!'

But I digress.

After a small pause in the action, Ivan comes back wielding a very big mallet and as the Trojan lurches into life, he gives it an almighty thump.

Wowing and fluttering as it valiantly picks up speed, the Trojan hits full 24-frame-per-second throttle. The pinging soundtrack rises and the oblivious cows continue grazing in front of the marvellous snow-capped volcano halfway round the wall. BASH into the metallic body of the beast goes Ivan's mallet. The cows jump, the mountain jumps and the music gets a fright. Everything jumps except the Dairy Board suits. They continue to watch without a word as they turn to face the film wherever it is in the room. But now Ivan has overdone it. The image has headed too far towards the other wall and the cows start grazing over there. Bash from the other side, and we hit the centre again.

The projection door closes and the screening continues. I'm glad the lights are off. I am laughing uncontrollably with a hanky stuffed in my mouth, and tears are pouring down my face. Leaving is out of the question. I have my legs crossed, hoping I am not going to disgrace myself. With my shoulders shaking, as *Cows, Computers and Customers* reveals gleaming silver milk-processing factories, I desperately try to think of something sad.

Unfortunately, something sad was available. Nick had not arrived. He was still in London, working on an animated film. I was coming to the conclusion that I was on my own. I was a single woman with a pencil and a Nikon camera with a couple of good lenses. Nick was always coming next month, then the next month, then the next month. And I was lonely.

John asked me one day, 'When is that ph-ph-phantom lover of yours coming?'

It had become a standing joke. I shrugged. They thought I'd made him up.

But then, so much of my British life was of no interest or relevance here. When I told anyone I was back after seven years away, the general response was to look incredulous and wonder why I had returned. Anyone arty was trying to get out of the quarter-acre pavlova paradise where everyone had a job for life and the arts were severely underappreciated unless they were in the service of tourism. No one understood why on earth I would come back if I had been doing all right over there, and I couldn't explain that it was the hills that had called me.

For the first time since my first year at art school, I was an independent woman. No husband, no boyfriend, and I'd fought for this. Now I wasn't so sure. I felt anything but at home in this trippy little white land of Rinso soap powder and everyone mowing their lawns on a Saturday. On the interminable weekends I took to wandering about and photographing stray cats sitting on mouldering concrete walls in empty streets. And clotheslines. I have a great collection of clothesline photos from this period. Private lives, strung up in public places.

Thank goodness for the Pacific Films shooting crew. I was happy in the van, sitting up the front in the middle between Rory and Crunch, listening to New Orleans rock 'n' roll and more outrageous rumours from Pacific. I was seeing the country as we travelled around the bottom half of the North Island shooting whatever came up and doing a particular Pacific Films thing called 'meeting the locals'. This involved going to the public bar of the most popular pub in town and bludging what we could – particularly locations – for the next day's shoot. I usually had my camera slung round my neck to take stills of this country I barely belonged to. Have Nikon, can travel.

But on one of my travels, I blew up the Pacific Films Holden.

John was negotiating with the Film Unit to make a television series he called *Crucible of History*. He was working with a World War One enthusiast to record the stories of veterans who had been in the War to End All Wars. And he had a job for me. Research. This involved travelling into the middle of the North Island to find veterans. I was dispatched with a list of vague addresses to travel alone across the North Island in Pacific Films' only production vehicle. The roaring eight-cylinder Holden Kingswood had travelled these roads so often, it could probably find its way without anyone at the wheel. They'd bought it to make *Don't Let It Get You.* By 1977 it was still going strong, with thousands of k's on the clock. I headed off to Taihape with a cassette-tape recorder to interview a World War One veteran who had survived that terrible ordeal and was still alive and chirpy enough to tell the tale. They were thin on the ground even by then.

I sat in the small house of this old man in his eighties who was living in what had been his family home. The ghost of his wife was ever-present as he sat on the grey rug thrown over his ancient couch and told me his experiences of the Battle of the Somme. I sat there in that little house with the occasional train woefully passing, listening to his tales of the horror, the blood mixed with mud, and the boys he left behind, as though it had happened to him only yesterday.

I was stunned. He had assumed that I knew much more about the whole sorry tale than I did, as he described terrible things. Hearing the stories of death and destruction, I found some of what he told me surprising. Mysterious. Like the fact that no matter how bad it gets, in the icy rain and rancid mud, the bully beef is always hot.

This is when I fall in love with oral histories. When the teller hits the present tense, you can tell that they are right there. Pure memory. I am transfixed, barely daring to move, checking that the little cassette recorder is recording.

Practised stories can be very entertaining, but they're not necessarily entirely true. Soldier's tales are disconcerting in that regard. In World War Two they went off to battle and came back to the

NAAFI – the Navy, Army and Airforce Institute – tent at night, having survived terrible things. But unless a soldier could find a punchline that made everyone laugh, they may as well not tell the story. The bar would be so full of tears you would drown. So find a punchline and stick to it. That's the soldier's tale.

John O'Shea had a repertoire from the war. Some of his tales were pretty risqué. One of his favourites was when he was charged with driving a military Jeep from the toe of Italy up to Rome after fighting ceased in 1944. He said there were three of them on this mission. The driver had a bet that in the time it took for the others to fill the tank and eat some food, he could score a consensual fuck. Guess who won the bet in John's story. Now it could be that it happened – not necessarily to John O'Shea, who, like me, cannot resist a good yarn told first-person – or it could be apocryphal. Something that nearly happened, or that they wished had happened and everyone told it as if it was them. Never the driver, always one of the others. When they came back home after the war, they built bars across our wee nation in order to drink beer and tell the tales, and laugh, all the boys together before they staggered home to the wife – blotto. (That's an interesting word, 'blotto'.)

But when I am sitting with this old soldier in the little house in Taihape, dimly lit by the single overhead bulb in his grey blanketed sadness, it is not the well-trod soldier's tale he is telling. His story is so present I swear I can smell rotting flesh.

It was hard to leave him. But I did, very late, getting little sleep in the damp motel room I had found in the rain. When I awoke, the sun was shining high in the sky over Taihape and I knew I had to skip breakfast and hit the road. I had hardly gone a few miles over the hills when, without warning, the old eight-cylinder roarer went clunk and the engine stopped. I coasted over to the verge as we slid slowly to a halt.

I turn off the radio and wind down the window. Birds are singing. The place is dripping with natural goodness. I can hear cows mooing.

I can hear the grass growing.

I clomp off back up the wet road and find a farmer digging fence-post holes and tell him my predicament. He downs his tools and throws open the bonnet. Smoke pours out. As I try to get it started, he watches the engine. New Zealand farmers know how to keep motors going. It's in their DNA. It dates from when there were rigorous laws restricting importing – you had to save money and get a special import licence, then wait for months for the vehicle to arrive by sea. The entire rural community kept their tractors going better than the Russians did after the second five-year plan. This farmer shakes his head. I can tell he knows what he's talking about.

Rory would have said, 'The fucking fucker's fucked,' or words to that effect, but this giant of a man just tells me, 'Your big end's gone.'

I have no idea what that is but I understand the Holden and I are not going anywhere today. I take the keys out of the ignition and clomp off after the farmer as he strides over the paddock to a nearby farmhouse.

The back porch is cluttered with gumboots of all sizes. My now-wrecked rainbow boots join the pile, and in wet socks I enter a scene of domestic bliss. In the lounge three children are working quietly on their home-schooling, surrounded by paper and crayons and books, and in the kitchen a radio is playing classical music while a woman stands at the bench stirring a delicious-smelling stew. The coal range is roaring, the windows are fogged up. I ring Rory back at Kilbirnie.

'The car has broken down.'

'Where.'

'Taihape.'

'Oh yeah.'

'There's a farmer who has had a look at it and he reckons the big end has gone.'

'Yeah?'

'I'll call a tow truck and get it towed into town?'

'Yeah.'

'And I'm chucking in this filmmaking.'

189

'Yeah?'

'I'm going to marry a nice mechanic and have children and cook roasts.'

'Oh yeah ...' A thoughtful pause, then, 'Well, don't do it in Taihape,' followed by a loud, gravelly laugh.

Now that I was working on something substantial, why was I constantly thinking of a way out? I guess this life I had chosen was too singular. That gang I had found – it wasn't really mine. I had gone from a communal house in Stockwell where the politics of housework were discussed daily to being one of the boys. But I wasn't. My name was not Bruce. They were great comrades. Plenty of laughs and rigorous in their craft, but this first year back in New Zealand I was a real fish out of water.

Not only that, but as I developed my technical skills, working at Pacific was a hair-raising adventure in crisis development. Being 'from London', I was supposed to know about everything already. Faced with a new challenge, I would bludge the accountant's car – never straightforward, as it seemed like he was permanently down at the bank – and head out to the National Film Unit at Miramar to find the men from my art school days.

Feigning a frustrated air, trying to make my unexpected visit seem more casual than it was, I would drop in and say, 'G'day. How do you do end credits around here?'

They would have already assumed that in London we did it better.

'It's like living in the Eastern Bloc. Bloody annoying,' they would say. 'We have to do it with Letraset and animation cells locked onto an animation board.'

'Where the hell do I get one of those?' I'd say, implying it was all so hard, away from the big overseas.

'Oh, you can have one of ours. Permanent loan.'

It wasn't theirs to give me, of course. It belonged to the Film Unit, which belonged to the government.

'Thanks!' And I'd get in the car with my ill-gotten loot, then I'd drive round the corner and make notes on all their instructions before I forgot.

In this way, I got to add credits and front titles to Pacific's educational films and the occasional television documentary that Bazza was still completing. Have a look at *Autumn Fires*, which he made with Martyn Sanderson. It's about Martyn's aunt, Olive Bracey, who lived in Hokianga. John O'Shea called this kind of documentary 'Pākehātanga'. I grabbed an old piece of wallpaper from my parents' place and laid black lettering over the top of the animation transparency. I was enjoying myself. When John Reid made a documentary about renowned weaver Dame Rangimārie Hetet, I loved drawing korowai from her inspired work to overlay the credits.

And, true to his word, John O'Shea fostered my growing interest in directing. Pacific Films was making a pilot documentary series they never managed to get off the ground called *Shoreline*, a *Country Calendar* of the sea. I managed to persuade them to make an episode about the toheroa season at Foxton Beach. Everyone was positive about this, toheroa patties in their eyes. Finally! My first professional television assignment as a director.

The documentary *Toheroamania* is told from the toheroa's point of view. This was mainly because every other idea I came up with, Rory would listen intently – 'Oh yeah . . . yeah . . . yeah' – and then say no.

'It's evening and the beach is emptying of people,' I'd say. 'There's a tall guy with a moustache wearing sunglasses and a hat. Bill Stalker in Mafia mode. He's driving a Zephyr. The boys are in the car sweating as the fisheries inspector, obviously suspicious, checks the boot for overfishing and undersized fish. To his surprise, there is just one sack of exactly the right amount of perfectly sized shellfish. This will tell the audience the rules in an entertaining way,' I told him, pleased with my ingenuity.

'Oh yeah.'

I continued. 'Bill Stalker, alias "Frank the fish", gets to drive off with the boys, gloating as the hubcaps clatter, full of toheroa.'

A pause, then: 'Can't afford it.'

There's a theory that restricting artists makes them more creative. (Ref. Lars Von Trier, *The Five Obstructions*. Every filmmaker trying to make films in Aotearoa should see it.) My ideas got more and more edgy, and cheaper, but got the same response. So I decided to put the opening sequence of *Toheroamania* into my department, where no one could say we couldn't afford it. There was a big old still-frame camera set up in the art room, so I drew toheroa and backed them with felt and did some paper animation. The little toheroa are singing away when a siren sounds and they dive. A Monty Python-esque hand comes down and grabs one. It screams as it is pulled up out of the frame. Cut to a kid on the sand: 'Look Mum – I got one.'

I was pretty pleased with my efforts, but I had only ever seen it from a dupe black-and-white print in the 16mm projection room out the back of the old pie factory. After constant terrifying experiences projecting 8mm, I was thrilled when the episode was finally scheduled to screen on TV One. It would be projected by the network. No big unruly ex-BBC tape recorder to activate. Sound in sync. I was coming up in the world.

'My film is going to screen on TV and I don't have to worry!' I told Maggie Kelly, who'd come over to toast my nationwide debut with me and my new boyfriend. He was a singer in a band. I was living the dream. A rock 'n' roll chick with a Honda 200 and a leather jacket.

We gathered around the telly, all expectation, slightly tanked. Just before the ad break, the announcer said *Shoreline* was up next.

Suddenly the house was plunged into darkness.

We raced to our fuse box. I looked down the street. Unbelievable. Not a streetlight was on. The power had gone out exactly one minute before *Toheroamania* was to hit the screens of the nation.

Electricity was restored in time for the six o'clock news, which solemnly told us what we already knew. The entire middle of the country had had a power cut.

*Toheroamania* was never rescheduled, and to this day I have only

The Prestons, 1919, with Granny Butler on the left and George on the right. Ed is the boy in the middle, in white.

The McDonalds. Tui is the smallest baby, with Elsie.

Tui, Granny Cressey, baby Ted and Elsie, 1941.

Ed and Tui,
1940s.

10 Ida St:
Tui and Gaylene,
Ed and Gaylene.

Gaylene with
Ted's f-hole guitar
at McLean Park,
Napier, and at home
on her trusty rusty.

Mr Hopkins' Standard Three/Four, Greymouth, 1957: Gaylene front
row, third from left.

Gaylene flying from Hokitika to Napier with a cabbage in her bag, 1959.

Jan, Tui, Gaylene and Elsie, 1964.

Gaylene, Elsie, Tui and Jan
dressed for church, 1961.

Tui, Ed (in his milk run overalls),
Jan, Ted, Gaylene in Napier, 1965.

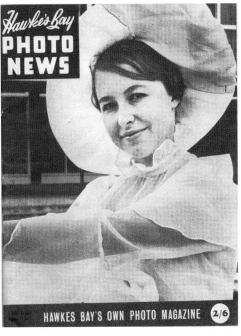

Miss Dyke's troupe, 1959: Gaylene in the middle.

Eliza Dolittle: Gaylene on the cover of *Hawke's Bay Photo News*, June 1967.

Bridesmaid for Ted's wedding: Ed, Gaylene, Jan, Tui.

Shirley Grace and Gaylene, Sydney, 1967. (Allie Eagle)

Art School capping float, 1968, promoting Mike Ward: Allie Eagle and Shirley Grace at top.

In the art school woods with ironed hair. (Kai Hawkins)

Wearing the wig in the Ilam print workshop.

Having a think. (Shirley Grace)

Elsie at Gaylene's wedding, 1968.

Gaylene and the mother of the bride.

Gaylene with Andy Dennis at his Harvard departure party.

The honeymoon photo, Taylor's Mistake.

Fulbourn Hospital drama group in their costumes for *Snow White and the Seven Dwarves*, 1969.

Cadaqués,
Spain, 1973.

That bath,
17 Stockwell Park
Crescent.

Girl about
town,
Cambridge,
1972.

Stockwell,
with Standerwick
the cat.

Christmas
orphans' gathering,
Stockwell, 1975

With the deaf
students of Brixton
College of Further
Education. (Nick
Kavanaugh)

Jan and Gaylene,
Tāmaki Makaurau, 1977.
(Shirley Grace)

Stills photographer,
*Middle Age Spread*, 1977.

Shooting the crowd at Marineland, Napier, for Pacific Films, 1977.

*All the Way Up There*, 1978, with the amended poster.

Bruce Burgess, mountaineer.

That jolly car, rerepossessed, 1980.

Music video with Rick Bryant and the Neighbours and friends, Blackball, 1982.

John Cressey's grave, Ahaura Cemetery.

Head above the crowd, Napier premiere of *Utu*, 1983.

Jan, Tui and Gaylene in the kitchen, 1 McVay St, 1984.

Gaylene and the Bolivisión on the floor next to Jonathan's legs and his cat Gools Gools, Roxburgh St, 1983. (Jonathan Crayford)

A supportive mate, Auckland 1983

Cannes Film Festival,
1983, in bespoke outfit.
(Thom Burstyn)

Monsieur Shelton's
assistant on the
Croisette delivering
invitations. (Thom
Burstyn)

Cannes circus
entertainer on the
Croisette. (Thom
Burstyn)

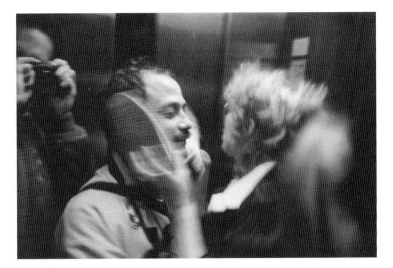

Hitting Baxter in
the lift.
(Thom Burstyn)

In the Cannes directors'
lounge with nouveaux amis.
(Thom Burstyn)

With Zac Wallace.

The *Mr Wrong* car, 1986. (*Christchurch Press*)

Jan Fisher (front) and Heather Bolton (right) rehearsing the correct way to hang washing in the wind. (Clare Clifford)

Filming *Mr Wrong* on Roxburgh St. (Thom Burstyn)

Gaylene, Gary Stalker, Trou Bayliss and Alun Bollinger. (Thom Burstyn)

Gaylene, Heather Bolton and Robin Laing. (Clare Clifford)

The Paramount ready for a party.

Filming *Kai Purakau* in 1987 in Okarito, with Leon Narbey.

Filming a Mainland Cheese ad for Pat Cox in Featherston, 1987.

Planting Chelsie's placenta, 1987, with little Sam Gruar in the foreground.

Acting lessons with Chelsie.

Everyone doing their best at the *Ruby and Rata* wrap party.

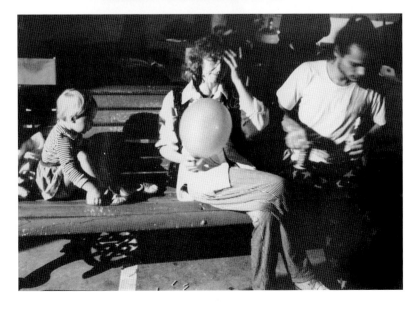

Scene 93 cont.

⑧ ⑨ ⑩

"Gidday sport"

④ ⑤ ⑥

Willie's P.O.V. of the room.    Pan with willie — Willie runs away

Gaylene's storyboard for *Ruby and Rata*, 1990.

Directing Lee Metekingi, who plays Willie.

Yvonne Rawley, Simon Barnett, Vanessa Rare and Lee Metekingi.

Gaylene and
cinematographer
Allen Guilford.

Graeme Tetley.

*Ruby and Rata* Q&A
at the Sydney Film
Festival, 1991.

Gaylene and Olive Oyl.
(Jenny Scown)

*Bread & Roses*, 1992:

Direction from above.

Geneviève Picot as
Sonja, centre, Chelsie
and Tui farewelling the
troops.

Gaylene and Sonja
Davies at pretend Kiwi,
filmed at Maymorn
Station.

*War Stories Our Mothers Never Told Us*, 1996:

Neva Clarke McKenna, 1940.

Mabel Waititi and her son Tukaki, c. 1944.

The *War Stories* women and Chelsie ready for a day of LA hijinks.

With Phyllis Diller in one of her Rolls Royces.

Gaylene
and Hone
Tuwhare,
1996.

Tui's famous
sausage
rolls.

Gaylene, Tui
home from
Rita Angus
Village for
a visit, and
Chelsie,
Austin St,
2004.

*Perfect Strangers*, 2003:

Alun Bollinger and Gaylene pretending to be all at sea.

Lining up a shot with Sam Neill and Rachael Blake.

The *Dauntless*, carefully beached.

*Home by Christmas*,
2010:

Ed, 1992.
(Kate Jason-Smith)

Tony Barry as Ed and
Gaylene as his daughter.
(Chris Coad)

Cast and crew.

Fires starting after the 1931 Napier Earthquake. (A.B. Hurst)

Hana Lyola Cotter interviewed for *Earthquake*, 2004.

Directing *Hope and Wire* in Atlantis, Christchurch.

*Hope and Wire*, 2014:

Simo Abbari as Youseff, Gaylene, and Bernard Hill as Len.

Joel Tobeck as Greggo.

Jarod Rawiri as Ryan.

*My Year with Helen*, 2017:

Helen Clark in Botswana, leading the UNDP.

Gaylene and Helen at the Athena Film Festival, New York.

Jacinda Ardern, not yet Leader of the Opposition, and Gaylene at the New Zealand International Film Festival Auckland premiere. (Veronica McLaughlin)

ever seen it projected off that dupe black-and-white print when we were checking the final cut.

Bad luck, Gaylene, but never mind. I was now officially a director.

About one week later, I got the sack.

It was a day like any other, as they say, when I arrived in the morning to a sombre mood at the old Pacific Films World Headquarters in Kilbirnie. People in and out of the former pie factory wear serious expressions and carry termination notices. I had been the last to arrive, so I was an easy choice. After all that flying by the seat of its pants, making corporates and commercials to haul in the cash, staggering on making quality documentaries for a network that no longer welcomed them, they had finally hit the wall. The entire time I knew him, John O'Shea had the banks snapping at his heels. He would go on to make several more features, but the golden years of Pacific Films were now officially over. What was the beginning of something for me was the end for them. And it had really been a total success for me.

I had found myself in that creative group I longed for. After *Toheroamania*, John referred to me as 'madame la director' in a French accent, which he could say without a stutter, funnily enough. But for me now, on this beautiful sunny Thursday, the remarkable opportunity of going to work in the morning and joining in whatever they were up to – filmmaking on the hoof – was over.

By the end of the day, the full-time staff of fourteen had been slashed to seven. We were given one week's notice. This really was a financial emergency.

On my final day, I was working at the big table in the art room that had been my domain over the last six months. I had done animations here and prepared graphics. And from the well-equipped darkroom, I had delivered black-and-white prints for the first season of *Middle Age Spread* for front-of-house stills to Circa Theatre.

On that late Friday afternoon I am quietly intent on spotting prints – a tedious, repetitive job involving a tiny watercolour brush and ink – when John enters and sits down. He doesn't speak immediately; his broad shoulders are slumped as he looks out the big picture window overlooking the bus depot across the road. I smile and keep working. It's a private moment. He's had a hell of a day letting people go. Some he's had working for him for years. I'm the least of his problems. The low sun through the venetian blinds renders the black art room golden-tiger-striped. Outside, trolley buses squeak and clatter, heading into town for a Friday shopping night.

When John finally speaks, he reflects on his younger days directing feature films that, by October 1977, before the country had a film archive, are barely remembered. He tells me of the time when he was up in the Southern Lakes shooting *Runaway*.

'We went up there into the a-Alps to a l-lake to shoot but the weather closed in. We waited three days for the light . . .' A long pause. '. . . I'm still p-paying for that . . .'

And I'm pretty sure, that evening twenty years later, he meant actual personal bank loans that had finally caught up with him.

By the time he is finished, the sun has set. All I can see is the glow of his cigarette. The streetlights have replaced the golden glow of the sun through the venetians. I can no longer view my work, but I don't turn on the light. In this strange orange-striped universe, I can't break the spell. By the time he stops, he has told me everything I need to know to sustain myself as an independent filmmaker in this country – this place that we both hate and love. I never forgot. And he never let me down. He gave me freelance work that saw me through until I was established as an art director on commercials in the new booming freelance industry. Having an income, aside from developing and making your own films, is rule number one in the sustainability stakes.

But to my everlasting regret, I think I failed John with the *Crucible of History* project. After recording on cassette tape the stories of those Great War veterans, John sent me off with a crew from the Film Unit to shoot an interview with an old man who lived in Ōtaki. He had not only been in the War to End All Wars, but had also been a bugle boy in the Boer War. Tony Brunt did the interview, and Bailey Watson was behind the camera. Now I know that with any interview, you just keep rolling whether you think it's very good or not, but I didn't know that then. The old chap was nearly a hundred years old and not very clear. Everyone was nervous, making the interview circumspect and stiff. The click of the film travelling through the camera gate got louder and louder in my head, and I became acutely aware of the crippling price of film stock. My inexperience ruled. I kept cutting.

When I went out to the Film Unit with John to view the sync rushes, it was so bad I could hardly watch it. Every time the old chap came to something remotely interesting, an insistent little voice rang out from behind the camera: 'Cut.' I squirmed in my seat. John never said much, but I know I certainly didn't help him in getting that project off the ground. It remains one of the few things I really regret. There is very little film of the surviving New Zealand veterans telling their stories, and a great series that would now be of tremendous value never got made. They say it's the things you didn't do that you regret. I know I couldn't have sunk the project singlehandedly, but it was a hard lesson and a hard way to learn it.

Once they have gone, they have gone forever.

# 15

# Thieves and Villains

Are we always nostalgic for a time when no one had any money, when we drank cheap wine and smoked just enough weed to stay uplifted, and when we got ourselves in and out of trouble? After I left Pacific, or, more accurately, after it left me, I was a lone ranger. A freelancer. I thought I was cool. I took photographs, drew posters, made up cartoons – anything to pay the rent, which was $25 a week for a little cottage in Kelvin Grove. My freelance work was really an extension of the cartooning and poster designing I had been doing in London, but now I was paid for it. Enough to run my motorbike, pay the rent and go to the edgy theatre and pub band concerts. I was still adamant that I would not join any institutions, and preferred to live the bohemian life that was to be had at the Te Aro end of Cuba Street. In late 1977, Te Aro was full of neglected cottages inhabited by the artistic riff-raff.

Cheap rent was the key. Finding a good place then was the same as it is now – you have to know someone who wants to sublet. A couple of directors from the Film Unit had stumbled on a great deal through the Ministry of Works. A new motorway was to forge through this semi-industrial part of town. Today it would be called 'mixed use', and gentrified, but not back then. The Ministry of Works had permission to buy up whole streets of colonial settlers' cottages so they could later bowl them for roads.

I lived at 7 Kelvin Grove, next to Maggie Kelly, who lived at no. 5.

At no. 10 lived the king of Kelvin Grove – Eric. A man of habit, he had been born there and intended to die there. Every day, he got up late, listened to the races, walked down to the TAB to place his bets for tomorrow, drank at the pub, and did the dishes for whoever was living at no. 7.

Eric had always done these dishes, he told me. It wasn't an option to ask him not to. He came with the house. He had a key and it was what he did. What could I do? No money changed hands. I had inherited him, along with a rental agreement that dated back to Stanley Harper, a former National Film Unit director, who was by now living in Paris and famous for having the longest Arts Council travel grant.

When I left no. 7, Sam Hunt moved in. I don't think Sam had many dishes to wash, so he and Eric drank together. This led to a serial argument about poetry that often went late into the night. Eric maintained that if it didn't rhyme, it wasn't poetry. Sam, of course, could quote at length beautiful verse that proved the opposite. Maybe Eric kept the argument going so he could listen to Sam's recitations while drinking beer at the kitchen table. In the end, to demonstrate that rhyming couplets were superlative, Eric wrote a long piece of doggerel about his cat. Once I had a VHS camera, I got him to read 'The Pensioner's Cat' on a little video I made about him.

Eric died before the bulldozers came in. The motorway didn't go through there in the end, but the houses were demolished and replaced with bland car yards.

I became friends with the union maids, a band of clever feminist strategists working within the male-dominated unions. The Working Women's Charter, sometimes known as the bill of rights for working women, was the focus of the Wellington Trades Council's women's subcommittee. The subcommittee even had a women's union choir, later to become Choir Choir Pants on Fire. I met Hazel Armstrong (now a leading health and safety lawyer) when she roped me in to work with her partner Bob Kerr to draw cartoons for the Cleaners' Union magazine, *Advance*. We became firm friends. Every union had a paper that was circulated among their members, so here I was back up to my elbows in cow gum but being paid for it. It was like old times – a cartoon collective to work with all night, as people came and went with copy for the paste-up. Hazel's enthusiasm for building a more equitable world was unstoppable, and with Therese O'Connell at the PSIS cooperative and Sonja Davies and Graham Kelly at the Shop Employees' Union, I was kept busy. Hazel often had photographic assignments for me, such as photographing night cleaners at work. I would find myself in very low light trying to get a decent shot, then I would ride out to Pacific Films, where I continued to use the darkroom, to 'cook' the neg to try to get an image worth printing. Cooking means over-developing the neg, which heightens the contrast but makes it grainy. Then I'd print on high-contrast paper, with the exposure lengthened. Warming the chemical baths makes the process more extreme. Hence 'cooking'. This risky approach became my speciality.

I was glad it was daylight when Hazel turned up at my office to get the Trades Hall caretakers' photograph taken. I stood Ernie near a window for his photo. He had been expecting to be in a proper studio, and didn't seem impressed. In the photo, this hard-working, hard-drinking union man is looking through the lens at this flibbertigibbet lady behind the camera, probably thinking, 'Call that a job?'

Never would we have imagined that my photo of Ernie would later become the image that stands for the Trades Hall bombing of March 1984. Locking up at the end of the day, Ernie picked up a suitcase that had been left unattended in the foyer. The suitcase had a bomb hidden inside it, and Ernie was killed in the explosion – a crime that remains unsolved.

It is thought that the bomb was meant for Hazel's boss, a staunch Liverpudlian named Pat Kelly. He kept a steady hand on the rolling strikes that the Cleaners' Union took on as more and more employers tried to squeeze their workers. Pat would introduce me ('This is . . . um, er . . . she's a progressive') to his old cronies down at the Panama, also known as the union's 'church', where they all went on Friday nights.

Pat kept a benevolent eye on the younger crowd but was stern about one thing. 'Don't take on the government, whatever you do. They will always win.'

His words were to echo in my head during the 1981 anti-apartheid protests, when I sometimes found myself, with Waka Attewell behind the camera, in the middle of police charges with everyone but me wearing hard hats.

After my star turn on *Shoreline*, madame la director waited for the phone to ring. When it did, it was from what sounded like a very noisy party. John Reid, a Pacific Films compatriot, was directing a film based on Roger Hall's 1977 play *Middle Age Spread*. His voice sounded a long way away.

'Bruce,' he said. 'Do you want to come up to Auckland and do a bit of set dressing?'

*Middle Age Spread* was one of the first local plays to be a hit, and John Barnett had found funding to turn it into a feature film.

I knew the play, having photographed the slideshow that was incorporated into the first production, directed by Michael Haigh. Circa Theatre was newly opened, and Roger's play starring Dotty McKegg and Grant Tilly had packed it out for a full season. Once again I'd found myself in the Pacific darkroom, this time in the middle of the night after the dress rehearsal, cooking the black-and-white Ilford negative. I wished I had opted for the design department at art school, instead of all that painting. I might have known what I was doing technically. Getting enough decent images for the foyer in time for the premiere performance the next day was almost more stress than I could handle.

After John Reid's phone call, I put my motorbike on the train and, for even less than what I had been earning at Pacific, joined the crew of one of very few feature films being made in the country.

The entire budget for the art department was $2000. My props person, Dorthe Scheffmann, and I would have to borrow stuff – vanfuls. Luckily, the whole production of *Middle Age Spread* seemed to be done during parties, where we could lean on our friends to borrow props. At every rowdy gathering, I ran into men I knew from art school, who cheerfully told me they had turned down the art director job at double my fee because the money was no good. This accounted for there being an art department of only two people. Me dressing sets, and Dorthe organising props. Undaunted, we boxed on, putting a coloured sticker on the bottom of every cup, saucer and plate we borrowed and storing it in a room at the production base. Dorthe kept a huge book that recorded the owner of every lace doily in the picture. When the producers decided to save money by letting Dorthe go before the film had completed shooting, I lost my rag. I can usually control my rage, but after a rushes viewing, in one flash of unbridled temper, I called the perpetrator out in front of everyone. I think the words 'pig', 'chauvinist' and 'male' may have escaped my lips, not in that order. In the ensuing silence, Frances Edmond, my sister-in-law at the time, dramatically crossed the room to kiss me on the forehead. Dorthe stayed on, and everyone got their props back.

It was a time of great expansion in the independent film industry. The new opportunities that had crippled Pacific Films fostered a lively independent sector, making commercials mainly. They hired freelancers for the time their skills were required. No tearooms needed. No sick pay, no holiday pay, no pension scheme, no paid downtime. Pacific Films' art director from London became a commercials art director, working with Geoff Dixon at Silverscreen Productions and Tony Williams at Tony Williams Productions. This involved a lot of ferrying of potted palms and hiring of white couches, but it paid the rent, and more. Gradually I mustered the confidence to start developing my own work. If the phone wasn't going to ring with the offer of a directing gig, then I would do it myself, as the little red hen says. I knew I didn't really know what I was doing, but no one else did either. Women are often found at the beginnings of things – until the men take over again.

The Muldoon era was a continuous battle. Wages were frozen and workers lost rights. At *Advance* magazine we were always trying to find a new approach to cartoons about the cuts. One favourite was set in an operating theatre with a scalpel-wielding surgeon who looks suspiciously like Muldoon, holding up a human heart, with the caption: 'But doctor, doesn't he need this?' I was on a continuous short deadline so I nearly didn't take the call when the phone finally rang. Warrick Attewell was on the line.

I had met Warrick, also known as Waka, when I was working at Pacific. A wunderkind of sorts, he had begun working in the camera department when he left school, and had made several independent mountain documentaries while still in his early twenties.

Waka had a mountaineering friend, Graeme Dingle, who intended to help a young man with cerebral palsy achieve his dream of climbing Mount Ruapehu. Hallmark, a small manufacturing firm from Hamilton, had made the gear and put up some money for a film. Waka knew that I had worked with disabled people in the UK. Could I make this unusual mountain film with him?

I hesitated. My problem was the mountain. I'm monocular and can't judge where my feet are going. I could climb up a mountain all right but I'd have real trouble coming down. Luckily, Waka didn't want me to go up there anyway. When it came to the shoot, he was happy for me to stay at base camp, out of his way. They didn't need two disabled climbers on their expedition. I was in.

We wrote a treatment and were offered $17,000 by TV One to make a twenty-seven-minute documentary. (That's how long a commercial half-hour was in those days. Now it is twenty-three minutes. If it feels like free-to-air telly is clogged with commercials, it is.) Before we left town to shoot, Waka and I stood outside the big tower in Avalon. The gear was loaded, the film stock actually paid for. We didn't have a contract, but we shook hands. Fifty–fifty all the way.

In his well-appointed office above the Hutt River, the television commissioner told us, 'Whatever you do, do not interview him' – referring to the young mountaineer. 'It will put the audience off. Just film him doing outdoor things backlit in the bush, and come back with pretty pictures to use as wallpaper.'

I knew we weren't going to do that. 'Wallpaper' is a television term for images that sit behind commentary – the voice of authority that talks over everything. I have trouble with that authoritative voice. Who is he? That was the question my three-year-old daughter asked me once, when we were watching a documentary about the beginnings of the earth. As the magma exploded and the red mud spurted up, the commentator said, 'There is no life here.' My daughter looked at me, puzzled. 'Where is he?' 'Who? 'That man.' 'There isn't a man there.' 'Yes there is, the one who is talking.' Precisely. Who is he?

The interview with Bruce Burgess is the heart of our film. It was Bruce's dream to go to the top of Ruapehu and it was for everyone else to support him getting there. We filmed a lot of preparation, then Waka took off up the mountain with the team, leaving me wringing my hands at the bottom. When they came back, Waka was tired and angry. Near the top, with a frozen camera, he had found himself running out of battery with a faulty mag. He was using his last frames to film Bruce struggling on his hands and knees towards the peak when a television news crew ruined his wide shot. They filmed the penultimate moment for the news, then left.

Waka had that empty feeling you have when you know you have shot the film roll to the very end. Risky.

Our editor, Dell King, used every frame we had of that ascent. For Bruce Burgess, the climb up the final yards to the peak is for him an entire mountain. Accompanied by stirring music composed by Wayne Mason, it's the climax to *All the Way Up There*. I don't remember showing the final cut to the TV commissioner, but by the time it screened on their network it had played as the short for *Middle Age Spread* in cinemas, and been embraced by audiences across the country. It was sheer bliss to watch this little documentary in the dark. Audiences laughed and cried, and I felt like finally I had made an impression.

I walked home with my father after a matinee. He was thoughtful.

He told me he was retiring. 'Why don't you have the milk run, love? It's the best run in Napier. You could have it done in three hours every day and have the rest to yourself. Steady money coming in.' He had seen the film and recognised the insecurity of it all. When I turned him down, he was resigned. I still had plenty of fights on my hands, though. No longer sheltered by the Pacific Films gang, I found myself fighting my corner. It felt to me like I couldn't get a hand-hold as an actual filmmaker, even in this 'fledgling film industry'.

When I arrived at the premiere for *Middle Age Spread*, I saw the posters for the documentary in the foyer alongside those for the feature. '*All the Way Up There*, a film by Warrick Attewell'. I had a flash of rage. Where was my credit? Waka and I had made the film together. He'd shot it and I'd supervised the edit with Dell. I was outraged, and said so to the startled man in a white suit hovering in the foyer. Waka backed me. The poster came down. This incident became a bit famous. Later, when Pat Robins was searching for a location for another film I was making she was told by an exhibitor that no way would they support 'that woman'. Apparently, according to him, I was a lesbian who came into his cinema, tore posters off the walls and screwed them up and stamped on them. Didn't happen.

But international sales did. During a lab screening at the Film Unit, a tweedy woman emerged from the dark. She was in charge of international sales on behalf of the National Film Unit. Would we like her to represent our film as well? She had sold the water film I had seen at the NFT in London. Diana Winn has no idea how influential she has been to my current situation. We had never thought about selling *All the Way Up There* offshore. What global networks would screen this little documentary of ours? Diana came back from the international television market, held every year in Cannes, with a sale to Encyclopaedia Britannica for North American educational rights, paying us three times as much as *All The Way Up There* cost to make. Our contract with BCNZ did not include any agreement about returns. This meant that Waka and I could share the proceeds. Success is often the downfall of creative relationships when it comes to doling out the dosh. Not in our case. Our hurried handshake outside the Avalon tower survives to this day.

I thought, 'Wow, this filmmaking actually works. You make a film, sell it, and with the proceeds develop and finance the next one.'

Sadly, once the network came to see the commercial value of the few independent productions they funded, they changed their contracts and that never happened to me again.

Nevertheless, I was able to concentrate on filmmaking more or less full-time. When we had secured all the funding for Bruce's dream, we had five thousand dollars left over from Frank Mahoney at the Department of Education. In a spirit of solidarity with the taxpayer, I gave it back. Everyone was shocked. You never give the money back, apparently. However, that act of naive honesty paid off for me when, a year later, I wanted to make my first fully independent documentary for my newly formed company, Gaylene Preston Productions.

It was a Friday afternoon when I went to find Frank at the beautiful wooden building, down by parliament, that housed the Department of Education.

My theory was that if I pitched to him around 3:30pm, he would be more likely to agree to fund the thing. I would make it easy for him by enthusiastically over-pitching as the clock ticked. He would not want to be late for his 4:10pm train to the Wairarapa, where he had a weekend cottage. It worked. My five thousand dollars was tripled, and with that funding I began pre-production for my first fully independent documentary.

Amid all the union work and discussions about the Working Women's Charter, I had decided I would try to make a series of short educational films, for use in schools, about work. I would follow seven seventeen-year-olds as they left school and tried to get jobs. It would be a one-hour documentary, screening at prime time on your favourite channel. I wanted to show how destructive the line of political thinking about 'dole bludgers' was; I wanted to show the complexity of family situations and to persuade people to think more kindly about those who were struggling and how devastating unemployment is for communities, whānau and the kids themselves. I gambled that at least some bright and breezy students would hit a big brick wall.

When I left Brixton in '76, the youth unemployment rate there was around seventy per cent, while in New Zealand the unemployment rate was marginal. In Aotearoa, it had always been possible to grab a job once you got out of high school. Civil servants carrying briefcases and wearing beige walk-shorts with white socks pulled up over bulging calves strode down Lambton Quay. Vacant smiling faces. (I was coming to realise that the Kiwi smile was a mask over clenched teeth. We all had to get on. We suppressed our resentment.) But a big wave of youth unemployment was building. In Muldoon's little isle of protected incentives, I knew it was the kids who were going to be hit first. I did not want to film tragedy, but I did want to sound a warning to the captive audience at home in their La-Z-Boys, if I could. Middle New Zealand, wake up!

Fired up with confidence from my meeting with Frank at the Department of Education, I began researching workplaces. Someone mentioned the railway workshops at Seaview. The foundry where they built locomotives had a glass roof fogged by years of welding, which produced a magical light that would be at home in a Caravaggio painting. On a beautiful autumnal morning, I headed out there on a location reccie.

For all its smallness, I love my Honda 200. On days like this, I feel like I am sitting in an easy chair, flying through space. On the motorway, I hear a low throb behind me. With a wave, Bill Stalker flies past on his yellow Ducati. He is famous not just for his acting in New Zealand's first television soap, *Close To Home*, but also for travelling from Oriental Bay to Avalon in just twelve minutes, door to door. I pootle on and turn off at the Petone exit.

I am travelling along the foreshore when, suddenly, from nowhere, the sky rains small steel barrels all around me. They fly through the air, hit the road, and bounce. There is nothing to do but drive through them, put my head down and hope.

205

A truck ahead has lost its load. Eventually it slows down and stops. So do I, as the last of the barrels wobble to the side of the road. Miraculously, none have hit me. Pale and shaking, the truck driver emerges. His face is grey with shock and his legs are shaking so much he can barely walk. He saw the whole thing in his rear-view mirror. We sit down on the kerb.

'Buy yourself a lottery ticket, lady,' he tells me, as I light a ciggie for him and he takes it with shaking fingers.

We sit there for a while, silently recovering, as the full extent of the fate we have just avoided sinks in.

'What's in those barrels?' I ask him.

'Offal.'

I laugh. If one of them had split open, I would have skidded and collected the lot on top of me and my bike. A true-life horror flick. It was not to be the only time in my life when fate would deliver me a happy ending.

Not so for Bill Stalker. A couple of years later, he was killed in a motorbike accident on a sedate Melbourne street. A freak accident. Though Elsie had predicted my good luck when I was born, after that narrow escape on the Petone foreshore I decided to sell my motorbike and walk for a while instead.

I waited until I was shooting *Learning Fast* to get proper wheels.

I had permission to film the sixth-form students at a middle-of-the-road state school in Masterton. I needed a car to go over the hill and back. Something big enough to carry a camera crew if need be, and reliable.

I walked up to the Basin Reserve to Windy Autoport, and bought a Austin Maxi from a chirpy fellow. The car looked all right to me. In the right price range (cheap). I took it for a test drive through the Mount Victoria tunnel and stopped in at the Kosmos fish 'n' chip Shop in Kilbirnie. Back when I'd had a job and an official midday break, this was my favourite place to get lunch. I liked to play the luck machine while they cooked my order. You put one cent into the slot and the wheel went round and stopped on your message for the day. *Your luck is in*, or *Don't bet on it*. On this auspicious day I asked the luck machine whether I should buy the car or not.

Around went the wheel in front of the fortune teller dressed like a belly dancer. The needle spun and quivered. It came to rest on *Stop worrying and start living*.

I had already decided to stop worrying and start living. My freelance income was patchy, but every now and then I scored a commercial to art direct and found myself in the money. I thought I was cool. Look Ma, no hands.

*Stop worrying and start living*. As I looked at the fortune teller in the Kosmos fish 'n' chip shop, I decided this meant I should definitely buy the Austin Maxi from Windy Autoport.

The minute I bought that car, my life fell into two chapters: before the car and after the car. Everything went wrong immediately. Before Christmas, the singer in the band announced he was leaving me. He said he wanted to be alone and got into a car with five other rockers and drove off, leaving me sobbing as I drove all the way to my parents in Hawke's Bay. The car overheated and cost a fortune to fix. My father's friendly mechanic said I was lucky it hadn't blown up and that whoever sold it to me was out to sting me.

At my parents' house, I was the poor, unfortunate single woman in her thirties at Christmas dinner. The one who 'didn't have anybody'. In the provinces, God's own country was for couples. My family treated me with a delicate care that made me feel like I had been in a terrible accident of my own making.

It was dawning on me that the fortune teller's message had meant: 'Stop worrying and keep walking.'

Back in Wellington, late for some meeting or other, I leapt out of the house one windswept Saturday afternoon to find the car park empty. I stared and stared at the space where I had left my car, as though if I stared hard enough my car would miraculously appear. Some local kids told me that a big yellow tow truck had hoisted it up and taken it away.

I phoned the police and reported it stolen. They told me that Windy Autoport had gone bankrupt and that my car was among many that had been repossessed in a swoop by the receivers.

'But that's wrong in my case. I'm all paid up.'

'Sorry, madam. Windy were not passing on your payments to the previous owner, so though you have paid them your car is not yours. It's a civil matter.'

'But you do know where my car is currently?'

'Sorry, we can't disclose the car park building. Your car is there with twenty others.'

I put down the phone and again looked out the window to where my car used to be. The wind blew a plastic bag across the deserted car park. I needed that car. I rang Windy Autoport. Silly idea. The owner was probably already on a plane to Sydney. I phoned Kearney's, the only company in town that had yellow tow trucks. No one there. I decided I would walk over and look in their yard on the off-chance.

Kearney's had had a busy Saturday. My heart leapt when I saw my car, locked behind their high wire-netting fence. It was sitting there innocently. I could almost reach through the fence and touch it.

The good thing about having an ex-boyfriend in the music business is that you usually know where he is on a Saturday night, because his band is advertised. I found him in a break and told him how he could have a go at making amends for dumping me.

After his gig, we went down to the all-night service station and bought bolt-cutters and a padlock.

The chain holding the steel gate shut comes apart with a satisfying clunk.

Gleefully, under the yellow street lights, revving the engine too high, I zoom my car out of the yard. We lock the gate behind us before making our getaway. Then we go straight for the most respectable person I know – my brother. He lets me store my car in his garage and tells me to find a lawyer pronto.

I thank my ex – who then heads back to his new life – have a mug of Milo, and go to bed.

On Sunday morning, every lawyer I knew was either playing tennis or out to brunch. I threw on some clothes and got ready to leave the house, but as I came down the stairs I saw the inevitable navy blue shadows in the frosted glass panel of the front door. I opened it and saw two enormous men in uniform, helmets on.

'Would you like a cup of tea?'

'No thanks. We are here to tell you that your car has been stolen from Kearney's yard.'

In cop shows the suspects demand to stay silent until they have a lawyer, but that was in America so I decided against it.

'I know where my car is and I don't wish to report it stolen.'

They looked at each other. Their helmets almost touched as they said in unison, 'Civil matter.'

'Well, it was yesterday,' I replied, confidently.

They asked if they could use my phone. I agreed, but once they were on the line I left the room and got on the extension upstairs.

One officer was talking to the sergeant on duty, who was not happy. 'I've got Kearney's beside themselves, trying to hacksaw into their own yard,' he was saying, 'and half the station's wanting me to bring her in for questioning. Put her on.'

'I'm here,' I say, and repeat that I don't want to report my car stolen as I know where it is.

'I've got Kearney's trying to break into their own yard.'

'I have the key to the padlock here.'

I heard a frustrated sigh on the other end of the line. 'Well, give it to my boys. We will need a work sheet and you'll have to make a statement.'

'I was told it was a civil matter yesterday.'

'There's men down here who think I should charge you with breaking and entering and theft. And if you hadn't locked the yard up again, I'd be doing that right now. I want you down here at nine in the morning for a statement.'

I got the distinct impression that if they had been able to find my ex to blame, they would have thrown the book at him. I know that if I had been Māori or Pasifika or an immigrant, my chances of getting away with any sort of direct action would have been zilch.

No charges, and I had my car. I got away with it.

My generation had a healthy lack of respect for authority. Mine flowed from my art school days and into women's liberation marches, the claim-back-the-night campaign, the fight for legal abortion, and so on. The late 70s and the early 80s involved plenty of protest, so it was no wonder that attitude permeated our independent filmmaking. As a group, independent filmmakers thrived on feeling excluded. John O'Shea's Irish rebel mindset was shared among the young ruffians of my generation who all knew about direct action. Government agencies wouldn't fund us, so we felt a certain entitlement to sneak our own facilities. There were no formal structures, and the institutions that did exist were not exactly welcoming.

I'd bought myself a VHS camera for Christmas in 1981. VHS tapes were too low-quality for the networks, but I was rarely without my Panasonic camera. It bridged the gap between my professional documentary-making, which demanded years of blood, sweat and tears, and the little 8mm films I had been making with Nick at Stockwell. I could use my VHS camera as a kind of sketch block – trying out ideas, making home movies and recording oral histories like the one I made about Eric, the king of Kelvin Grove. I filmed a dramatic anti-nuclear march through central Wellington. Artist Debra Bustin led the Nuclear Horror Show in 1983, a noisy, carnivalesque piece of street theatre, with huge puppets of Muldoon and Reagan and papier-mâché missiles swaying among the office buildings on Lambton Quay. I recorded the show as one long shot that shows everyone going past for about thirty minutes.

I didn't have the time, the gear or the inclination to spend long days editing my VHS footage, so I devised a way to shoot that edited in the camera. It was intuitive and not always successful. But without realising it, I was giving myself a homemade film course, the only course I've ever had. It has stood me in good stead. We used 16mm film stock during the Springbok tour protests. Affordable VHS arrived at LV Martin's the following Christmas. I sometimes wonder how our visual history of that time would be understood had we all had VHS cameras then.

There were about four women independent filmmakers I knew of at that time, and one was the Māori activist filmmaker Merata Mita. I had seen the 1980 film of the police siege at Bastion Point that Merata had made with her husband, Gerd Pohlmann. Shot by Leon Narbey, *Bastion Point: Day 507* is a landmark documentary that only gets better with time.

Merata called me over to her house on Cricket Avenue in Tāmaki Makaurau. She wanted to document whatever was going to unfurl around the forthcoming South African rugby tour of the country, as the everyday racism in Aotearoa surfaced into hatred. Every filmmaker I knew was poised. We knew that what was about to happen would reveal everything sitting under the smiling complacency of the mainstream culture. This anti-racist campaign would hit where it hurt most. The national religion. Rugby.

Merata wanted to make something special. I did too.

She said she had been working with men on her films and was sick of it. I didn't ask why. Making films can wreck even the best creative relationships. You never know the amount of blood on the tracks when you see a film. Some of the best ones have the worst making-of stories.

After the success of *All the Way Up There*, I could see that pooling everyone's efforts into one film for theatrical release would be the best way to make a strong, uncensored anti-racist statement. Merata agreed. Getting our films screened in cinemas was not easy, but it was preferable to the editorial interference to be had at the network. In my experience making activist films in Britain, collectives would often argue in editing rooms for years, and sometimes the films wouldn't even hit the screen. Merata and I agreed: one film from all the contributed footage would be made, and it would be her first feature.

Complete creative control would rest with the director, Merata.

Brave plans, with a very small amount already raised from the National Council of Churches. Merata and Gerd covered important planning meetings in Tāmaki Makaurau Auckland. My job was to hit the streets with Waka, shoot what we could among the protestors, and maintain the kaupapa among the many filmmakers who stepped up. Compatriots at Vanguard did the heavy lifting.

When all the dust settled, and the blood from the split spleens and broken heads had flowed downstream, with Annie Collins editing, *Patu!* emerged, and made a big contribution to changing the conversation about racism in New Zealand. Completed in 1983, it carried the Geoff Murphy-inspired tagline 'You may love it, you may hate it . . . you may even <u>be</u> in it'. The audience stampeded into the dark to spot themselves. When they didn't, they often confronted me afterwards, since I was among the many filmmakers who had recorded the protests.

'I wasn't there, and I did a lot. I led my division.'

'I know. But you asked us not to film you, so we didn't.'

I would usually receive a long, sad, withering look.

1981 was a busy year. In the middle of all this, I went to Australia to complete the lab work on *Learning Fast*. In a taxi from the airport, as I slumped in the back seat, the driver turned round and looked at me keenly in the rear-view mirror.

'You're a Kiwi, aren't you.'

'Guilty.'

I thought he was going to make me say 'feesh and cheeps', to which my reply was always 'Champagne.'

'You've got some terrible racial problems over there,' he said.

No reply from me. Of course we did. I was exhausted. We inched towards town in the hot traffic while he went on a major rant about 'the Maoris' and how much better off 'the Abos' were in the equivalent of reservations. Something snapped. I realised I had a choice. I could get out of the taxi and walk. Or I could wake up. I woke up, and had a huge argument about whether New Zealand and Australia are racist countries all the way into town. It's the conversation that is important, even if you never seem to make much headway.

Between all the upheaval here in Aotearoa, shooting protests every Wednesday and Saturday across the land, I had also developed a short script for the International Year of Disabled Persons. I had an idea for a feature film. It would be about a series of heists carried out by a young woman with Down syndrome, her bodybuilder boyfriend with an intellectual disability, and a genius with cerebral palsy in a wheelchair. They escape the institution they are in and hit the road. The loot from their bank robberies is given to the disadvantaged and no one suspects them because they are not taken seriously. I still haven't made that film.

But when I was offered some money from the Disability Council, as it was then known, I conceived a short drama about a blind radio announcer, a deaf dress designer and a film critic with cerebral palsy who, together, witness the robbery of a cinema. There are clues. The designer notes down the number plate of the getaway car because it has blocked her in; the radio announcer is bumped into as the robbers run down the street; the film critic sees the whole thing but is knocked to the ground in the ensuing panic, leading to an ambulance being called as people think he is having a seizure. Everyone sees only their disabilities, and the vital clues are ignored. The parts were played by Chris Orr, Lorraine Schriener and George Theobald.

Closing with short interviews of the actors, *Hold Up* won an Australian Teachers of Media Award for Best Overseas Film for under twelve-year-olds, and played on TV here. It also won Best Overseas Film at the Rehabilitation Film Festival in New York.

But during the making of it, I fell out with my sister, who was writing the soundtrack. One minute we were talking about a music cue, and the next, some misunderstanding in 1966. She stormed out, and it took a while for us to recover. The music is really good though. Blood on the tracks.

# 16

# Bulletproof

After I stole my car back, I considered myself bulletproof. By August 1982, I was down in Blackball shooting a music video with Rick Bryant and the Neighbours – the time when Alun Bollinger and I found the Cressey grave in Ahaura. The Arts Council had forwarded just enough cash for me to pay for food and accommodation for everyone, so I set off with great enthusiasm. The band were booked to do a knees-up with the Topp Twins at Blackball Hall, and we had booked out the Blackball Hilton – a colonial hotel full of single beds, faded pink candlewick bedspreads and a cracked washbasin in every room. A speaker hung above every door: the current owner had wired the place for sound and blasted the Grateful Dead and the Doors to get everyone up in the mornings.

When AlBol and I drove into town at eleven one night, I worried that we might be too late to book in. But I needn't have. The joint was jumping. Music blared, people were dancing, the whole place was lit up. We were handed jam jars full of beer.

'Who's the party for?' I asked.

'You,' they told us.

Word of our shoot had travelled and helpful locals wanted to join in. Everyone had something to contribute – a car, a costume, free labour. Each car came with a set of instructions about what to tell the traffic cop if we were pulled over. We were warned about

'Sydney Dave', who always rode his motorbike on the wrong side of the road. 'You can hear him coming miles off,' I was told reassuringly. 'Just switch sides until he's gone past.' When I met Dave himself, he proclaimed through broken teeth, 'Never had an accident. It's karma.'

Money for the shoot was tight. I'd bludged the camera, and a commercials crew travelling from Queenstown up to Wellington, through the kindness of Geoff Dixon at Silverscreen, dropped off top-of-the-range gear, on the understanding we would return it afterwards. This camera dolly and small crane were pure pleasure when we used it to shoot the band robbing a bank in Greymouth and tricking the local bobby, played by Rick, who had once done time for smoking a joint. Putting a police hat on and twirling a truncheon really appealed to him. The whole town of Blackball got into it.

But with no money left, it fell to me to get everyone back home, along with all that shiny gear.

We could put two thirds of the gear in Brian Kassler's ute and fill AlBol's station wagon with rest. At Picton, everything could be loaded onto Brian's ute. But I still had to get us over Cook Strait on the ferry, while paying for one vehicle, and with only four people ticketed. That left another ten.

I grew up with the idea that trains and ferries could always be negotiated. I owe it to the great-grandfather who smiled down from Nan's wall. From childhood, I understood it was not Robert Holmes who built the Raurimu Spiral but Edward Cressey, railwayman of Cobden.

We gather very close to the ferry terminal while Brian loads everything onto his ute. I go to find the harbour master at the Picton wharf. He's up above the terminal in a glassed-in office.

'We've come to film the commercial,' I tell him.

A look of puzzled outrage passes across his features.

'Nobody told me.'

'It's just some small inserts – we're travelling with a skeleton crew.'

'Who sent you?'

'Oh . . . um . . . I don't remember his name.'

'Was it at Head Office?'

I nod. 'It was a man,' I tell him helpfully.

'What did he look like?"

'He was wearing walk shorts.'

'Did he have thinning hair and glasses.'

'Yes . . .' I say, trying to sound as uncertain as possible.

'Bloody Gary.'

He calls out to someone else in the office. 'Would you believe it. Gary again. Unbelievable.'

I leave with the appropriate paperwork and report to our anxious little band waiting below.

'Do we have to carry a whole lot of gear on and pretend?' they ask with dismay.

'No. Just carry the camera and a couple of flecky boards. Maybe a light stand.' Flecky boards are very big and very light.

When Brian tries to drive his completely overloaded ute up the ramp to the ferry, the wheels won't go round. Several railway crew help lift it on board.

'What you got in there, mate? Lead?'

'Pretty much,' Brian says.

We make a very funny-looking film crew as we are welcomed on board. Once we are sailing through the Sounds, we try to make ourselves scarce. The camera assistant wants to know what to do with the camera.

'What do you need to do?'

'I need to give it a thorough clean,' she tells me.

'Do it in the purser's office.' Which is what she does as the boat forges through the waves towards home.

A couple of very stoned hippies on board like the look of us and will not leave us alone. We try to avoid them, but they persist. Just before we enter the Wellington Heads, they disappear.

To my horror, as we berth, an announcement comes over the tannoy. Would all passengers please not immediately disembark as the police are coming on board. We hold back, only to see our unwelcome fellow travellers arrested and marched off the boat in handcuffs. A couple of stowaways, we are told.

There was a film brewing at home that I knew had a decent chance of helping that racist Aussie cabbie and at least half of the Pākehā in New Zealand to confront their prejudice. After *Goodbye Pork Pie*, Geoff Murphy had polished a script he had been working on for years. Based on oral histories gathered by James Cowan in the 1934 book *Tales of the Maori Bush*, Geoff had conceived a rollicking Western set during the New Zealand Wars. This film was ambitious, international in its scope, uncompromising in its exploration of the Māori–Pākehā abyss – and a truly entertaining story, bound to be a popular success.

*Utu* is probably the seminal New Zealand film. It stars Zac Wallace, a unionist warrior and veteran of Paremoremo Prison, as Te Wheke, the rebel leader who calmly submits to corporal justice meted out by his own people according to ancient rules of tikanga Māori.

The producers asked me to document the shoot and make a one-hour TV documentary to support the theatrical release. I jumped at the chance. It was a dream project.

I was given complete creative control of *Making Utu*. All my mates were up there working on the shoot. I scored a deal with Mitsubishi to provide a brand-new station wagon and had the camera bulging with 16mm Fuji colour film stock provided free from their head office in Tokyo. With my friend Tungia Baker as my production manager, off we went to Napier and got cracking.

It turned out to be one of the hardest shoots I have ever done.

The first problem was my cinematographer. With 16mm negative in the camera, I like to end-slate, which involves having the film crew settle in with the camera lined up and observe. Only when the scene feels like it is revealing itself do I silently signal to 'roll camera'. If we are doing it right, people in the room can't tell the difference between the times when we are shooting and not shooting. Having a camera crew around is very intrusive, no matter how you do it. To make three people and their gear disappear in a small room is not easy. End-slating is a good way to achieve authenticity. It can be pretty stressful though. Being poised, while not actually shooting and not missing anything, is nerve-racking. But it means that less film stock travels through the camera. The downside is that it takes three times longer to sync sound with picture later when the print gets to the cutting room.

As I was the producer and was paying the assistant editor to sync up the material, I didn't see that end-slating posed any problem. But my cameraman did. He had been trained at the Film Unit where end-slating was deeply discouraged. They never had to worry about the cost of film stock. Anyway, it all came to a head. I told him that I loved his framing but he had to end-slate. He refused point blank. Impasse. After only a week's work, I had to sack my cinematographer.

After that, every cameraperson who came to Hawke's Bay to shoot *Making Utu*, apart from AlBol, wanted to join the camera team on the big movie itself. I kept losing them to the extra units that *Utu* seemed to be growing weekly. There were other problems too, mainly that none of my erstwhile mates wanted to be filmed. They were all doing jobs they hadn't done before and didn't want to be recorded in case they were doing it wrong.

At the beginning, I'd had the idea that I could ask all the owners of the land we were shooting on about the history of that land. Naive. The last thing that landowners, Māori or Pākehā, wanted to talk about publicly was the history of the land they stood on. Pākehā, because following the Land March in 1975, the established landowners of places like Ngāmatea were more aware that they were under suspicion of having stolen it. Māori, because they were living with this history every day and knew which whānau in their iwi had fought with colonial troops and who had sided with the so-called rebels.

The rollicking Western that Geoff was making was exploring this history under considerable controversy. He never seemed to lack confidence. With Merata Mita at his side, he forged on. Wi Kuki Kaa, one of the most experienced Māori actors of this time, arrived from the Sydney stage. He was brilliant playing the second lead, Wiremu, who has thrown his lot in with the colonial troops and is constantly underestimated.

In one scene, Colonel Elliot and Wiremu are playing chess.

```
Wiremu: Mon dieu! Check mate.

Colonel: How is it that you, Wiremu, a
native aboriginal of Aotearoa, speak such
good English though you have never been to
England?

Wiremu: I speak French but I have never been
to France.
```

As the shoot continued through a punishing winter and Ngāmatea became breathtakingly beautiful and snow-clad, I was freaking out under three layers of blankets in my little caravan. I still had no real access to anyone much and was just shooting whatever I could. While editor Simon Reece cut sequences back in Wellington, many of which bore no real relationship to one another, I was under extreme pressure to find a narrative structure. I was going crazy.

These days, the 'making of' film is a sub-genre. They are sales tools. Directors are interviewed later, once they have recovered some sanity. Actors praise the genius script, and they are all happy families. *Making Utu* was to screen for a commercial hour on mainstream television, and I did not want to miss this opportunity to get something meaningful into the sitting rooms of the nation. Rollicking Western *Utu* might be, but I saw it as a vehicle to say something more.

Terry Crayford arrived on his motorbike to join his son Jonathan, already a magnificent piano player, who was working with Geoff's son Matthew in the art department. I filmed the band in their costumes on set, rehearsing 'Oh! Susanna', the old folk song by Stephen Foster. This became the device I needed. It would be a non-narrative documentary. It would be experimental but still screen to the mainstream.

By structuring the band's performances around the commercial breaks, the themes were energised. Geoff had only one stipulation, which was that we not film rehearsals. He thought they always looked naff. But he gave us free access to the film itself. This presented a breathtaking opportunity. Going from the cameras and the pony clubs and the taped hats to the band sounding terrible as they rode in on the orchestral score by John Charles, the transition to the actual film takes your breath away. It's a 'through the mirror' journey. *Making Utu* shows the genial camaraderie of a new film industry at work, enjoying every minute of making something revolutionary. *Utu* is even more of a terrifying miracle if you see how it was made.

And everyone I know and love is there, including a very pregnant Shirley Grace bent over her large-format camera, photographing the cast on long exposures to emulate the photographers of the colonial misadventure. With days to spare, she put down her camera and headed out from the bush to give birth to her second son, Sam.

The young piano player, Jonathan Crayford, sneaked into my heart during the shoot. I think I had already fallen in love with his beautiful piano-playing well before I fell for him. *Utu* has a subplot that culminates in a grand piano being thrown from a building. As the film shoot followed the piano being moved around Hawke's Bay, Jonathan's music was all over my soundtrack. When it came to completing the documentary, Jonathan, though only eighteen at the time, composed all the music. By the time I had completed the film, we had bridged the age gap and got together.

But the best thing for me was that when it came to shooting my own feature film, it was the *Utu* whānau who helped me realise it. There is much to be said about the meaning of the word utu. Very simply put, utu means reciprocity.

# 17

# A Primo Possie

At this point in my life, I still hadn't made that movie. The one that would screen in a cinema near you. *Learning Fast* had screened to some acclaim at home, but there were no international sales. When I screened it for the ABC, the film commissioners watched it and enthusiastically reported that they would like to make one of those for themselves – still, no sale. The global reach of the Gaylene Preston Productions catalogue had become a bit limited. Well, speaking truthfully, you could say non-existent. I was on the brink of giving up filmmaking and getting a real job. God knows what.

I like filmmaking. It's the one thing I feel like I'm any good at. I love the thrill of sitting in a dark cinema with everyone looking in the same direction, reacting together. You get to know your film when you sit with it in an audience. That's the buzz. Hearing people laugh, hearing when they choke up. The sound of sobbing is like angels singing. Movies are the feelies after all is said and done, and a way to change the world for the better. Make 'em laugh, make 'em cry and leave them with something to think about. Plus, as a creative medium it's not lonely. Not like sitting here trying to write this down, wondering which word works where. Help is always available when you are making a film. There are always other creative people on the job to get you out of the jams you've invented for yourself.

But filmmaking, more than any other art form, is a business, and in 1983 I was on the brink of not very bankable. At all.

I wanted to join the proper film industry. The one where they have meetings on the balcony and sign deals over white tablecloths in restaurants, toasting one another with champagne before sauntering off to dally on the red carpet before a premiere. I wanted to eat oysters au naturel and choose the lobster with the mornay sauce.

I accepted a job with the New Zealand Film Commission sales arm to go to the only market that really mattered: the 1983 Cannes Film Festival.

They would pay my fare and help me find a cheap hotel (very cheap as it turned out) and I would assist Lindsay Shelton in the office, whatever that meant. 'Oh you're nicer than the others,' Lindsay told me, by way of explanation when I asked him: why me? Actually, there weren't any others. This was the very beginning of everything and all of the other possible candidates were men who were unlikely to pick up a clipboard or deliver a flyer, no matter how much you paid them. After my hotel and airfare were paid for, I was 'pro bono', as lawyers like to say, but I was happy to be there and prepared for my great leap forward.

Cannes feels like a small provincial town wrapped around a farmers' market, like so many towns dotted around the South of France. The famed Croisette is not that different from Marine Parade in Napier, and by the time I arrive the place is already full to bursting. The circus is in town. You can't walk down a footpath without being pushed out onto the road. As my taxi inches along, I get a great view of the madness.

I soon find that in Cannes, a cup of coffee will set you back the equivalent of NZ$10, and forget eating in a restaurant. 'So, I'm gonna be on the bludge,' I think to myself as I go to find our HQ.

Monsieur Shelton is completely at home here. The New Zealand Film Commission has a third-storey office on La Croisette on a corner overlooking a bar. The office is housed in a well-appointed marble apartment, the bedrooms converted into offices. All the furniture is chrome and white leather and what isn't silver is gold. The kitchen is already stacked with publicity materials. Reception is a lounge with a wall of glass doors that open onto a lawn on the roof of the bar downstairs, forming our own backyard. From here I can see all the way down to the Grand Palais one way and almost to the Carlton the other. Marvellous. 'A primo possie,' as my father might have said.

The office is already bustling, and Lindsay is wondering where we should put up our posters. I suggest we erect a revolving clothesline on the far corner above the bar and peg all our posters on the line. They'll go round in the breeze, optimising visibility and promoting our unique way of life. He thinks I'm joking. He is unfamiliar with the beauties of the iconic Hills hoist. I'm quite serious. No one has heard of New Zealand.

Lindsay gives me the key to the apartment so that I can open up in the mornings. 'Whatever you do, *do not* give this key to Grahame McLean,' Lindsay tells me in a stern voice. As my fingers curl around the key in my palm, neither of us know that Grahame McLean, one of New Zealand's most prolific film producers, is already *en residence*.

The first time I open up the apartment in the morning, I find Grahame making his bed in Lindsay's bathroom. He has been locking the door and sleeping in the big pink art deco bath during the day and 'entertaining' in the apartment by night. He does deals in the marble lounge and hangs out there with well-known regulars of the Cannes night circus. Every now and then Lindsay complains that his bathroom lock is stuck, and scurries off to use the common lav. That's because Lindsay's bathroom is not just busy by night. By the afternoon, people are smoking joints behind the heavy pink door, with the industrial-strength fan switched to high.

Early on, the office receptionist wrote down the brand of cigarettes she smoked so that I could arrive every morning having bought them for her. She was really the local fixer. She always knew a man (her husband, or a brother-in-law, or an uncle) who could organise whatever we needed and charge us double, which was apparently better than the going rate, which was triple. The first time I bought her cigarettes, I felt like an enabler. The poor woman could hardly breathe. She'd stagger into the kitchen to have coughing fits. The second time she asked me to buy her cigarettes in the morning, I told her as politely as I could that as a former smoker who had quit with difficulty, it was against my principles to buy cigarettes – at all – for anyone. To say she was extremely put out would be an understatement. Volcanic eruption.

From then on, it was war.

Trouble among the women staffing the office was not a good start. My personal politics got in the way at every turn. I was finding the fawning sycophantism of Cannes impossible. How the hell would you ever know what anyone was really thinking if all anyone did was tell lies to one another? Everyone was 'charmed'; they 'loved your movie' but hadn't seen it. They threw parties that weren't actual parties where you might meet someone interesting to talk to. The purpose of these parties was to 'do the room', which involved meeting and greeting and having the same conversation over and over again. Schmooze city. I just couldn't conform. I found everything disturbing and/or demeaning.

One day, Lindsay sent me down to a suite in the Carlton Hotel to deliver some invitations. Off I trotted, jaunty as all get-out in my new suit and pink shoes.

I'd decided on this working costume with great care. I needed something that I could put on in the morning that wouldn't get me thrown out of parties at night. Cannes has a strict dress code. The men all wore the same clothes every day no problem, so I'd asked a designer friend to make me a suit too. He got into the job with total enthusiasm. The suit had classy pleated trousers, and a double-breasted jacket with broad shoulders, over a pink cotton shirt and a thin knot tie. I think my friend had a crush on David Bowie. Jonathan made my shoes. Comfortable shoes you could hurry in were essential, and these were soft as a glove, and a beautiful pink. Wearing them meant running was never a problem. In this multi-purpose uniform, I was ready for anything.

Which was lucky. I needed to be.

I was not a young virgin groupie here. At thirty-five, I was in the band. I knew what it was like trying to socialise in the film industry back in New Zealand, and I didn't think it was going to be any more edifying at Cannes. *Goodbye Pork Pie* is almost a documentary to me. A snapshot of the gender gap of the time. In that film, the bet is: 'I'll be hanging out of her by the time we reach Whanganui.' He's not talking about the car.

Those guys were my mates by day, then we would get fuzzy stoned after work, and towards the end of the night the direct question might be posed: 'Wanna fuck?' The offer could easily be declined with a laugh. But this was Europe, where I knew a young woman could get seriously hassled. I'd been to Italy, where it was not uncommon for some bloke to randomly pull out his erect penis right in front of you on a street, as though it was a compliment. And I'd been to Paris, where one night my friend and I beat a hasty retreat from a street market as the male stall-owners beat tin pans loudly, because we were wearing our skirts too short for them. I'd been on the Paris Metro. Garlic breath and wandering hands.

In my suit, wearing a Venetian fedora at a jaunty angle, I could cut a male silhouette when I walked home at night, so I'd be left alone and save on taxi fares.

As I headed down the Croisette to the mighty Carlton, clutching my official deliveries, I felt truly sophisticated and cosmopolitan. I passed Nagisa Ōshima, the great Japanese filmmaker, strolling with his impressive wife and family in their exquisite kimonos on their way to the Grand Palais screening of *Merry Christmas, Mr Lawrence*. Celebrities were everywhere, acting like they were normal people. And if it wasn't the real ones, it was the fakes. On one footpath I hit a complete logjam that flowed out onto the road. A woman was dressed as Marilyn Monroe. Her face was caked in clown-quality make-up. She had the wig, she had the beauty spot, she had the frock. She did not have the knickers. An industrial fan on the side of the road was blowing up her skirt, as in *The Seven Year Itch*, to the delight of a paparazzi scrum clicking away. Coins were cascading into her suitcase. Some of it was tinkling to the ground as boot boys wriggled among the legs of the crowd to pick up every franc.

The Carlton Hotel is an icon of wedding-cake architecture from the great old days. You could imagine Zelda and Scott hanging out on the terraces, champagne drunk, the wicked wit cutting like ice. But I was taken aback to see a two-storey cardboard cut-out of a nearly naked woman caressing a gun, legs akimbo, bedecking the main entrance. Octopussy. She was gigantic. The sight made me distinctly uncomfortable. I daren't look up. Nobody else seemed to be worried, as they wandered under her implied cardboard twat. Well, I had already caused enough of a fuss back at the office with the cigarettes incident, and I was beginning to feel like my skin was on the wrong way round, but I just didn't like it. I didn't like it because of what it meant to me as a woman trying to get a toehold in this bloody industry.

The Cannes Film Festival projects an international brand of sophistication, art films, serious filmmakers, razor-sharp critics. Here, art, business and global entertainment intersect in a garden of beautiful clothes worn by glamorous sophisticates at arty black-tie premieres on the red carpet in front of the Grand Palais. All this is very true, and terrific to be part of. But I was quickly finding out what I really, really didn't want to know.

The overwhelming driver of the festival, the thing that sends the international film industry crammed onto the Croisette for those crucial festival weeks, is money.

Dirty money. Mafia money, in some cases. Instant gold. This is the industry that will launder your cash and it can do it fast and in great quantities. It's a money hoover. And in 1983 it's low-level, medium-grade smut that's doing the business. At the TV market, the big seller was naked Jazzercise on the Playboy channel. On the co-production board, some desperado looking for partners suggests 'getting it up down under'.

'Probably an Australian,' I think charitably.

\*

226

Cannes in May 1983 was no place for a girl with auteur aspirations. The place was littered with ordinary-looking men with big-breasted beauties on each arm, leaning all over them as they sauntered down to their next screening. The more powerful the man, the more the women surrounded them. Starlets, leaning in.

But I just felt lonely. Really lonely. And invisible. My uniform disguised my feminine side, so I wasn't getting hit on, but I didn't feel like I was a filmmaker either. I felt like a pale shadow. No one wanted to meet me, it seemed. I stood in the jambon sandwich queue ($15), silent, as everyone chattered on around me. They all seemed to know one another. How could I be taken seriously as a member of the gang, this big gang of proper filmmakers, if no one knew I had joined?

'I'm a filmmaker!' I wanted to proclaim.

In this silent world in the middle of the noise, I began to question why I was so hung up on that.

I was in the game because I had something to say. I was a feminist, wasn't I? Where was the influence of the great women thinkers of the 1970s in our cinema? Shulamith Firestone, Gloria Steinem, Germaine Greer? Nowhere that I could see. Feminist ideas had seeped into experimental cinema that screened to tiny audiences in lofts in Soho. Unspooling to the converted. But film is a mass medium, and if feminist films couldn't crack in, then how was the overwhelmingly male-centric storytelling ever going to change? Where was the great gender-consciousness-raising going to happen if not in the most wonderful and compelling storytelling medium ever invented?

The very beginnings of cinema began in peep shows on flickering paper. The medium is all set up to encourage us to sit back and watch. But audiences were being turned into voyeurs. How does showing rape onscreen actually stop it from happening? I badly wanted to make films that were in opposition to the films I was watching. The world wasn't going to change if privileged women like me didn't take on that mission. I needed to make my first feature or die.

So I go and have drinks that I can't afford with the Laings. Robin and I met in the jambon queue. She is here promoting her husband's latest feature film, *The Lost Tribe*. They aren't finding it easy, as the entire New Zealand Film Commission sales arm is completely preoccupied with organising the after-party for the *Utu* premiere. Being an Official Selection in Un Certain Regard is not only a coup for its director and producers but also for its sales agent, New Zealand Film Sales. Money is being spent to pull out all the stops and make the most of the opportunity. It's probably why Lindsay has an assistant this year – the worst assistant he's ever had, no doubt, but in my head I am an unpaid volunteer and entitled to a rather more independent path than he may have envisaged.

To his chagrin, with the *Utu* premiere just a few days away, I announce firmly that I will be helping John and Robin for the afternoon and will be unavailable for other duties. We madly Sellotape flyers to lampposts (illegal, but everyone is doing it) before overheating and going to a bar, where I invest my entire life savings in a double gin and tonic. This makes me cry but John and Robin don't mind.

Things are descending into chaos. I have regressed to my inner naughty fourth-former and I'm not alone. With the stress of releasing the first great New Zealand movie into the world, we all need an outlet. Once Lindsay is away on business and reliably out of the office for an hour or two, it's my duty to alert the team that the coast is clear. With Robin Murphy and her partner at the time, Kelly Johnson, who plays Lieutenant Scott in *Utu*, we have parties in the pink marble bathroom, getting stoned and singing into the shower head. Kelly has an idea for a film promotion he wants to do if he ever goes back to Cannes. It consists of a big inflatable penis he can float offshore among the yachts to advertise a film he will call *Dorko*.

In all this madness, I was beginning to realise that filmland was a tiny global village, population approx. 2000, ninety-nine per cent of whom were middle-aged white men. That's how many producers it appeared to me were actively making a film at that moment. The few women 'vice presidents' tended to be wearing very high heels. Me in my suit and hat trying to connect with them was ludicrous.

The Cannes market is not a friendly place for an actual filmmaker, particularly one who makes documentaries. Documentary was what everyone in the industry said they liked to watch best, but their makers, until recently, held very little status in the distribution industry. And was I a director or a producer? You needed to be one or the other, not both. They lauded auteur filmmaking up at the Grand Palais, but underneath, at the Market – no, you couldn't be both. Kiss of death. Not seriously in the business. An English-speaking colonial girl who thinks she wants to make a feature film is an impossible apparition. Also, I was Monsieur Shelton's assistant, everybody knew, and therefore I was not a filmmaker. The very scheme that had got me there was the very thing that held me back.

I had a card I thought would be funny and cheeky that I would whip out for a bit of a laugh during meetings with the movers and shakers, which I was sure I would have. They would find me fascinating and my ideas pitch-perfect. I had this card tucked into my hat band. It said: 'If you can't convince 'em, confuse 'em.' But I felt like I had accidentally confused myself.

There was a Belgian paparazzo on the Croisette that year who decided I was somebody. As in, 'somebody', in disguise. Telling him to go away and that he was wasting his film just made him more persistent. He had his eye out for me and my suit and hat for the entire festival. He whizzed around on an ancient Vespa. His gold business card said 'Baxter' and on the other side just 'London. Paris. Rome'. Wherever I went he would follow, clicking away. We all told him that I was, strictly speaking, a hanger-on, a lowly assistant to the New Zealand sales branch, and that, yes, I'd made a documentary about *Utu*, and yes, other films in New Zealand, but they were not at the festival and what he saw was who I was. The more we tried to convince him, the more fascinated he got.

One night, I was attempting to get into the Australian party down on the beach. They were celebrating the premiere of Peter Weir's *The Year of Living Dangerously*. They had a lot more money for their parties than we did, the Aussies. Their governments have always understood how valuable their film industry is for them. Their party was resourced. Heaps to eat, prawns galore, good champagne. Theirs was a hot ticket. A hot ticket I did not have. These days it's just about impossible to get into a prestigious party you don't have an invitation for, but in those days, if you arrived late, security could be pretty slack. The trick was to blend in and head to the food table fast.

With John and Robin Laing, who did have the all-important bit of paper (though theirs was addressed to Mr and Mrs Loins), as night fell I snuck down the stone steps on the sea wall to the beach below. Outside a big tent, the party was lit by tiki lights, like a classy barbie.

Halfway down, safely in the dark, I heard a voice ring out from the gloom. 'Prescott!' And suddenly we were blinded by a camera flash.

My favourite paparazzo had spotted me and was sure this was going to be his great scoop. The other paparazzi heard Baxter's delighted cry and joined in. Caught in the glare of popping flashbulbs, pinned to the spot with no escape, we tried to look entitled and descended to the beach. Seeing the excitement, the Australian reception committee – who were in the middle of their first beer after a long night – pulled themselves together, the women shoving their shoes back on. They leapt to their feet and welcomed us with double handshakes. They were thrilled we could come. Gradually, as we went down the line, it sank in that we were Kiwis, and their fulsome welcome turned to puzzlement.

There's a photo taken by cinematographer Thom Burstyn of me in a lift, hitting a pleased Baxter on the head with my soft shoes.

'Prescott, you are full of sex,' Baxter is saying.

'Baxter, you are full of shit.'

He probably didn't even have film in his camera. But here's a note to Baxter, just in case he should be still living and setting eyes on this book. If you're out there, Baxter, and you've kept the negs, send 'em on over.

Baxter got us into the Directors' Club though. It was a secret spot on the middle floor of the Petit Palais. Everyone in there seemed to be spending the festival lying around under a pall of smoke, reading the daily trades and slagging one another off in that very shruggy way the French have perfected – not committing to being thoroughly nasty while implying terrible things. But hanging out in there made me feel connected to the great and glorious past of real French filmmaking. Maybe Agnès Varda would turn up and slap them all.

With the arrival of Zac Wallace and a one-of-a-kind Egyptian make-up artist named Wagi, brought to France specially to apply Zac's moko, things started to feel more normal. That moko was designed by prosthetic make-up artist Bob McCarron to look like it had been chiselled into Zac's skin. It took time to apply, and once it was on Zac didn't want to take it off. There, in the circus among the clowns, among the grubby Marilyns and the tawdry Bardots, Zac cut a striking figure as we walked to the New Zealand Film Commission party to publicise this great work.

The party was already in full swing as we made our entrance. It was small but well attended, flowing through the apartment and onto the lawn. Very convivial, as Grahame McLean could attest.

Zac had it all planned. As we were going up in the lift, he pumped up the veins on his forehead and leapt out straight into the official party with a full-throttle pūkana. 'Yahhhh!'

As one, all assembled headed for the walls.

'You want a scary movie, then I'll give it to you,' Zac seemed to be saying.

As Zac performed a haka, gold bangles rattled in fear, schmoozers and posers and caped imposters shivered in their loafers, the ice in their drinks clattering. They stared at him, wide-eyed, as he glared back. Just as the tension reached fever pitch, he threw his head back and roared with laughter. A huge sigh of relief. Here in this place of crazy publicity stunts, it was still possible to really scare people.

For me, Zac's entrance distils the very thing that *Utu* is about. It sums up the heart of the cultural conversation around the great colonial present. People with money and power facing the unknown other, fearful as the culture they have subjugated rises up. Acted out at a party in the South of France. Etched in my memory forever.

The day dawned for our Grand Palais moment, and I was delegated to look after our star, while the producers and director were doing business. This was a task that was absolutely fine by me as, by this time, having observed the shoot as a documentarian, I knew Zac. We enjoyed each other's company. He was staying at the Hôtel Du Cap, at that time the primo possie for all the stars and their agents.

Sitting out on the balcony of the hotel restaurant, eating a steak tartare that cost the equivalent of my hotel for the week (courtesy New Zealand Film Commission), we squinted out beyond the white tablecloths to the azure sea sprinkled with the floating pleasure palaces pulled in for the festival. Zac told me about the Paremoremo riots in 1965. The riots had happened when he was in prison and the prisoners took over. Something about all that shining glass must have reminded him. Men had ripped metal poles out of ceilings to use as ramrods to break unbreakable glass, trying to escape the fire that was coming for them.

We talked about Paremoremo as we sipped champagne alongside the stars and their handlers. Was that ice or diamonds clinking in their drinks?

Then it was our turn on the red carpet, and all the flashing bulbs were for us. Oddly enough, Baxter was nowhere to be seen.

The film went down gangbusters. It was a great screening, a real triumph. Afterwards there was a terrific critical reception. Geoff was hailed as the new Kurosawa, and the important American film critic Pauline Kael wrote a review that opened doors to Hollywood. Afterwards, we all went back down onto the beach to host the post-screening party. Zac and Wagi disappeared to do a quick moko touch-up, and I went down there to help. It was my job after all.

The party was to celebrate that wonderful achievement. Held during the afternoon, it wasn't as glamorous as a night-time party and, compared to the Aussie bash, it was small cheese. The weather was hot but grey and a sultry wind was blowing. The idea was to announce a deal that would see *Utu* distributed into the United States, and for the world press to meet the star and the film's director. At great expense, sheltered under a long awning, they had spread out the latest New Zealand chardonnay, lamb chops (hardly cooked, how the French liked them), bite-sized pavlovas and Heineken beer. I was always hungry at Cannes, but visitors came first, so no one touched a morsel.

We stood around waiting for the press to arrive. We could see them up across the road above us outside the Carlton. There gathered roughly fifty members of that brave brotherhood, huddled in a press stakeout. David Bowie was arriving, apparently. But after that, they were bound to come over the road to eat a chop and hear about our magnificent movie. That was the plan.

I was lurking by a foot pool at the base of the sea wall. When swimmers go up to the hotel from the beach, they are encouraged to soak the sand off their feet before climbing up to cross the road to go into the hotel. Idly passing time, I had my camera wound up and was filming some scene setters.

My camera was a little clockwork 16mm Bolex that I had used when I was making *Making Utu*. I'd loaded it with film stock and thrown it in my suitcase so that, even though I had delivered the documentary by then, I could record the historic moment when *Utu* screened in Official Selection. I used it to do time-lapse. You could easily take stills with a Bolex, but it's basically a clockwork camera that you wind up and it shoots a couple of minutes of a ten-minute film roll. Invented for Abel Gance, the great French filmmaker of the Silent Era in the days of hand-cranked cameras, it was designed to be wound up and affixed to the back of a horse. This particular Bolex I held in my hand was affectionately called 'the Bolivisión'. There is barely a film shot in New Zealand before 1980 that didn't have at least a small contribution from this clever old camera.

As I sat there, I looked up and saw a comely bleached blonde woman stride out onto a first-floor corner balcony of the Carlton, where she began to slowly strip. At that moment all the paparazzi

233

forgot David Bowie and trained their sights on this spectacle. What do you call it when a woman stands brazenly naked, her arms outstretched, her nipples facing the sky on a wedding-cake hotel balcony overlooking the hotel entrance, while a giant cardboard cut-out of Maud Adams as Octopussy, legs akimbo, gun in hand, is seductively winking to an army of cameramen?

The woman disappeared, but very quickly reappeared between Octopussy's legs and walked across the Croisette, pursued by a stampede of the world's press. Edy Williams, though not young, was a staple of the festival and she had a new film out – *Chained Heat*. They followed her down the concrete sea wall steps like they were the children of Hamelin and she was the Pied Piper. Within seconds, down at the foot pool, I found myself surrounded by jostling cameramen all trying to get a good shot as Edy lay down in the water, à la *From Here to Eternity*, shaking her bosom and rolling down her bikini bottom seductively, revealing well-toned buttocks. The sound of film running through the camera gates was deafening. I was hemmed in and couldn't easily get out, so I set the old Bolivisión rolling when, without warning, a boot boy – he could have been no more than sixteen – in leathers and piercings leapt through the throng and landed right on top of Edy.

The kids come down from Nice during the festival to do a little light robbery and a bit of what we now call disrupting. He was simulating sex, missionary position, with his full weight on her shoulders, and in his humping enthusiasm he didn't seem to realise or care that he had pushed her right under the water. She began struggling, but she couldn't get her head up, even out of this shallow water. Because she was being filmed by every major news outlet in the world, she kept smiling.

I look around to see if I am the only one aware of what is happening. Edy is still under the water but her smile has grown into a grimace. The boot boy is oblivious as he plays to the cameras. This is a very long minute.

There's a reflex that happens when you are drowning and it's very silent and still. Drowning people don't actually splash around. It kicks in at a certain point and it's very dangerous.

The paparazzi all have their eyes to their viewfinders. Is anyone going to drop their camera and jump in to save her? The guy is a hulk. I realise that the more difficulty she gets into, the more valuable that footage becomes and the less likely they are to stop filming and help.

I had gone to the MIPTV, the television market in Cannes, a few weeks earlier with one sole purpose in mind – to find out what could be recorded on a hundred feet of 16mm film that would return the most cash. The truth was appalling, but in retrospect obvious. The one thing that was absolutely failsafe – you could name your price – was real death on camera. The more shocking, the better.

As I stand there clutching the Bolivisión, surrounded by the incessant clacking of film stock flowing, I realise I am the only one without a network or a boss expecting a scoop. I am also the least likely to be able to drag him off her. Just as I am about to jump in, with gargantuan willpower she pushes him off. Gasping for air, while miraculously still looking alluring, she stands up. He looks like he's getting ready to punch her. Then she is out of there, back up the steps to the Croisette, the rampant media tribe following. A bit of uncommitted pole-dancing up a lamppost, and then, clearly shaken, she retreats to the hotel.

David Bowie has arrived anyway, and the media wander off to do their official assignment. Show over.

In New York state a few weeks later, someone will phone a TV news station to tell them he intends setting fire to himself at a certain place at a certain hour, and they will turn up and film him doing it. He will live to tell the tale, then sue them.

Down at the beach, the wind has become quite brisk in the late afternoon around the New Zealand Film Commission table. The odd Australian journalist has arrived and is sculling back the Heineken.

The expected announcement of *Utu*'s distribution deal did not eventuate. Neither did the deal. There are many possible reasons why –

but they are all a shame. The New Zealand contingent and associated wives hoed hungrily into the cold lamb chops once everyone realised this was it. A fully tattooed Māori warrior, star of a movie in Official Selection, was no match for a topless woman in bikini bottoms as far as press profile was concerned. And therein lies the problem.

As my time at Cannes came to an end, I was beginning to feel a bit more at home. I unpacked a beautiful jacket my mother had bought at Beath's in Greymouth just after the war. It was the New Look of 1947, the year I was born. It had leg-of-mutton sleeves and was tucked in at the waist. I had a pair of slightly ruched trousers my friend Janet had made from silky silver, red and black striped material I had bought at Evans's on Cuba Street – the most amazing fabric shop in the world. You sat on a chair at the big worn wooden counter as huge sharp scissors scrunched their way effortlessly through anything. The whole outfit cost me half a crown.

With my mother's black ebony necklace at my throat, and wearing low-heeled red suede boots, I had an unforgettable red-carpet moment.

I stood next to the legendary Italian actor Marcello Mastroianni for a full five minutes. And it was just as thrilling as it sounds. He was wearing a white linen suit and I was going in to see the premiere of the film in which he starred. One minute I was just standing there, the next minute, so was he – right beside me. A flock of Italian fashionistas then surrounded us, so I just stayed put. Everyone thought I was with him and asked no questions. They all spoke Italian and were far too engrossed in one another to worry about me. He didn't seem to mind me there. Most successful actors I have met are less than themselves off screen, but not him. We exchanged a glance and I felt like he knew me. That's the power of the great stars. There's a conspiracy with the audience that binds you to them for life. I savoured this delicious moment and, as they all fluttered into the cinema, I blended in, then melted away.

That's all you ever really have to do. Blend in and enjoy the ride.

# Part III

# 18

# Wrongs and Rights

Ripped paper figures are falling from a billboard and landing on the wet footpath in front of the cinema. *Danish Dentist on the Job, The Broccoli Patch*, and various body parts of buxom broads flutter to the ground, a haphazard pile of tits and bums beneath the ladder I'm holding.

Tearing the past off the hoardings of the local porno picture-house is a bit of a task. We are replacing all the light bulbs around the front of this gone-to-seed old girl in order to hold the opening of the New Zealand release of my first feature film, *Mr Wrong*. Call a film that, and what do you expect? Men in raincoats are coming out from the afternoon session and taking a casual interest.

It's 1985, and soft porn is one way to keep an old cinema open in the afternoons, and these guys are the regulars.

I have been making my first feature film for the last two years. I'm thirty-seven years old and with my producing partner, Robin Laing, I owe the New Zealand Film Commission $200,000, which is due to be paid back in a fortnight or crippling interest will ensue. I have no money, and no idea how to pay the debt, and we have just agreed to buy this mouldering theatre, giving the owner/manager $6000 a week for two weeks, in order to release our movie that every distributor in the country has turned down.

How did a nice girl like me get into this position? This is serious.

*

239

That moment on the red carpet at Cannes was unforgettable. It made me realise how easy it is to scam your way into the film industry. And Cannes that year was full of scammers, that's for sure. Maybe one of them was me.

I had ruled out real death on camera, obviously. And naked Jazzercise was not my bag. But genre films were doing an okay trade. Jean-Luc Godard apparently said all you need for a movie is a gun and a girl. (He meant with not much on – the girl.) Plenty of films were doing great business using that very formula. But when I told my staunch cousin Maxine that I wanted to make a thriller about a woman who buys a haunted car, she said, 'I hope you're not going to just make another film that exploits our fear. It's already bad enough.' Good point, cuz.

My mother had given me a book by the English writer Elizabeth Jane Howard. Uncharacteristically, she suggested that the story would make a good film. She'd never said anything like that before. When I read the book, I agreed with her. That too was unusual. With my before-the-car and after-the-car life, I over-identified.

But screaming women in thrillers do not contribute to our confident ownership of the street. If you are sitting around watching people who look a bit like you being stalked by murderous villains, or worse, beaten to a pulp and hacked up while trying to get away in diaphanous underwear, how is giving the gun to the girl liberating? And why do we keep watching these movies? There's a psychological theory that we are drawn to things we are afraid of, to help mitigate those fears. That's probably why horror movies and thrillers do so well at the box office. You have to admit that women look good in their undies, but while screaming and waving their arms about? Women in these films often don't seem to know how to run. In 1983, I wondered: how is yet another film about a female victim contributing to the global good of humanity?

After the festival, I went to Britain and had a cup of tea with Elizabeth Jane Howard, and bought the rights to her story. She said I was only the second person who had been interested in buying them.

'Who was the other?' I asked, as we sat under a laden quince tree in her idyllic summer garden.

'Alfred Hitchcock.'

'Why didn't he make it?' I asked her, with a flicker of worry.

'Oh, he died, dear,' she said, and passed the corned beef sandwiches. 'You can have no restrictions,' she continued, 'but there is just one thing I would ask. Please don't change the ending.'

It was the only thing she was adamant about.

In her short story, the main character, Meg, dies watching the knife of the killer pierce her ribs. He tells her to lie back and enjoy it, that death is the best ecstasy of all. It was the only part of the plot I wasn't sure of – but Elizabeth Jane Howard was.

There was something about that story that had me in its grip. It had mystery, suspense and, if I fleshed out the character of the ghostly Mary Carmichael, a sisterhood across a divide. It had got under my skin, and I thought it could work low-budget, but with that ending, wasn't it yet another contribution to the problem of female victimhood?

This was not the only philosophical problem I faced. The challenge for a feminist filmmaker in 1983 was to appeal to mainstream audiences but have something to say. Be fun and scary – while also having a main character slightly like me, while dealing with the threats that come her way. Vulnerable and too nice, but strong at her core. A real Kiwi woman who could wear Farmers pyjamas and sensible undies. A character who was modern and less masturbatory. Where better to get away with it than in New Zealand, where feature filmmaking was barely established and there was a tax incentive that fuelled the financial packaging of films into a dollar fire that was basically a licence to print money?

Everyone was doing it. Gearing up. The script goes in here and the money goes round and round and pops out there worth five times as much. This complicated financial system seemed to greatly energise men with Parker pens and gold-embossed business cards. It all came down to Scrubbs Blakeney, the first chief executive officer

241

of the interim New Zealand Film Commission.

The Muldoon government of 1977, which began out-of-control lending while running an economy slightly to the right of Romania, was setting up the last Stalin-like five-year plan outside China. It was called 'Think Big'. In New Zealand we always give things uniquely personal names so they can't easily be traced to any kind of sensible debate going on anywhere else, like Rogernomics, for the great Chicago Business School theory of economics, monetarism. Anyway, in 1978 the New Zealand Film Commission Act was passed, a momentous piece of legislation that made the country one of the last places in the world finally to fund filmmaking. The overwhelming driver for this was not what you might expect – the need to tell New Zealand stories on the big screen. No, it was foreign exchange. The country was on its knees for it.

Bugger that argument about culture – it was filthy lucre the government was after. The country was going down the tubes after Britain had joined the European common market. No more butter and little frozen lamb carcasses all tucked up in big refrigerator ships speeding to the dinner tables of the Midlands. Even the most closed political minds at the Beehive were scanning the globe looking for something to export. By then, every back bedroom in Te Aro and Ponsonby had a Steinbeck in the corner, and bins full of film hanging hopefully. A Film Commission was well overdue. Hence the bunch of dissatisfied ruffians, labelled the 'fledgling film industry', who were unacceptable out at TVNZ and were carting around their Bolexes, insisting they were independent filmmakers. By 1978, they got some traction.

It has always been believed in this country that all creative people are hapless and unruly and don't understand business – that they need help with money. This assumption, like many strongly held assumptions that never change despite evidence to the contrary, is codswallop, as Nan would have said. Financiers making money out of money = easy. Filmmakers making money out of stories = unbelievably difficult.

But, in this case, there was a very lucky, unlikely, dodgy appointment made: Scrubbs. Who was the genius who'd suggested him? John O'Shea? Bill Sheat? David Gascoigne? Scrubbs had been a merchant banker in London, until he became disillusioned and came back to New Zealand in the early 70s. He landed a film credit as the caterer on Roger Donaldson's trailblazing *Sleeping Dogs*. This made him extremely qualified to run the first taxpayer-funded organisation for Kiwi filmmaking – the New Zealand Film Commission.

And it really did get films made. Scrubbs was devoted to the gang – Roger and Geoff and Vincent and Sam and Lloyd and Larry et al. If only every film administrator were more devoted to the gang than to their official bosses, we filmmakers might not be the paranoid bitter self-doubters that we are today.

Well before I was winding up the Bolivisión on the beach at Cannes, Scrubbs had found a loophole in the tax law that was originally an incentive to attract investment in fishing, and applied it to film. Along with a lolly scramble at the 'blue chip investment' firms, this ignited an explosion of Kiwi filmmaking – *Utu* was but one. They are great movies, folks. Everyone was in on it. One moment no one had even heard of film investment. The next minute – boom! Everyone had a financial package fatter than the script.

But after a few financial years, once the walk-shorted flagon-carriers along Lambton Quay had chewed their pencils at the IRD, they were horrified. It was all money out and virtually none back in. A whole industry had exploded into life on tax money. Lots of it. Panic ensued. There were six months of high-level talks between government officials, financiers and the Film Commission. The fledgling film industry wasn't very organised, and no one took them seriously anyway. As doors clanged shut on the money stream, they were more interested in fighting amongst themselves and looking for who was to blame. The Muldoon government closed us down. The tax incentive for fishing boats that Scrubbs had found was no more. Full stop. Our brave new industry was outlawed before it had really begun. Filmmakers were suddenly the bandits. I became Zorro's little

243

sister almost overnight. So much for the fixed smiles down Lambton Quay. They are assassins.

But in 1983, if you had registered a feature film in development, there was still a possibility of using the mechanism for another year or so. I didn't have a feature in development, but I know when I see an opportunity about to disappear. Before I left for Cannes, I officially registered the working title *Truth Dare Promise*. I thought that name could cover almost anything. I became a very late, somewhat empty-handed passenger on the last bus leaving for tax-incentivised feature filmland.

When I was up the ladder on Courtenay Place, surrounded by torn falling figures and preparing for the New Zealand theatrical release of *Mr Wrong*, I should have been happy. I'd managed to make a movie that hadn't been interfered with creatively, and I wasn't even French. But almost from the moment when I sat down to write the screenplay, there was trouble. You should be careful what you call a film.

For a start, I had no idea what I was doing – but neither did anyone else. As it turned out, this was not an advantage. There were probably about three screenwriters in the country, and the only one I knew was Geoff Murphy. He said it was hard to assess a script when the filmmaker hadn't made a film before. I had, but Geoff didn't count documentaries, where writing happens during the edit, and where the filmmaking process is one of distillation. Drama is an entirely different process. Life does not already exist in the frame; it must be constructed, piece by piece. When the film works, life inside the frame bursts out to imply a whole imaginary world that exists outside the frame.

Geoff suggested that he write a draft, and I was only too happy to hand the pencil over. In Geoff's draft, the Hillman Hunter became a Mark II Jag, and he invented a 'night of terror'. Predictably, I changed back all the character changes he had made. However, by the time he took off to direct *Quiet Earth*, he'd given me a new structure that would survive to the screen.

In my lonely little writer's room, I grappled with the characters. How to translate Meg, the young middle-class English wallflower who buys the haunted car, into a recognisable central character who the home crowd could care about? They needed to care enough to be terrified for her. So I needed to Kiwi-ise her. Make Meg the kind of country girl we'd meet in the supermarket on cheap Tuesdays, who wore gumboots and could fix a fence but was out of place in the city. Who was going to help me write this script? I felt like the Little Red Hen asking for help.

Graeme Tetley was working with Vincent Ward, writing *Vigil*. When I approached Graeme to give me a hand with writing *Mr Wrong*, he made time. Fortunately. He wrote all the scenes I couldn't, and turned Wayne Wright, played by Danny Mulheron, into a genuine young man who wanted to be a beekeeper. And this is where the script started getting funnier – in a low-key Kiwi way. We began to enjoy ourselves immensely. I had found a co-conspirator in Graeme. We were both up to the same tricks. Nothing was complete until it amused us. And nothing amused us more than making a point while getting the audience to laugh, or scream.

As the writing was getting funnier and the plot scarier, the heart of the film was getting stauncher. *Mr Wrong* had the potential to say something serious and useful around self-defence for women.

New Zealand has a dark history of young women who set off hitchhiking and never arrive, and I kept thinking about them as we worked. Unsolved hitchhiker deaths are everywhere. I'd done my share of hitchhiking – it was our favourite mode of travel when I was at art school. It was fun. We'd been inspired by the bold romanticism of Jack Kerouac's *On the Road*, but every single young woman who set out and disappeared was a dark shadow over our entitlement.

Self-defence classes for women, run by Sue Lytollis, were becoming popular – I did one. It was empowering. How could I get one thing that might save a woman in a bad spot into this bent genre comedy thriller? How far could I take the social realism? Was this a bridge too far?

We had other creative problems – big ones. The script assessments from the Film Commission were bad. Worse than bad. Every single one sent me into decline. Nobody seemed to get it.

'She needs to be a skater.'

'Is it supposed to be funny?'

'The car was good, could be the next industry joke.'

All this written down and now carefully stored in Ngā Tāonga.

I didn't dive under the duvet when I read that last one. I rang Jim Booth, who had taken over running the Film Commission after Scrubbs left to produce *Utu*. I told Jim that the writer of that searing 'script assessment' had, one night within living memory, pinned me against the wall in my own home and I'd had to fight him off. I suggested that this highly esteemed script assessor may have over-identified with one of the boyfriend characters in a scene recreating that event.

'Jesus Christ, it's a village,' said Jim.

All this rejection was stoking the fire, though. I was getting madder and madder.

There had always been practical problems. Before I went to Cannes, I asked just about every producer in New Zealand to climb on board, but they all turned me down. No one wanted to touch it. One of them said, 'Train up a mate.' So I took that advice and asked among the wives – they were the ones who were doing a lot of the spade work after all.

The Robins sisters, Pat and Veronica, were key organisers for the Blerta films and *Utu*. They cooked for a crowd of kids and typed up scripts and project-managed for their husbands, Geoff Murphy and Bruno Lawrence. I asked Veronica if she was interested in producing, and she was horrified. Pat knew better. When I met Robin Laing at Cannes, and saw her good humour as she helped to promote her husband John's film *The Lost Tribe*, I decided to pop the question. Initially she said no, but before we parted company she gave me her business card. 'Wardrobe/props' was crossed out, and on the back she had written 'Producer' (characteristically in pencil).

After leaving Cannes and securing the rights, I had a romantic notion that I would hunch over my little typewriter and bash out a script in New York, like the greats at the Chelsea Hotel. I had friends from my Stockwell days who now lived in an apartment on the corner of West Broadway and Canal Street. Their small room on the roadside was always vacant, because I was the only person they knew who could sleep through the noise of trucks bouncing towards the Holland Tunnel at three in the morning. I loved New York and the loft scene there in the late 70s. Every party was performance art. But after six weeks I was too hot, the cockroaches were huge, and I was homesick.

I was also missing Jonathan. I'd hoped he would join me in New York, but when that wasn't possible, I gave my spare ticket to a B.B. King and Miles Davis concert to Ralph Hotere. That was a great way to end my time in New York. It was in the Rainbow Room down in Harlem. B.B. King warmed up the audience for Miles to ignore. When he played Cyndi Lauper's 'Time after Time', the crowd took a breath in that huge packed old theatre. Time stood still. Neither Ralph nor I ever got over that moment.

Robin heard I was home, and rang.

'When do we start?'

But her climbing on board had an unexpected effect.

Robin was even less a part of the gang than I was. This meant that, without a man in sight, we were raising money for a film with no financiers to do real business with. No one trusted us. Paradoxically we were possibly the most honest hustlers ever to cross their path.

Everywhere we searched for money, we knew that as the doors closed behind us the phones would start ringing. 'Do those girls know what they're doing?'

What they really meant was, 'Do they know how to play the game?' Obviously not, if you are excluded from the court. When we went to meetings with the Snooty Face and Biggsys of Queen Street, there was a lot of small talk, nervous touching of ties, and glancing at the door before someone said, 'Is this everyone?' When we nodded, there would be more touching of ties and adjusting of papers. They were waiting for the man to arrive so they could have a real conversation. We were not basking in a sea of enthusiasm. However, I was getting used to being the only woman in the room.

I'd become an alternate member of the New Zealand Film Commission – if someone couldn't come to a meeting, I got to fill their place. So I was often witness to some wily weirdness. It is true to say that the Film Commission has served filmmakers much better than the governments that have under-resourced it. But at the time, sitting at the table could feel like watching bulls in a china shop. I wasn't supposed to know anything, being a lowly documentary-maker, but when I have offered up three sensible suggestions in a row and been kindly patted on the head, a switch clangs in my brain. I turn into a fox terrier. I knew it was really annoying – I annoyed myself actually – but someone put me in there to represent, so represent I would. If every time you open your mouth no one wants to hear what you say, or if they listen politely so they can cross off your opinion as having been 'taken into account', then what's the point of being there? It was explained to me that, strictly speaking, I was not representing anyone but myself. But as the only woman filmmaker, I felt I could represent the opinions of the downtrodden and dispossessed. I wasn't the only one who wasn't in the gang. Every now and then I decided to play the game, but I never felt very good about that afterwards. Being 'good' equals keeping quiet on things you care passionately about. It leads to low self-esteem. Most of the fledgling film industry didn't really agree I should be there anyway. One established commercial filmmaker told me he thought my selection was ridiculous. He said this to me like I wasn't there and he was down at the pub with the boys, which we were at the time. So obviously he didn't think I was representing him.

While even caped poseurs with half-baked ideas seemed to be getting funding, Robin and I continued to struggle. When we finally scraped together a couple of sympathetic script assessments (thank you, Dame Fiona Kidman), we still had time to apply for production funding to get the film finished before the tax incentive expired. I knew from the meetings I had attended that it was never a flat no. It was always a 'Yes, but'. With this hole in the fence, filmmakers could massage their deal as they hurtled towards pre-production.

In a trailblazing decision, the Film Commission turned us down. A flat no. This they had never actually done before.

The letter informing us had a black border aspect to it. In his favour, Jim Booth took Robin and me out to lunch to explain. He said nobody knew what the film was. 'What's it a film like?' That was always the burning question. For example, is it *Arsenic and Old Lace* meets *Goodbye Pork Pie*?

I find 'What's it a film like?' impossible to answer. Couldn't think of one. Then there was the issue of genre. Was it a comedy, or a thriller, or a ghost story?

'Well, it's a thriller.'

'But it's funny. Is it supposed to be funny?'

'It's a comedy thriller.'

'But it's got a ghost in it.'

'It's a comedy thriller with a ghost in it.'

As he shook his head sadly and looked a bit hopeless, I ran for the ladies' loos to cry. Jim advised Robin to find a man to join the production team. The most composed person at that lunch was Robin's four-year-old daughter Chloe, who spent her time building intricate cities with the cutlery. She attended most of our meetings. I thought she would become an architect with all that tableware building. She didn't. She's a film editor now.

Angry is good. It fuels the fire. Sad is bad. When I'm sad, I just withdraw under the duvet. On the bright side, it's quiet under there. I reviewed the situation. The 'If only's surfaced first. If only I had been a back-up singer. I could be on the road with a band, and bugger the lot of them. I believed that the last boyfriend who left me did it because he was sick of me trying to make films all the time. If only I didn't want to make films all the time. It's a pest. Jonathan was much more supportive, but everyone has their limits.

In those days you typed your scripts on an electric typewriter, if you were lucky enough to own one. Some had a key that used white ribbon to make corrections. The patched-up paper original would be photocopied at great expense, and that was all you had. But at this black moment I was considering assigning the entire script to the fire. And then the phone rang.

Jim had been busy. A producer who could help! He had a deal with a millionaire from somewhere in the middle of the North Island (all that milk) and he could send the first instalment Thursday. We just had to sign something called a heads of agreement document. I had no idea what that was, but this was the best news since the police had decided not to charge me with breaking and entering when I stole my car back from the tow yard.

'Send it down.'

Signed it.

Beware the fairy godfather. I knew that – but you only ever find out what you know already, don't you? The heads of agreement document was full of wherebys and wherefores. It seemed to have a legal 'if' in every clause, which made it look innocent enough. 'Standard practice,' we were told, and who could afford a lawyer anyway? Not us, we were on our knees.

Note to those at home contemplating signing a legal document of any kind. GET A LAWYER. Without their say so, SIGN NOTHING. But here in May 1984, with our backs to the wall and the big clock ticking, we sent the signed document up north, and the pre-production money started arriving.

We set up a production office in a rundown warehouse in Oak Park Lane and started contracting crew. Robin then had to handle the fact that the guys, though they were perfectly happy to work alongside me when I was art-directing, weren't feeling so confident about me directing them. Although in my head I was the most brilliant filmmaker since Robert Altman, and at the time one of the most experienced filmmakers ever to make a first feature in the country, they didn't feel comfortable.

I'd produced and directed five documentaries by now: *All the Way Up There*, *Learning Fast*, *Making Utu*, *Hold Up* (which included drama), and I'd helped with *Patu!* Plus, *All the Way Up There* and *Hold Up* had won international awards. And I had production-designed a feature (*Middle Age Spread*) and heaps of commercials. But this was not worth a hill of beans in this tiny town. Many people I really admired turned me down – they read the script and in various kind ways told me they thought it was 'a bit silly'. To be fair, we were working in the middle of a closing-down sale. Anyone who could stand behind a camera in any capacity had a job. That clock kept ticking.

It was actors who kept me going. They liked the script. A moment's grateful silence for actors. They are the bravest people I know. You can ask them to do something that you would never ask any other living soul to do, and they give it a go. (They may complain about it afterwards, but that's another story.) The actors came to my auditions and made that worrisome script glow. They leapt about the place, forgot their words with nerves, cried, and did all those terrific things we love them for. When I found Heather Bolton to play Meg, the script leapt into focus. It *was* going to be funny – and if I came at it on the right trajectory, I could scare the pants off the punters while they were still laughing.

Hindsight is a great thing. I'm sounding far more certain here than I was. But Robin kept doggedly making the calls and signing up crew. I had met Canadian cinematographer Thom Burstyn at Cannes when he was supporting the promotion of *The Lost Tribe*. It had a moody look that could fit. Undeniably a terrific cinematographer, he even agreed to our pathetic fee. So did Alun Bollinger, a long-time collaborator. Albol is one of the greats of New Zealand cinema and a good mate. I asked him what he wanted to do, light or operate – he said he didn't mind, so I got him behind the camera. His intuitive eye and our close history give *Mr Wrong* an immediacy that enhances the suspense. A suitable key location was found just down the road from where I lived in Roxburgh Street. We bought a Mk II Jag and, with a first assistant director who never understood what the hell I was doing, and a crew of Bindy Crayford (the first female gaffer in New Zealand), Matt Murphy and Jonathan Crayford doing special effects, Robin Murphy in the art department and her mother, Pat, production-managing, we lurched into it.

Every now and then, the money was late – but generally it arrived. I knew the cashflow was dodgy. This way of financing was about to become illegal any moment anyway. But there was too much smiling and covering of mouths coming down from the folk up north to feel entirely confident. We decided to just keep going until someone told us to stop. No one did, but it got to the point where I would just get up every morning expecting the whole thing to grind to a halt. I'd concentrate on shooting the schedule every day and live to face tomorrow. I still don't know exactly how Robin managed to keep the show on the road as long as she did – you'd have to ask her. She may not tell you.

One day it was in the news.

*Mr Wrong*, 'a Wellington film currently shooting on Mount Victoria', was being halted by a financier neither of us had ever heard of, Toa Woodbine Pōmare. We got Jim on the phone. Our heads of agreement document had apparently been sold by the Te Kūiti millionaire who'd owned it. He had fallen out with the Queen Street crowd and presumably didn't need the licence to print money anymore. He'd flicked it to another financier who did. And that financier was busy injuncting the film in the High Court. Spookily reminiscent of what had happened with Windy Autoport.

The Film Commission – you will remember they'd said a definite 'no' – had, when the money slowed from a drip to nothing, forwarded us a kind of short-term commercial loan that they offered overseas productions to fill gaps in cashflow. It was called a star loan. We had one. Now the new proud owner of our film wanted some of that ol' star loan too. We advised against it, and Jim agreed. We never met

Toa Woodbine, but by this time we were suspicious of guys who wanted to help, and after he had taken his slice off the top, how much of it would trickle down to the screen was not disclosed. Ages before the one per cent arrived on this planet, I had never been a fan of the trickle-down theory. If it was an actual thing, it wouldn't be called a theory, would it. It would be called a factor. Even by 1984, I'd only ever seen money trickle up.

By some weird stroke of God's pencil, Toa Woodbine and his partners decided to sue the Film Commission as well as Robin and me. We learnt this, along with everyone else, from the six o'clock news on National Radio on a Tuesday. We decided to call a crew meeting, and tried to explain. Their eyes glazed over after a while, then some bright spark said, 'Does it affect the next shot?'

'Hmmm. Well, no.'

And they all stood up and someone got the clapperboard out.

Every morning tea, lunch and afternoon tea time was spent on the phone conversing with our 'stakeholders'. The Film Commission didn't like being sued. Particularly over a film they had turned down flat. The commissioners weren't filmmakers; they were lawyers. And now, they were mad. They went to war with great gusto on our behalf. They rode up on their chargers and rescued us . . . from ourselves. You will recall that they were generally put there by government officials to teach the filmmakers about real business, so a case in the High Court was something they could certainly take on – with alacrity. This meant Jim Booth had full permission to get the filmmakers in question deeply into debt very quickly. Before every pay day, he sent over the ten-page star loan legal document that proved Robin Margot Laing and Gaylene Mary Preston owed a growing sum of money back to the Film Commission, due date in August 1985. They were bailing us out, but I had become a born-again contract reader and every clause said, 'You must pay this back by the due date or crippling interest will be charged.' I kept refusing to sign, then after long phone calls I would fold.

Never a borrower nor a lender be. That was my upbringing. I drove Robin and Jim crazy as our debt quickly grew past $100,000 and kept going. To give you the context, our location house was valued at $27,000.

Every payday now, our crew were worrying. They would sidle up in ones and twos waving their weekly cheque and ask in a conspiratorial fashion, 'Am I supposed to bank this?' That's the *Mr Wrong* crew for you. Once they'd committed, they were in for the long haul.

When we had nearly completed the shoot, we received a different legal document. Our godfather in the north was urging us to sign over the rights of *Mr Wrong* to his production company to protect us. Who from, it wasn't entirely clear. There was a 'Don't worry your pretty little heads about it' vibe that had worked for me once, but now just didn't cut the mustard. You do learn; it's crisis development.

So here was another document I wouldn't sign. And not because we couldn't afford a lawyer. As it says in a Hitchcock film, 'If it don't gel, it ain't aspic.' My intuition was kicking in and I was learning to listen to it. Normally, the rights would have correctly been handed over to the financiers before a single frame was shot, but because of the headlong runaway train the film had been, none of this had occurred. This meant that I still held the rights – and now, considering that we were up to our elbows if not our necks, I wanted things to stay that way. My sunny lunch with Elizabeth Jane Howard under her quince tree in Hampstead felt like years ago.

I had a funny feeling that once I signed them over, we, the producers, would lose any vestige of control in the situation that we thought we had. But these rights evidently needed to be 'protected', i.e. separated from the company that was making the film. Apparently. I didn't quite understand how that would work, but legal advice had been 'strongly given' . . . up north. Quite a bind. What to do? And my head wasn't entirely clear to think about it, because we were still shooting and my commitment to the actual ending of the story was looming. By the time I had watched rushes, I was working six fourteen-hour days a week. I was with Ringo when he said he'd had a hard day's night. I hadn't had a day off for weeks. Praise the goddess I'm a good sleeper. Make your films when you are young. Or fight for better working conditions.

When I was living in London, we got worried that the gas man might spot our marijuana growing in the atrium, so we moved the crop, but not to our own backyard. We grew it in the garden of a very good friend of ours. We knew it was safe from marauders over there at her place in Clapham, because she hated the stuff. So my lifetime rule of thumb is: don't give anyone anything to look after if they might like it for themselves. Applies to lettuces, tomatoes and also film rights.

I racked my brains to think of someone I knew who already had a company not associated with *Mr Wrong*. Someone who knew the film trade, who wouldn't want the rights, who wasn't a lawyer who could get struck off, but someone who would never hand them over to any legal beagle no matter how many court cases they might be threatened with. Someone who might even enjoy the fray, should it eventuate. I woke up one morning with the solution. My mechanic, Andy Grant of Mickey Mouse Motors, hated the establishment. He could keep an angry letter exchange – with, say, the Wellington City Council on some tiddly planning issue – going for years. He was as staunch as you could get and pretty cluey in the ways of certain producers, being a partner in the Acme Sausage Company. It was he who kept the yellow Mini going as they shot on the back roads all over New Zealand for that other hit movie you will know. During morning tea time, in our usual preferred private conversation spot – the upstairs loo – I ran the plan past Robin.

My solution to our current dilemma was to sign over to Mickey Mouse Motors the whole rights document. All twenty-seven clauses of it. Worth a try, she agreed. I whistled up the road at lunchtime to call him.

'I don't want the rights to your poxy movie, Gaylene,' was his first reaction.

'I know. That's why I want you to have them.'

A slight pause.

'Well, how much are they?'

'One dollar?'

'Far too fuckin' much.'

He agreed after I promised to bring him fish 'n' chips next time I saw him.

Back down the road to shoot the last shots of the day. There is a real advantage to having your key location close to home.

We prepared the documents immediately. Andy Grant insisted that we filled in his 'occupation' as 'alchemist'. He signed; I didn't. Into the middle drawer it went, ready to produce in a twinkling should it ever be needed. It never happened of course. After we finished shooting, a guy arrived at the production office to serve a writ. I wouldn't accept that either. Ever since Windy Autoport had stolen my car, I was as brave as tigers.

After a court case to allow us to continue filming, and another to allow post-production, it all ended up in the High Court, with Hugh Rennie defending us. He was the only man in New Zealand who everyone agreed knew the foggiest thing about copyright law. This was by now February 1985, and we couldn't take the completed film out of the country without being slapped with an injunction. By this time, those financiers had moved on to other things, like hurricane housing in the Pacific. That was the big money-spinner now, evidently. No lawyer representing them arrived to present their case, paradoxically making it harder for Hugh to get the injunction lifted. The judge looked perplexed. With that secret forelock-tugging code that lawyers do in court, Hugh suggested he speak to the judge in chambers.

After a five-minute adjournment they returned all smiles. *Mr Wrong* could be designated officially as perishable goods, and we were herewith ordered by the High Court of New Zealand to get it to the market immediately. That, we were only too happy to do.

When it hit the Cannes Market that year, New Zealand Film Sales signed deals for sixty-seven territories, including the United States. *Mr Wrong* remains the only film in the world, that I know of, officially registered as perishable goods. Thirty years later, I ran into Hugh at an airport. He commented that *Mr Wrong* was the longest-lasting piece of fresh goods to leave the country.

I have often pondered on what the outcome would have been had the original case left the Film Commission out and been a claim against the producers only. God is indeed a woman.

During that court case, Robin and I were invited to the meetings held at Hugh's offices, around the very long, very shiny table. At the first one, he went around the room pointing. 'I will represent you, you, not you, not you, you,' and so on. The 'not you's were the fairy godfather and his lawyer from Hamilton. If I hadn't hung onto the rights, I have a funny feeling that those long shiny table meetings between the Film Commission and Hugh Rennie may have proceeded without the producers in the room, who everyone agreed to a man were innocent.

'You girls haven't broken the law,' we were assured, and Robin and I – in between feeling very grateful to every single one of them, including our friend in the north – congratulated each other on having maintained girlhood status at the grand old age of thirty-seven. Was the warm wind about to blow through our hair?

# 19

# Walking the Plank

Well, no. None of this, absolutely none of it, had prepared us for the next major barrier. No warm wind. A very slow cold one. And it came from exactly where we least expected it. We couldn't find a distributor to release *Mr Wrong* into New Zealand cinemas. How could my cousin Maxine see my sacrifice and pain if she couldn't slouch down to her local picture house, pay her money and see the bloody thing? (It wasn't just her I was worried about, obviously, but family comes first.)

Distributors loved their movies, especially in those days, to have Tom Cruise in them. The cinemas were full of major movies from everywhere else – and contributed to the Kiwi crowd suffering a huge self-hating cultural cringe when it came to hearing their own accent on screen. To overcome this deep insecurity caused by the Hollywood takeover of every living room and cinema in every small town in the country, releasing local work successfully was almost impossible. Very few films not by Roger Donaldson or Geoff Murphy triumphed at the box office. But *every* local film that managed to get made at least got a release. It was unheard of in 1985 to be locked out of your own cinemas. At the time, government rules around distribution made it easy for two companies – Kerridge and Amalgamated – to dominate the market unchallenged. A distributor sat at the board table of the Film Commission from where he could shake his head sadly and call everything we made 'a dog'.

'Oh, that was a dog, this'll be a dog.'

Truth is, local films come onto the local circuit without the benefit of millions of offshore dollars already spent on publicity. They don't have Tom Cruise in them. They have John Bates or Donna Reece doing the heavy lifting. Releasing a local film is hard work – particularly when the audience in those days was unforgiving of any local film that didn't click. We care more about our own culture. We get sadder when something doesn't work. But if you don't have the promotional money – the press and ads budget – to run a good campaign, you have to have a lot of resourceful, energetic friends. That's how *Goodbye Pork Pie* thundered up and down the country and *Smash Palace* caught the local imagination, making Bruno Lawrence a local star. But *Mr Wrong* didn't have a part for Bruno, and Sam Neill had ridden the silver rocket to Australia and beyond, where he continued a beautiful career. There were no lead roles for Kiwi women that could have made them stars, which meant we had no women's marquee names.

By 1985 Kerridge and Amalgamated were in the habit of putting local films, no matter how promising, into their cinemas a couple of weeks before the school holidays. This meant that whatever business the film did, when the Disney film arrived off the screen it went. Cinemas tended to still be single screens, so that would be that. Distributors always prove what they know already. If it's 'a dog' but it's doing good business, it's still outta there for Disney. All that heartache and pain buried, come the school holidays. 'Next.'

But, knowing all this – love the one you're with. We started with Kerridge. We screened a print to them in Auckland in their screening room. Dead silence. They sat like stones. Not even a slight titter. Sad sighs when the lights came up as they scurried back to their offices to leap on their phones and tell everyone how bad it was. Slightly better reaction from Amalgamated. Joe Moodabe said there were some good shots there. 'But . . . no.'

By this screening I have a pretty good idea what the outcome

259

would be, and have already shown the film to Bill Gosden, the director of the Wellington Film Festival. In those days, the fledgling film industry experts considered it 'non-commercial' to screen your film in the Film Festival. According to the five people who thought they knew, only the pointy-headed who liked reading subtitles went (entirely untrue), and your film would be tainted by those challenging words – 'art film' – forevermore.

That festival had been my saviour when I first came back to Wellington from Brixton and was suffering life-threatening culture shock. I was delighted to find that I could go and see a heap of films I would have had to stand in a queue for hours just to get an advance ticket for in London. All I had to do was turn up and buy a ticket at the box office before the show and snuggle in – well, in those badly heated old theatres, I learnt to take a rug and a scarf and woolly hat before basking in the pleasure of the light on the screen.

The Film Festival brought good films from everywhere, documentary and drama, and screened them the length and breadth of the country. At a time when freighting heavy prints in metal tins was expensive and challenging (watch *Cinema Paradiso* if you haven't already to see what I mean), this chain of festivals leap-frogged a programme to all the main centres.

Pacific Films virtually closed down their operation for the fortnight of the Wellington Film Festival, and we all just went to the pictures. Bliss. I saw films by Frederick Wiseman and Agnès Varda and, wonder of wonders, actual Australian films. Until very recently it was hard to see an Australian film in a cinema in New Zealand. Unless they had a Hollywood deal, we didn't see them. It works the other way round as well. They didn't see ours. Thanks to the festivals, hope for cultural understanding was fostered. I love Australian films, so when it was announced that *The FJ Holden* was screening and the director was going to be present, I was in boots and all.

Michael Thornhill wasn't entirely sober when he introduced his film. Swaying slightly, a tinny in his hand, he glared at the audience and spoke slowly, as if to a bunch of ten-year-olds.

'All those who are media here, put your hands up.'

A couple of brave souls raised their hands.

'Yeah? – well – here's all I've got to say – if you like it – great – and if you don't – shuddup!'

Refreshing. Muscular and flawed. Like his film.

But back to *Mr Wrong*. In our darkest hour, it's Bill Gosden we turn to. Despite a lukewarm *Variety* review from Mike Nicolaidi (who later made it up to us big time), Bill got it. Not only that – he liked it. He understood exactly what it was up to and greeted it enthusiastically. Enthusiasm. This was new and good. He wrote that *Mr Wrong* was 'a thoroughly spooky good time' and programmed it. Five o'clock on a Saturday. I was a bit put out. Why not a more prestigious slot, like opening night? But he wouldn't budge. And he was right too. The best festival directors know their audience.

When we turned up outside the Embassy Theatre (capacity of around 800), the crowd in the foyer was a scrum. I thought the doors hadn't opened, but the theatre was already seating, and the teeming throng were the punters who wanted to get in but who hadn't booked. Of course, most of them were my mates. A full house can be stressful for a filmmaker. It's a rule of nature that the people you care about most are the very ones who turn up late without a ticket. Some were holding $10 notes above their heads, a bit like auctioning seats on United.

I was absolutely knocked out. After the many rejections, this was the opposite to a hairball in your throat. But no time for tears as the start time approached. *Mr Wrong* has a stunning musical overture by Jonathan Crayford, so everyone could finish their ice creams and listen as the lights dimmed. Let the show commence.

Sharing your film with the first audience is a terrifying and thrilling experience. You sit there facing the screen, but you would be better with a chair beside the screen watching the audience.

The first Auckland screening of our little comedy thriller was a week earlier, in the mighty Civic in Auckland. The Civic was not as mighty then as it is today. Along with all the great theatres, it had fallen into disrepair. Its gold paint was peeling and the blue lights in the panthers that guard the ornate proscenium arch had been dark for years. To get onto the stage I had to walk a wooden plank over the yawning dark of the orchestra pit. Balanced on the railing at one end with the other on the stage, the paint-splattered plank wobbled the second I put weight on it. Could I come around the backstage area? No. There was a fire curtain up. At this moment I was grateful that I hadn't accepted any of those pre-screening whiskies I had been offered. I walked that plank with my heart in my mouth, wondering how the hell I was going to get back once the film started. It seemed to take forever to get to the stage to turn to face that first expectant crowd.

I did not feel like Michael Thornhill. I felt small and silly. How could I have been so audacious as to think I could present myself as a proper filmmaker – one of the gang? I wasn't Roger or Geoff or Vincent. What if those smiling excited faces turned to not excited at all? I was convinced they wouldn't like it. All indications were that this could be my first and last sortie into dramatic storytelling. Should we have stationed people on the doors to lock them all in? However, just when all seemed hopeless, those childhood elocution lessons kicked in. You put your feet on the ground, and you breathe and slow down. I can't have been very convincing though. One article in the *Auckland Star* described me as 'a skinny little bookworm in blue jeans'.

And they also described the film as having a standing ovation. I must admit it was pretty awesome. The crowd began laughing early on and the laughter grew more and more hysterical, until at one moment towards the end the Civic erupted in a big laugh followed by an ear-piercing scream. The sound of grown men screaming in the movies was something I hadn't heard before, and I'm here to tell you there can't be too much of it. The rest was a blur. I thought that some people were sitting down clapping while others were standing up to put their coats on, but once it was in the *Auckland Star* – a standing ovation it was ever after.

Joe Moodabe had said that if it did all right in the Film Festival, Amalgamated would look at distribution. 'At last,' I thought. 'At last we will get this film all the way to Invercargill.' We steamed down the country in the festival, packing it out all the way to Dunedin. But no. Amalgamated said that we had 'stacked the audience' (meaning we filled the seats with our friends), and anyway, now too many people had already seen it. This is just plain silly – well, it was in the case of *Mr Wrong* – but those sentiments live on today. You need to know that distributors still hold very firmly to these opinions despite all evidence to the contrary.

By July 1985, though Lindsay Shelton had sold *Mr Wrong* all over the world and we were completing the US deal, we were still on our own as far as our home territory went. However, there was one stone left unturned. Masters Cinemas was a very small chain, owned and operated by Lang and Maureen Masters. They had two theatres in Christchurch and one in Wellington. Not exactly a national reach, but beggars can't be choosers, can they? Their Wellington theatre was small with no street front in Cuba Mall above a Jazzercise club. It was managed by Kerry Robins, co-producer of *Goodbye Pork Pie* and *Utu*, whose sisters, Pat and Veronica, I have told you about. Being married to Bruno Lawrence and Geoff Murphy, they worked tirelessly for their husbands. They mothered the Murphia – the tribe of Murphys, Robinses and Lawrences who continue to populate crew lists. Kerry took on *Mr Wrong* with enthusiasm, if not a little guilt. He was vaguely implicated in the episode that got us tied up in the High Court.

Nevertheless, Kerry is whānau, and had been instrumental in making *Goodbye Pork Pie* an enormous success, and I was sure he would make *Mr Wrong* a memorable splash – even if it was with only one print in one cinema. The marketing budget was pretty well non-existent but, fuelled by our Film Festival success, Robin and I managed to line up a veritable tsunami of national-reach publicity, including the cover of the *New Zealand Woman's Weekly* for Heather Bolton. A date was set. Friday September the 13th. On top of the *WW*, we

263

had an article in the *Listener* with a good review, and I had designed and hand screen-printed a hundred posters with Chris McBride at the Media Collective. We had three thousand flyers printed with the opening date on them, ready to go into letterboxes. All set.

When the phone rang, I was putting flyers in envelopes to post to schools. Kerry sounded shell-shocked when he delivered the bad news. The cinema was closing immediately. The Jazzercise club had bought it. Masters was closing up shop at the end of the week. I put the phone down and just sat there stunned for a very long time.

There was only one place left – the Paramount on Courtenay Place. On the bright side, it was well-positioned, and it could take six hundred-plus punters. It came alive at Film Festival time, but for the rest of the year it sat sadly on Courtenay Place, screening soft porn in the afternoons. It was owned by Merv Kisby who had a second, more successful, suburban cinema in Brooklyn. The Penthouse was one of the last family-owned and run cinemas in the country. But Merv was put out. He wasn't happy that we had put our film with Kerry. Not that he had uttered a word to make a bid. But when the Masters deal fell over, he wasn't in a hurry to return our calls. We just couldn't get to talk to him. His office was sympathetic, but he was clearly not answering our phone calls or coming to our party. Time was ticking by and there was only one option left – we were going to have to make him an offer he couldn't refuse.

We needed to buy his cinema for a week or two and get this film launched. It's called 'four walling'. Not unheard of, but hugely risky. The producers rent a cinema for a season and take the financial risk. They cover all costs and pocket the profit – if any. We were running out of options fast. We had to secure the Paramount for Friday the 13th. The date was in black-and-white in the *Woman's Weekly* and the *Listener*.

I knew Merv was a gentleman of habit. Every weekday at five o'clock he would cross Courtenay Place to go to his friend's record shop. They'd lock up and go to the pub.

At quarter to five one wet Wednesday, I lurk behind the record stacks. His mate knows I am there with no intention of buying, but what can he do? I hunch down and wait. Sure enough, in comes Merv. I leap out and greet him like a long-lost friend.

'G'day, Merv! I've been trying to reach you,' I say, with more confidence than I am feeling.

Caught on the spot, he mutters a gruff hello.

'You will know we are looking for a theatre to screen our film in. How much for the Paramount for two weeks, starting in ten days?'

Merv doesn't really want our film in his cinema. We will be a nuisance, he is sure. But the thought of some actual cash is too much for him. He names an astronomical sum. By this stage I would accept any price he utters.

'Six thousand dollars.'

I stick out my hand and look him in the eye, beaming, 'Done.'

He hesitates, then shakes on it and immediately goes into reducing what we are buying. We could have his projectionist and one ticket-seller person. That will be it. We'll have to look after the cleaning. Cleaning? The least of our worries. All that floor-scrubbing and dusting of dressing tables we did for our mothers in our childhoods was going to come in handy after all.

Next morning, he hit the phone.

'Do those girls know what they're doing?'

You can be pretty sure what the answer was.


So that's how I ended up holding the ladder pulling down *Danish Dentist on the Job* from the Paramount front hoarding to replace it with our brand-new billboard for *Mr Wrong*. We tested every light bulb while a small army of schoolkids did a letterbox drop of Mount Victoria – it was our friends who wanted to see it when all was said and done – and every journalist that turned up to interview us wanted to know why we were launching this festival hit in the porno picture house. So we told them. I got a letter from Sir Robert Kerridge asking me to cease and desist from spreading misinformation about them in the media. He was fairly famous for never putting anything in writing, but this letter was from him not a lawyer, because he knew I hadn't. I had just broken the big secret deal that keeps us filmmakers in pubs complaining – if you do them down publicly, your next film has no show. That's the fear. Well, given how hard it had been to make this one, I wasn't thinking of making another, so I was fearless. But the bullies rule. The Weinstein factor.

The day we opened, we went down to the cinema half an hour early to find a queue already stretching to Cambridge Terrace. Holy cow. We're in the money. But when we got to the top of the stairs, there was hardly anyone seated. Merv's box office woman was multi-tasking, selling a ticket then rolling an ice cream, selling a ticket then rolling another ice cream. We pulled up our sleeves and quickly mastered the ancient Kiwi art of making chocolate-dipped ice creams, and the session started almost on time.

The film took off, and everyone did indeed have a very spooky, very good time. We returned $11,000 plus that week, and grew the take in the second week. Merv took our film on, and we even ordered a second print for his far more respectable Penthouse.

I was thrilled about this. The Paramount had two very old carbon lamp projectors that were antique even for 1985. This means that the light fades over time, and if the projectionist isn't onto it, the screen can go entirely black. This happened a couple of times during our Paramount season. I found out by accident. My neighbour, Meriol Buchanan, an actor I knew, plays a small part in a scene where she turns up to buy the car but her dog won't get in it. She got a couple of complimentary tickets and went with her daughter, who worked in the industry. I came across her at the supermarket and said how much I had enjoyed her performance. A cloud crossed her face, then she said, slightly querulously, 'I suppose that was an artistic decision with that scene, to not see me. An artistic decision, the sound but no picture.'

During the screening, the screen had slowly faded, going black just before her scene. It lit up again immediately afterwards, when the projectionist replaced the carbon lamps. If the film wasn't haunted, it sure as hell had a life of its own.

The other thing about the Paramount projectors was that they worked in parallel with one another. When one twenty-minute roll ran out, the other projector took over with the next one. This led to a lot of film handling. Sometimes the beginning and end of print rolls would sparkle like sandpaper. The Penthouse, on the other hand, had a platter. The film gets loaded onto one huge horizontal plate and hangs in space as it winds through the projector gate before rolling onto the other plate. At the end of the process the film is ready to be threaded up for the next screening. Far less damage. No rewinding, no handling. I hadn't seen the second print, so I went up to the Penthouse to check it the first time it screened.

I slouched in my seat among an excited six o'clock audience of suburbanites, looking forward to the first time I would see the film without a roll change at twenty minutes. Away we went. I was feeling really pleased with how it was looking when, right at the roll change moment, the image froze and *Mr Wrong* melted in the gate and burnt.

Silence. The lights came on. I leapt out of my seat and went up to the projection booth, where Merv was none too gently hacking at our pristine print to splice it together and shove it back onto the platter.

'It's never happened before,' he told me.

I hate it when someone tells me that, but this is what he said happened. He is indeed a man of habit. After he set a film going and all was well, he liked to eat an apple. When he was finished, he always threw the core out a little top window in the projection room onto the street below. In this case, the core had bounced on the window frame, ricocheted back, hit the film hanging on the platter and dislodged it, so it stopped. Hence the freeze and burn. Heath Robinson, eat your heart out.

Should we, right at the beginning, have had the film blessed – before it was even a mark on a piece of paper? Was the title a jinx? Was the ghost of Mary Carmichael actually embedded in it? Well, if it was, she has a great sense of humour. The film travelled the world, and I heard that dogs in the cinema at the Munich Film Festival growled at the screen every time David Letch – who played the villain – came on. And when it went wrong, it always went right. A young distributor, Mark Christiansen, picked up the film and it screened in the Academy Cinema in Auckland for seventeen weeks, 'right up the arse' of Kerridge, according to John Hart, who ran the theatre.

I popped in to see him during the season. We were chatting in his foyer when his ears pricked up and we heard that laughing, blood-curdling scream emanating from the cinema.

'They'll be out in twenty minutes,' he said, and put on the coffee pot.

# 20

# You Must Remember This

It's a sunny morning at my parents' home in Tītahi Bay. Chelsie is playing with her grandfather, who is good at finding jellybeans in her ear, and Tui and I are cooking in the kitchen. When 'You Must Remember This', the theme song from *Casablanca*, comes on the radio, she sings along with a misty look in her eyes.

'Oh, this was a very special song for me during the war,' she says. A pause, then, 'Between your father and I.'

I went out to Tītahi Bay often after my parents moved from Napier to Wellington when, to their delight, Chelsie was born, and alongside my brother's two young ones they found themselves with three growing grandchildren in the district. It was a big move at their age – both in their seventies – but they found a lovely spot in Onepoto with a stunning view of Mana Island. My father joined the local bowls club and introduced his new pals to his demon homebrew. ('Only ten cents a bottle.') And Tui joined the local church, where one of her old friends was the vicar.

Les Church and his family were part of theirs. Much younger and with more progressive views, Les got to know Tui when he was curate at St Luke's Church in Napier – a dear little wooden structure where the flowers were fresh every Sunday and they did outreach programmes for the elderly. It had a pedal organ that as a teenager I had pumped along playing patchy hymns for Morning Prayer, when I couldn't read the music because I was going through a period of not wearing my glasses.

Ed was a confirmed agnostic, and Tui usually kept her church and home life separate. Knowing Ed often shared his views freely on sight of any man of the cloth, she took Les under her wing and brought him home. While Tui made a cup of tea in the kitchen, Ed took Les for a tour of their lovingly maintained garden. There was a small concrete pad down the back where sheds used to be.

'Do you know what's under there, Les?' says Ed.

'No,' Les replies.

'The last curate who tried to convert me.'

That was it. Friends for life.

When Ed was dying, he rang Les. 'Les, come over, I've got a job for you.'

Les arrived wearing overalls and carrying a pruning saw, thinking that Ed wanted him to cut back the pōhutukawa that was blocking light from the back bedroom.

'No, Les. I want you to bury me.'

As he died, I observed the care and attention that Tui and Ed paid one another. Their marriage was not what they would have called 'lovey-dovey'. They were very different people, my mother by her own admission a worrier, and my father disposed to keeping life as simple as possible – his own and everyone else's. Theirs was a marriage that got better as they got older. They were still calling each other 'Mum' and 'Dad' long after we'd left home, still working hard at their milk delivery business, still keeping in touch with their old friends while making new ones – usually younger than them. When they retired and moved from Napier to Tītahi Bay, they quickly became close to the young couple next door, just as they had in Hawke's Bay. They understood the concept of loving the one you're with, well before that song was written.

It had not always been so. The stress and strains were more obvious in the Greymouth years, when the war still sat like a dark cloud over the little house in Ida Street. Tui could get restless. She often said she would have left him after the war if only she had the 'rights'.

'In those days, Gay,' she told me on more than one occasion, 'women had no rights. If you left him, he got the children, the house, and everything else.'

She told me she had really wanted to be an interior decorator rather than a mother. In her dream life, she had no children and a glamorous husband – one more likely than Ed to smoke a pipe and write poetry, drive a Wolseley and take her to Paris for holidays.

As I listened to 'You Must Remember This' in the kitchen that day, with Tui misty-eyed, I thought – interesting. *Casablanca* didn't come out until 1943, when Ed was Missing Believed Killed. How was this song so special to Tui, and with whom? Was the handsome prince that Tui lived alongside not just a romantic fantasy, but real?

Her innocent remark fired me further into an investigation that resulted in two feature films and took the next twenty years. A filmmaker in the family is not necessarily an asset.

After *Mr Wrong*, I began collecting women's stories of World War Two. I thought I would make a TV series, set in a big old house somewhere like Newtown, where a cast of seven young women would share their lives one episode at a time. I lodged the cassette tapes of these interviews at the New Zealand Oral History Centre, which had been housed recently at the Alexander Turnbull Library. Broadcasters Judith Fyfe and Hugo Manson had got sick of throwing good research tapes into the bin every Friday at the Broadcasting Corporation of New Zealand, so they began a collection that grew into a treasure trove of recorded memories, which then became the New Zealand Oral History Centre.

I needed to talk to Judith.

'Judith. I think my mother has a war secret of a romantic nature and I am wondering if I could commission you to do her oral history.'

'Certainly not.'

'I can pay you.'

'Definitely not. We get a lot of families asking us to do this and it is totally out of bounds.'

Judith Fyfe sits implacably before me, sipping her cocktail. A woman of outstanding style that is matched only by her razor-sharp brain, she is indefatigable. It's a definite no.

I persist.

'But it's such rich territory. So much was forbidden in that period, and then the war came along and roughly half a million Kiwi men left on big ships, and roughly 100,000 American servicemen turned up on R&R. The women have kept their secrets. That whole generation has been by and large very quiet.'

Judith takes another sip of her cocktail and looks out to sea.

I take a larger one of mine.

Judith is a big thinker. She is aware that most of the women of this generation – those in Elsie's time, who saw their husbands and lovers off to World War One and their sons off to World War Two – have died by now, 1986. She agrees this is rich territory. The 'Women in World War Two' oral history collection is born. We thoughtfully clink the ice in our respective glasses and order another round.

I hatch a plan. It's going to take a bit of fundraising. Judith will manage the project. She will train a small band of experienced women oral historians and we will ask them to interview their aunties. We want stories from their ordinary lives. What dances did they dance? What did they get up to on a Saturday? Where did they work during the week? I will help her get some dosh, from God knows where – but Judith knows about secret Internal Affairs stashes, little bags of money that can be applied for if you know where to look.

And Judith will interview my mother.

Along with many others, that interview is stored in the Oral History and Sound collection at the Turnbull. Gathered over several years, and including stories from Māori women, some speaking in te reo, Chinese women, and European immigrant women, it is an invaluable legacy collection.

I was happy after *Mr Wrong* finally took off. It had stimulated discussion about women and fear. And women had even come up to me to tell me with delight that they had the same Farmers pyjamas as Meg. I felt like the world had opened up, and that I could do what I liked. I began to research that secret space of 'during the war'.

It is then that my dear friend the radio delivers me a gift. I hear Sonja Davies reading her autobiography, *Bread & Roses*, on the radio. Her description of watching young women dying in Wellington Hospital due to backstreet abortions is searing. I listen closely and see it clearly in my mind. Her tales feel very recent to me, even though in Aotearoa we have, to a degree, achieved abortion law reform. Why make these stories up, when here they are written by someone who was there? Screen stories told from historic events must hold some resonance in the present moment, otherwise why tell them? That TV series I'm mulling is all laid out before me. With the hundredth anniversary of women's voting rights in New Zealand approaching, I think it should be easy to gain traction with the funding bodies.

I meet Sonja to talk it over. She is tiny, because of her lung issue. A fierce campaigner for workers' rights, this little beak-nosed woman stood apart and campaigned for the rest. The underdogs. Preston–Laing negotiates the rights to her story.

*Mr Wrong*, for all its difficulties, took exactly one year to make, from scriptwriting to shooting. I assumed that Sonja's autobiography would be similar. We could select the key stories, and off we'd go. Not so. It took years. Translating that book into compelling drama was quite a mission. Every film I ever make, I set off thinking I can do it fast. Still haven't learnt.

Much of Sonja's story is about illegitimacy. Born out of wedlock into an otherwise establishment family, being an outsider within the establishment gave her a very particular place to stand. Over her lifetime she had finessed a crusading strength that she used for the common good, particularly women. She was the confidante of prime ministers and was often the only woman in the smoke-filled, whisky-fuelled back rooms at parliament, where the gang of five – there's

273

always a gang of five – made the important decisions. Sonja knew her own mind and could be extremely persuasive.

I chose to concentrate on the time during World War Two when she was coming of age as an agitator and when she had contracted the tuberculosis that nearly killed her. Sonja wanted us to find a woman to write the screenplay, but I felt that Graeme Tetley had the right experience and, more importantly, the right politics. His feminism was ingrained. His creative process and mine were sympathetic. When Sonja didn't entirely agree with something, she would say very little but she would raise her head up, which caused her chin to become more prominent. And Sonja had her chin out on our choice of screenwriter.

It was with a certain amount of trepidation that Robin and I found ourselves sitting in a Willis Street café waiting to introduce Sonja to Graeme.

When the two of them met, Sonja picked at her food and gave Graeme the once-over. Graeme didn't say much. His head receded into his shoulders. He looked like a cactus. If he retreats any further, I thought, Sonja will remain equivocal. She could take up a position and never budge. She would just hold it and wait for everyone to come round. In these situations, I often find myself overcompensating and talking too much, so I was trying not to. Fortunately, Sonja's great gift for rapidly finding common ground, a gift every successful politician has in spades, saved the day. In that gloomy café down Willis Street, with the tyres hissing on the wet road outside, Graeme and Sonja began a conversation that lasted the rest of their lives.

It was more than mutual respect. Graeme told me that when he was with Sonja Davies, he was aware that he was in the company of greatness.

She was indeed a great woman. Not only did she have the common touch and a strategic brain, she also possessed great tenacity. She didn't pull the ladder up behind her; she took people with her. She looked to the future and encouraged women to come up through the ranks. She was instrumental in encouraging Georgina Beyer – the world's first openly transgender person to be elected a mayor – to become the world's first openly transgender member of parliament. Helen Clark would have had Sonja's ear when she stepped up to lead the parliamentary Labour Party in its hour of need. Without Sonja, there would be no Helen; without Helen, no Jacinda. It's a chain. When women work together – not necessarily on a personal level but a systemic one – everyone can get somewhere.

As we worked on the scriptwriting, I couldn't find the centre. Sonja's book is a series of anecdotes; it does not accumulate dramatically. These anecdotes insist on being episodic, which is death to television drama. I began to flounder, taking Graeme with me. What was the story really *about*? Well, Sonja Davies obviously – her life. But the last thing to assume – especially when making a biographical portrait – is that the audience is as interested in your subject as you are. Never the case. The storyteller has to make them interested, suck them in. And a film has to be about something. Something beyond just the external conflicts faced by the central character. The best biographical investigations find the flaws that reveal internal disharmony. Internal conflict is where real drama lies. Universal. Sonja's story does not dwell on her internal disharmony but concentrates on the difficulties of social change.

There was also the problem of finance. Raising money for a story featuring an unknown peace campaigner was proving taxing. As we grappled with the project, Graeme gave me five pages of a little television drama he had conceived that had been turned down by the network, called *Ruby and Rata*. I think Graeme showed me his script because he was feeling undermined and needed support. *Ruby and Rata* didn't have the creative problems in translation that *Bread & Roses* had. It was a serious comedy about two women who lie and cheat on one another in order to get by. It critiques the mean neoliberal economy that turns everyone into customers and clients, leaving no room for the very young and the very old.

Leaving executive producer Dorothee Pinfold pitching *Bread & Roses* at international TV markets, Robin and I signed Graeme to write a film: *Ruby and Rata*. We would let *Bread & Roses* sit for a while, and maybe clarity would miraculously reveal itself after time had passed.

It was a day like any other. You know that something horrible is going to happen when you read that in a book, don't you. In this case, it was not my world that came apart on that day, but Graeme's.

One sunny afternoon, he rang to tell me that his son Jonty had had a terrible accident. A clever student of marine biology, Jonty was his father's joy. Spirited, thoughtful, funny and brave, Jonty was at Victoria University and had a holiday job in a warehouse. He and his mates were playing around, skylarking on a forklift, when somehow Jonty was thrown up against the low concrete ceiling. He broke his neck very high in his spine and was now in hospital unable to move. As Jonty hovered between life and death, I joined Jonty's friends and parents pacing the corridors of Hutt Hospital. Jonty became the first person to survive such an injury in Aotearoa, and Graeme's life changed overnight.

As Jonty was learning to live his second life, I gave birth to a daughter, who grew up in parallel. At nearly forty, I had been blessed by getting pregnant with Jonathan. By the time Chelsie was talking, Jonty Tetley was finally clear of his tracheotomy tube. Somehow Graeme and I bonded even closer, as his son and my daughter consumed our time. Graeme's script was written in the early hours. I'm pretty sure it was a comfort.

Keri Kaa had become a good friend of mine. If you were friends with Tungia, you got Keri too. What a gift she was. To the whole community. A talented educationalist, native speaker, writer and bossy cultural bridge builder, Keri was the right person to regularly read what Graeme was writing. What followed were long afternoons of laughter and serious talk forging our kaupapa. Not just for what the film could say, but the process of how to go about it. She made us bold. More confident in our pakehatanga. Rata and her son Willie were characters who could easily be misconstrued as negative stereotypes.

Actually, in this dramedy, all the characters are stereotypes. But as they are all out for number one, the stereotypical aspects cancel one another out.

In *Ruby and Rata*, Pākehā Ruby is in her eighties and wants a live-in helper she doesn't want to pay, and Rata is on two benefits and on the move with her truant, arsonist seven-year-old son. She scams her way into Ruby's downstairs rumpus room, now called a studio apartment by Ruby's nephew, who is posing as a land agent, and together they deal with the new age as best they can. The only character who is completely honest while being robbed and put upon is Ramesh, who owns the dairy down the road.

Chelsie was two and a half when we set out to Auckland to shoot the film. Leon Narbey was director of photography, with Rob Gillies designing. Ngila Dixon designed the costumes, and Jonathan and I settled into a rented house along the road from his sister Bindy – our gaffer, and mother of two little kids, Bonny and Jack. Jonathan and I would work on the film – he would compose the score, and I would co-produce with Robin Laing and direct. It was going to be ideal. Chelsie could go to Playcentre around the corner with Bonny and Jack and be looked after by Shirley's daughter, Aimee Gruar. Women can make movies with their families and live happily ever after . . . hmmm. Not so easy. Happy families are often a myth, and mine was falling apart. I developed a lump in my stomach which took years to go away. But *Ruby and Rata* would live.

Casting was difficult. Where was our Ruby? There were very few eighty-year-old actors in New Zealand. We offered the part to a couple of English ones, but they were not happy to fly so far from home. Yvonne Lawley took on the part with gusto and became the only professional actor in the core cast.

Finding Rata was harder. Di Rowan and I must have auditioned every Māori and Samoan female actor in their thirties in the country. No one was right. The talent pool was small, and most female actors, because of the lack of lead roles in an emerging film industry, were theatre folk, and most Māori or Pasifika women seemed to be doing their PhDs. I had a class problem. When I auditioned Aimee's friend Vanessa Rare, I knew I had found her. Aimee and Vanessa were members of the Auckland street girls, a staunch gang made up entirely of women. Vanessa rose to the challenge along with broadcaster Simon Barnett, who plays Buckle, Ruby's conniving social-climbing nephew.

But we still had not found our seven-year-old.

I visited many schools looking for Willie. I had a little two-hander audition script that was good at sorting those who could inhabit a character and those who could not. Again, no one felt right. It was during pre-production, when I was busy drawing storyboards, that an assistant visited a holiday programme run by Lee Metekingi's grandfather. Lee was found behind the building truanting from his own moko's classes.

Lee turned out to be one of the best actors I have ever had the privilege to direct. When we offered him the part, I sat on the back steps of the beautiful house we had bought in which to stage our film in Mount Albert. Lee was excited, but I wanted to warn him – without dampening his enthusiasm – that film days are long and boring, and this was to be an eight-week shoot.

'Why do you want to do this, Lee?' I asked him.

'Oh, it will be a new experience and good for me,' he said, a response that sounded parental.

'Yes, but it will not be a new experience after the first week. It will be old and tedious after that and sometimes you won't be in the mood. What do we do then? You'll need a better reason to get you through.'

He thought for a moment.

'The money. I want a computer.'

'Great, Lee. When all is lost and you are completely over it, think of that computer.'

It was plain sailing all the way. At first, there was worry that he wasn't really doing much, but every night when we watched rushes that kid was dynamite. He holds the film together. It was right towards the end of the shoot, when I suggested a direction to Lee, that he responded for the first time: 'That's silly.' I realised we could have had that conversation for every set-up. Lee Metekingi is also the only actor I have worked with who wanted to know the lens for the shot. When the film came out, he won Best Male Performance at the 1990 New Zealand Film Awards. A huge hoo-ha ensued, as often it does. It's hard for adults to compete against a brilliant child performance. Sadly, Lee didn't act much after that. I wish he had carried on. Perhaps he didn't get parts because on the small monitors in audition studios his performance was lost. I haven't seen him for years. Lee, if you are reading this, I hope you are still brilliant in your own world. You deserve to be.

After my public shaming of the local distribution industry during the release of *Mr Wrong*, I was warned that my films would be blacklisted. Happy to tell you that this was not so. If anything, I felt a new respect.

*Variety* reported that two female 'helmers' were leading the box office in New Zealand when Jane Campion's *An Angel at My Table* was released, and our little serious comedy was invited to film festivals all over the world. In Sydney I stood on the State Theatre stage – a temple to the golden age of cinema – feeling about two inches tall, having a lively discussion in the Q&A about land theft, private property and indigenous rights. These are the deeper themes of the story. In 1991 I did not expect to be having this discussion with my Ocker cousins. Through the festival I received a message from the English director Mike Lee, who asked me to supper. He was sure that I had used an improvisational technique in *Ruby and Rata*, and seemed a bit put out when I had to tell him that every word of the dialogue was from the script delivered by unschooled actors, one of whom is seven years old. I didn't know that he did not like being quizzed about his own famous techniques, where he has actors largely improvising the script. He humoured me, and I had a valuable film masterclass from one of the world's best.

Screenings were always referred to as 'warm', but outside Australia *Ruby and Rata* was not picked up for cinema distribution. The

Miramax guys wearing their *Eat Fuck Kill* badges at the Toronto Film Festival were unlikely to make any offers, and the best that ever came our way was a half-hearted suggestion from someone that we pursue Disney for the remake rights.

I have never really thrived in filmland. I was only ever offered what I could refuse. I was only too happy to come home to my dear little girl, who I did not want to grow up in Los Angeles. I rather arrogantly said that I wanted her to think that coke only came in a bottle you could buy down at the dairy. Besides, we had that TV series to make.

Sonja entered the Lange government in 1987 at the age of sixty-four and became a busy and conscientious MP. When she gave her maiden speech, she remarked that one member of the opposition kept calling her 'granny': 'To that member I say that to me that is a badge of honour, and one that he will never attain.' Much laughter in the House.

By the time four episodes of *Bread & Roses* had been written, I wanted Sonja to read them. I would bundle up the scripts, trudge the circular corridors of power at the Beehive, and hand them over personally, swearing her to secrecy.

'For your eyes only,' I would whisper sternly before I scurried out.

I didn't realise how much reading an MP has to do. Under the mountains of reports and endless memorandums of understanding, our scripts were not exactly top priority. After a few weeks of enquiring, she finally confessed to not having read them.

'But it's okay. I gave them to my Greek taxi driver to read.'

She always called him her 'Greek taxi driver'. He would wait outside parliament at all hours to drive her back to Eastbourne, where she lived. He was 'devoted', apparently.

'What!'

'He's got more time than me. He likes to read them while he's waiting for me at night.'

'What did he say?'

'He thought they were all right.'

Not exactly the feedback we were craving.

A production date had been set, and I was really keen to have Sonja's opinion. Translating a book full of anecdotes into a dramatic story that gives characters emotional arcs is a job that needs surgically precise story-engineering. This was to be a television series that could first screen in cinemas. It would be a suffrage centenary event, and a dramatisation, not a fictionalisation. We had rules, such as no amalgamations of characters and no amalgamations of scenes. The tools we used were good character writing, and we allowed ourselves to slightly rearrange the order of events to enhance the narrative. That was it. So I wanted Sonja's opinion even if she didn't like what we had done. We had subtly, I hoped, changed her life story. She had signed over all creative control, and I felt a strong responsibility to at least know her thoughts. Giving our precious fourth-draft scripts to taxi drivers, no matter how Greek or devoted, was not going to do the trick.

One morning I wake up to hear on the radio that the member for Pencarrow has broken her leg and will not be in the House for some weeks. Sonja's health has always been a matter of public scrutiny, because she is known to have very little lung capacity.

I ring Sonja. She is bored stiff. Can I come out and bring lunch? What a good idea. I find her holed up in her little flat overlooking the sea with her leg up in plaster like Jimmy Stewart in Alfred Hitchcock's *Rear Window*. She is completely my captive.

'Are you sitting comfortably?' I say. 'Then I'll begin.'

And over the next few days we eat French bread and cheese, drink red wine and laugh a lot, and she gets to listen to the dramatised version of her life. Brilliant. I can tell when she's getting bored, and when she's engaged. When that chin goes out, I know we have a problem.

'What are you thinking, Sonja?'

'It's fine.'

'Is there a problem?'

'No. It's just that Charlie didn't care about any of that.'

281

'How do you mean?'

'He didn't mind if I went to ten meetings a week.'

'Well, where am I going to get the dramatic tension here?'

'Oh, it was from the woman next door who had to babysit. She totally disapproved.' Then she tells me a searing anecdote not in her book. Nothing she suggests makes her character more 'likeable'.

I make notes. We'd have to scratch our heads harder, Graeme and I. Inevitably it gets better. Never the obvious thing. That's why I like working from actuality. The truth is elusive, but really it is not only much stranger than fiction but usually more interesting.

While we were shooting *Ruby and Rata*, Dorothee and Robin cobbled together the finances for *Bread & Roses*. When the independently owned and operated TV3 had launched, a new arm's-length funding mechanism had been invented. Independent filmmakers with a broadcaster attached could apply for funding. So we did. Over at New Zealand on Air, the board was split. Jim Stephenson noticed that all the women were for it and the men against it – so he changed his vote, and we were through. Once men notice the gender imbalance, they are only too happy to help. A gender-conscious lawyer in 1991 on the New Zealand on Air board – on such luck do our fates rest.

# 21

# Art and Accidents

In 1955 a group of women sat on the railway line at Kiwi, a deserted place in the backblocks behind Nelson, to protest against the railway lines being pulled up. They sat on the rails every day from nine to five to stop the railway workers from doing their job.

It was the first all-women's protest in the world that was not specifically about a women's issue. At five o'clock, the railwaymen, who didn't agree with the line being pulled up, were only too happy to shut up shop and not return until the next day. This meant the women, most of whom couldn't drive, could get their husbands to pick them up and drive them for an hour and a half back to Nelson so they could cook dinner (a little late) and prepare the school lunches. As long as they were back on the railway line by five to nine the next morning the protest could continue. It is a tale – sometimes funny, and revealing – of women's power.

No one knew what to do with them. Ruth Page, who led the action, was the only woman who could drive and owned a car as well. She was a National Party stalwart who drove a Morris Eight. She wore a tweed suit and shook hands with the policemen who came out to Kiwi to ask them to desist. The men would be smothered by kindness – offered a cup of tea and a hot scone and, if they weren't careful, they'd find themselves sitting on the line too, having accidentally joined the protest. These large men had no idea how to handle such gentility.

As the news spread as far as the London *Times*, a locomotive was driven at the women to shoo them off the line. They didn't move. Especially harrowing for the driver who, after the third attempt, threw his hat in and quit working for the railways forever.

Eventually, all of the women were arrested and charged with being on a station platform without a ticket. A tiny charge but one that they all pled guilty to, wanting to take the protest to prison by not paying their fines. When the local MP took the hat around without asking them, his gesture was met with the wrath of the disregarded.

This protest is Nelson folklore. When *Bread & Roses* was finally completed, I knew I had to go down to Nelson with Sonja and present a screening before anyone else saw it.

Even though Sonja has not lived there for decades, when you walk down a street in Nelson with her, the traffic stops. On a deserted late Sunday, when we are walking along a suburban street, a car stops dead in the middle of the road, engine running. A man gets out and runs over.

'You're Sonja Davies, aren't you?'

He's about twice her size.

'Yes,' she says, in that way she has of making it plain and not particularly interesting.

'You helped my father take a claim to the tribunal when our family was at its lowest ebb, and he got his compo,' the man says. 'That was a turning point for us all and we never looked back. I was ten at the time and I just want to thank you on behalf of our family.'

Nearly in tears, he stoops and takes her hand in both of his and shakes it gently. On this balmy late afternoon Nelson street, time stands still.

Sonja takes all this in her stride. It is like what I imagine travelling with the Queen Mother might have been like, minus the pomp and circumstance.

I am a worried woman though. This screening will be nerve-racking, not only for the usual first screening reasons. At the packed

Suter Theatre, my concern is that we did not film the Kiwi sequences at Kiwi. We chose a different location, close to Wellington, on the Wairarapa line. Maymorn looks a little like Kiwi, enough for a general audience not to notice the difference, but this screening will have people attending whose combined knowledge of the protest is far greater than mine. I also know that the locomotive driving at the women to scare them off the line is a larger model than was ever in Te Waipounamu. I had opted for an accurate-looking location but the *wrong train*. I'm expecting trouble during the Q&A.

Sonja takes a seat among her old comrades. I watch from the back, gauging the audience reaction.

To my relief, it goes well. The audience laugh and listen and don't appear to be bored. A generous, warm screening. But when the credits roll, no applause. The names roll past in interminable silence. My heart has started beating firmly in my mouth. The lights come up, but no one moves. That silence is nearly more than I can bear, then the cry goes out.

'Three cheers for Sonja!' and the place erupts.

In the foyer at the party afterwards, a woman with the bluest eyes I have ever seen fixes me with a steady gaze. She wears a floral dress that shows off her brown sun-tanned calves and sandalled feet. She carries a leather bag full of papers. I pick her as a researcher and local historian. Here we go, I think to myself. The train issue is steaming up the rails in my brain to swamp me in apologies. But she surprises me.

'You didn't film the driving lesson here at Tōtaranui Beach, did you?'

The driving lesson is a scene near the end where Sonja and her husband, Charlie, have a huge row while he is trying to teach her to drive.

'No. That was shot at Peka Peka in Kāpiti.'

'I knew it wasn't shot at Tōtaranui,' the blue-eyed woman says with some satisfaction.

Now, to me Peka Peka and Tōtaranui are both sandy beaches.

There are waves, there's sand. This was an easy location choice. What is she on about?

'The sky was the wrong blue.'

And of course she is right.

Every time I pass Tōtaranui Beach now, I notice that the sky is indeed a different blue there. A blue with much more red than yellow. A special blue that is completely missing at Kāpiti.

That's the home crowd for you.

*Bread & Roses* is about an outsider becoming an insider on her own terms.

The full impact of internal disharmony in character-based storytelling was hammered home to me when Sonja, in her autobiography, becomes pregnant to an American serviceman and has to hide it in order to keep working. In our television series, once Sonja was pregnant we could have lovely long scenes where people talked about everything under the sun, and the audience would still stay worried. They know she's got a problem that is right inside her and isn't going away – in fact, it's growing. No need for big bangs, huge rows, yelling and screaming and crying and shaking. The scenes are intimate and quiet. The audience is leaning forward, riveted. Wherever Sonja goes, whatever she does, this problem will not leave her. In storytelling terms, it was pure gold. I have never forgotten that lesson. Internal disharmony drives drama.

Three and a half hours of drama based on the life of a student nurse who contracts TB and lives not only to tell the tale but to become an activist leader needed to have deeper themes. The lives of women during the 1930s and 40s were well described in Sonja's book. But life isn't tidy, and three and a half hours of screen time had to hold together seamlessly.

Watching it in the lab theatre, I knew it would work projected into a larger space than people's sitting rooms. The scenes are written short for television, but I filmed as many of them as I could as one-take action. That way, though *Bread & Roses* was four one-hour

286

television episodes, in the cinema the drama is not too cut about, and accumulates. This made the shoot difficult, because I spent a lot of time blocking. Choreographing the camera and the actors into long tracking shots was demanding on both actors and the camera team. We would take two and a half hours of a three-hour schedule to shoot one shot in four or five takes, then we would race around capturing close-ups to offer editing options for cutting between takes if we had to.

The crew hated it. The first assistant director especially hated it. The first AD coordinates all the departments over a shooting day, so the scene isn't lit and the camera ready while the actors are still in make-up. In 1992, here in New Zealand, first ADs like to be able to ring the production office an hour after call time and report that the first shot has been done. This rarely happened on *Bread & Roses*. Actually, on hardly any of my films. If the first AD is not sympathetic to or does not understand the director's creative process, then it is going to be a hard slog for everyone.

Unfortunately, in those days of film production in New Zealand, my explorative approach, where I took time to find the life of the scene, was viewed as not having 'done my homework'. This wasn't how they were used to shooting television. They were used to making an often static wide shot, opposing mid-shots, and finally short close-ups, where often the actors, having 'saved' their performance, had done it too many times and were dry. I came from a much more fluid documentary tradition, but I couldn't explain effectively what I was up to. I was intuitively finding it. Working with Allen Guilford lighting and Alun Bollinger operating was always a pleasure, because they worked intuitively too, but the crew were not happy.

I was evolving a philosophy about cutting. Every time the shot cuts to another, the tension is cut too. I believe that if the shot is held, particularly if tension is building, the audience is trapped in real time and can't get out until the shot cuts to the next. It's a tiny nanosecond unconscious event. Every cut either dissipates suspense or amplifies it. Hitchcock knew this. He is famous for the fast cutting in the shower scene of *Psycho*, but it is his use of long shots – where he traps the audience and won't let them out, like in *Rear Window* and *Rope* – that really makes him the master of suspense. And suspense applies to all storytelling. While *Bread & Roses* wasn't a thriller, it still needed to keep the audience in and not let them out. *Bread & Roses* would not be 'cutty'. (That's what it was called at Pacific when a film had an edit that was strained. 'It's just a bit cutty.')

Over several weeks, the group dynamic got worse and worse.

The crew would arrive, then sit around while Alun Bollinger, Alan Guilford and later Leon Narbey and I worked with the actors and the key grip to achieve a whole scene. This could take a while. If after several takes I felt that there wasn't a whole shot that would stand on its own, I would call for cut-ins. Right when we were about to wrap and move on, suddenly they would find themselves racing around, sometimes fighting the light. Why couldn't I make their day more regular? The general opinion was that I was coming at it unprepared and that I changed my mind all the time. I could hear it on the hand-held radios broadcast to the department heads every day, about ten times over.

'She's changed her mind again.' Et cetera.

I worked for fourteen weeks in that environment. I was undermined and let it upset me. The grumbles on set got worse and worse. Then, one day, the whole thing exploded with a very big bang.

We were eating lunch. It was a beautiful balmy sunny day. Leon Narbey had joined us for the second shoot. He and I were sitting between two trucks parked at the back entrance of the warehouse we were using as a studio and production office. We had baffled the old building with swathes of underfelt hung like curtains across the wide truck bay in order to record clean sound. Helen Bollinger, our costume coordinator, was facing me as we discussed the afternoon requirements for the knitting. Whole scenes included knitting. Continuity knitting isn't easy. On *Bread & Roses* it had become an exacting science, because we shot out of order over four episodes.

There was a very short loud bang. My world turned silent. Helen turned grey, lifted out of her seat and in slow motion flew backwards through the air as a runner hurtled past from the other direction, landing heavily on his shoulder on my table as the world returned to normal speed. Like a radio tuning in with a high whistle, my hearing recovered. Everyone was yelling. Helen was standing up and pointing to the props truck.

'There's someone in there,' she screamed.

I turned to see a big black mushroom cloud rising from the truck that I had seconds before been sitting alongside. It was on fire, belching black smoke from its canopy.

All I could think of was to get Paul Sutorius. Paul would know what to do. He was a former rugby player and fireman before he took up film editing. I ran into the warehouse through three layers of carpet-felt curtaining and, disoriented, in my panic, found myself in the 1930s set for the surgical ward at Wellington Hospital. I fought my way out as more bangs could be heard – and there was Paul, on his way to the scene. I don't know what I wanted him to do, but when I told him to come with me, he did.

What we saw when we emerged back through the carpet felt was chilling. Heroically, our gaffer had leapt into the burning truck and driven it a few yards away from the building. Our electrician was standing in the burning canopy, throwing out small expanded steel barrels, which bounced around the forecourt. Leon Narbey was hosing down the smoking fuel tank under the truck, his feet in sandals. Others were behind fire extinguishers, attempting to get the blaze under control.

Would there be a body in there? Just as I was preparing to go in, a crew member crept out from behind the building. Wearing a pirate's eye-patch and a full machine-gun belt, having blackened his front teeth, he had been preparing a practical joke for later, using gunpowder while smoking. His wooden box full of gunpowder had caught fire and blown up. Solid shards of splintered rimu had penetrated three layers of carpet felt. Fortunately, above head height. Only seconds earlier, three actors had got up from eating their lunch on the back of the truck, put their dishes in the pile and wandered inside. A little later and they could have been killed. Those little steel barrels were half full of aeroplane fuel. If one had exploded, it could have taken out the back of the building and us with it.

The emergency department at Wellington Hospital had heard the bang, called in extra staff and waited for the injured to arrive.

Everyone was grey with shock, but the most shocked people I saw that day were the police forensics team in white protective clothing, some hours later, picking through the remnants of that explosion. The largest special effect in *Bread & Roses* is when someone boils the kettle for a cup of tea. The explosives in the back of the prop truck were left over from other productions. We had been rattling down the motorways and back roads of greater Wellington carrying the equivalent of two decent-sized bombs. As Helen and I watched the forensic experts gingerly picking through the charred remains that thankfully were not body parts, there in the middle of the concourse, still smouldering, was our knitting. All of it. Wrecked.

We went home and got out the wool and the needles, then laughed and laughed until we cried.

A culture of practical joking, drinking and drug-taking pervades the film industry worldwide. In 1992, the local industry was full of talented larrikins. They came from the edges. They worked hard and played hard.

But every day, I was dealing with the bad vibes on set then going home at night and crying in the bath. Once a negative dynamic gets entrenched, it is hard to turn the ship around. I sat in the editing room and cried. I went for long walks and cried. I seemed to be leaking.

It wasn't just the making of *Bread & Roses* that had punctured my heart. My personal life had changed completely. I was now a single mother of one.

It seemed to happen all in one week, but of course that was the accumulation of a year's worth of shifts and tensions that felt like they were happening beyond my control. Jonathan decided to move out, leaving me heartbroken and puzzled. My feelings had not changed, but his had, and after a period of hanging on that seemed to do more damage, he floated off. During this time, my father went into hospital for a routine prostate operation and emerged with a liver cancer diagnosis and a devastating prognosis. I was grief-stricken. But I did what I always do when life gets tough – I plodded on, one foot after the other. Every day was an anxious, repetitive dream.

I organised childcare for Chelsie, I travelled the road to Tītahi Bay where my parents lived, and I sat with my father as he faded. I had come to rely on both my parents for childcare and now turned to Jonathan's father, Terry, and Terry's partner, Janet, for practical support. It does take a village to raise a child. Mine was the grandparents on both sides, and though times were difficult, they did not desert me.

Following the Nelson screening, we premiered *Bread & Roses* for the crew and cast at the Paramount in Wellington. That old theatre had been given an upgrade by then, and its porno matinees were well over, but in 1993 it still had the 16mm projector that screened occasional films for the Film Festival.

*Bread & Roses* was due to be released into cinemas through the 1993 Film Festival. We were screening it in two feature-length parts. We must have been the last 16mm cinema release in the world. Pure madness. The projectors were old and rickety, and the projectionists were well and truly over 16mm.

But Jim, the projectionist at the Paramount, was a complete fan. Jim loved Sonja, and he loved my work. Before the screening, I went to see him to make sure the film would be presented at its best. We checked the matting for the frame; we lined it up so that the permanent inbuilt focus problem at the theatre was minimised; meticulously we even went through the routine for turning out the lights and pulling the curtains open. This was to be an unusual cast and crew screening, because so many of Sonja's friends were now leading the country. The governor-general, Dame Cath Tizard, would be in attendance, along with all accompanying gold-roped equerries. Everything had to be perfect.

The crowd is a-buzz in the foyer drinking their free wine. We are raising money for Women's Refuge, and everyone is enjoying themselves, perhaps a little too much. Sonja's grandchildren are here, and Sonja is surrounded by everyone she loves, except for her daughter Penny, who is ill and can't travel. Viceregal protocol imposes strange rituals on public performance, making it necessary for everyone to be seated before the governor-general arrives. Our crowd is far too pleased to see one another to take any of that seriously, and the governor-general and her entourage have to circle the cinema block several times before everyone is seated and ready for her.

After Robin has thanked the investors, and the cast and crew, I give my speech of welcome, managing to remember the officials in the right order with the right titles. Satisfied that everything has been done to make this night a success, as the lights go down I take up my usual position near the door at the back. I always do this during a screening, so that I can pace outside if I get too agitated.

The lights go down in the right order, but when the film comes up it's in the wrong place.

The image is diagonally crooked, falling off several degrees to the right. One side is badly out of focus. It's a *Cows, Computers and Customers* moment, but worse – a horror show, a worst nightmare. I run for the exit and into the foyer, where I yell at the innocent child cleaning up the ice cream counter, who opens the door to the projection box. I thunder up the wooden stairs, followed by Richard Bluck and John Laing, and burst in on Jim. Startled, he leaps away from the projector and hangs against the wall, eyes bulging with fear, like a man facing crucifixion.

'*Turn it off!*' we shout.

Someone does. Jim hovers in the shadows. While our audience has been drinking their free wine in the foyer, Jim has been having a nervous tipple in his projection box and must have knocked the projector. All that careful placement – wrought asunder. I leave them to rewind the film and line up the image as best they can, and clatter down to the auditorium.

The lights have been turned on. A cinema with all the lights on loses its mystery. It's just a big scuzzy old room that needs painting. All artifice is destroyed. There is still excitement in the air, though. In a sense, the audience has been catapulted backstage to the secret place where the magic is built. Everyone is excited, in a slightly tremulous way – not quite knowing how to be respectful while containing their amusement. This mishap is a great leveller. Strangers talk to each other, and later I hear of one couple who met at that screening and went on to get married.

It takes five long minutes before I get the signal that we can begin again. Once more I go to the front.

'Your Excellency Dame Cath, honourable members, ladies and gentlemen, this is what we call take 2.'

Thanks to Richard Bluck and John Laing, the image is now square – not perfect, but acceptable and mostly in focus. As the lights go down, I slump in my seat and breathe slowly.

I have begun to relax. Things are going well.

Ten minutes in, to my horror, a lanky figure lopes past me. It's Jim. He has deserted the projection box and is heading up to the screen – a man on a mission. He fumbles in the curtains and disappears behind the film, which is still playing.

Suddenly all the lights turn on, then off again, followed by the hum of the air-conditioning running down. Jim has become so nervous about his mistake that he wants to make sure the sound is perfect. As he strides back towards us in the dark, I seriously wonder if I might put my foot out so that John Laing can rugby-tackle our perfectionist projectionist before he causes any more mayhem.

I am reminded of the Fulbourn librarian's question: 'Apart from that, Mrs Lincoln, how was the play?'

*

Despite all that the Paramount threw at us, it was a great screening. Every actor who appeared – and there were heaps – was justifiably proud, and even the grumpy crew were surprised and pleased with their work. The audience was bowled over. *Bread & Roses* was something they were ready for. The film has rich colours and a Vermeer aesthetic. Alan Guilford lit for depth in the frame. Designer Rick Kofoed provided layers. If you don't have width, then depth is key. Robin and I were careful to extend the care we had spent developing the script into the research required to provide authenticity on the screen.

Sonja and Dame Cath spent much of the screening talking loudly. 'That's Ginge. Do you remember that cat? They couldn't get a ginger tabby, so they had to use a plain one.' They went on and on, to the amusement of everyone around them.

After the lights came up, in the scrum of well-wishers surrounding Sonja, along came Jim with his flyer for her to sign. He grinned broadly.

'I'm your biggest fan,' he told her.

Out went the chin.

'Yeees . . .' she said, dubiously, as she signed the flyer.

In this case, my heart was swelling with pride at what Robin, Dorothee, Graeme and I had accomplished. I don't usually immediately like anything I have done, but when we watched *Bread & Roses* that night, I saw it as if for the first time. That is a blessing. You might have to wait years for that special screening when you experience your film as an audience might.

Meanwhile, at Tītahi Bay, my father was dying. He was taking this in his stride, but was annoyed. He had been pretty confident that he would see the year 2000, and here he was in 1992 with liver cancer that was going to curtail that idea. He told my brother, 'A man gets sick for the first time in his life, and he dies.'

When he was in the cancer ward at Wellington Hospital, I went up to see him one afternoon. 'What a bugger eh, Ed,' I said.

He pointed at the man asleep in the bed across from him, 'See that bloke – he's seventy-two.' He pointed at another and in a horrified whisper he exclaimed, 'He's sixty-eight!'

Then he sat back behind the terrible striped curtains.

'I'm eighty-one, love, I've had a good innings.'

Chelsie began running her own campaign. With so much change going on, she had become an assertive four-year-old. One day, during a tantrum, when I had tried every trick in the toddler-taming book, I raised my voice and asked in desperation, 'Chelsie – what is the matter?'

Immediately she crumpled.

'I don't want Ed to die,' she wailed, and I realised that the calm, organised surface I had so carefully constructed above all the chaos had left her out. I had never taken her up to the hospital to see Ed. She had continued to visit as usual at Tītahi Bay, where we could maintain a degree of normality with her two doting grandparents.

I rang Ed on the landline in the cancer ward.

'Do you think it would be all right to visit? She needs to talk to you.'

'Bring the little one up,' he said.

We walk into the ward, this place of silent invasion. Men lie on beds behind curtains, some sleeping fitfully. Chelsie goes straight to her grandfather, who lies on a high bed. She climbs up to sit on his stomach, a painful place for her to settle but he doesn't flinch. She looks him in the eye.

'Ed, I don't want you to die.'

She is with every fibre in her little body beseeching him not to leave her. He returns her gaze.

'Well, I have to, love, you see, because it's my turn.'

She considers this and relaxes slightly.

'Oh,' she says, thoughtfully.

'Yes. Because I'm the oldest.'

'Oh.'

She's disappointed, but not distraught.

'And I will go over there, and I will get everything ready to meet Tui when it's her turn, and then your mother when it's her turn, and everyone else.'

'Oh,' says the little girl, who has had to grapple with this 'turn' idea all year at kōhanga. She understands.

I am in tears, so I leave them and go to the visitor's kitchen to pull myself together and make us a cup of tea. When I return, they are playing a game and giggling. The moment has passed. Everyone back on track. Him to go home to die in his own bed.

After Jonathan leaves, I decide to move house. Too many memories of setting up a family, only to have it crumble in the walls of the place we called home. It all happens in one crazy week. I am packing up, knee deep in five years of living together, when my mother calls. She has managed to keep my father comfortable at home with the help of the local hospice. His physician has told her he will be dying within twenty-four hours. They are certain. I leave Chelsie with her father, now living across town, and travel to the little house in Tītahi Bay, where my parents have lived three gloriously fulfilling years near their grandchildren.

The oncologist and his nurse have been, my mother tells me. During that visit, my father sat on the edge of his bed, looked directly at the doctor, and said, 'I've had enough, doc.'

The doctor asked him again. He repeated, 'I've had enough, doc.'

The doctor then turned to the nurse and said a number relating to the dose of morphine to be administered. She looked up, alert, and carefully repeated the number. The doctor repeated it back to her, and thus did my father have his passing peacefully managed.

A few hours later, I hold his warm hand as my mother paces the room.

'Go, Ed, just go,' she murmurs, hardly bearing to look at him as the space between each breath he takes becomes unbearably long.

With a sudden whoosh that I swear touches my nose, the spirit leaves him – so present that I find I have turned to see where it went.

Outside, Mana Island shines in the late evening sun. My brother and sister are on their way. Jan is in the final mix for Leon Narbey's second feature, *The Footstep Man*, which she has written the music for, and can't leave. I hold Ed's hand to keep it warm for her. When my brother arrives, he takes over. I leave and sit on the deck and watch the sun set over the island. The colours are psychedelic. A big peaceful wave breaks over me.

When I tell Chelsie that he has died, I say, hoping to cheer her up, 'He'll be playing bowls with God.'

'No, no,' she protests.

'What, then?'

'Chess.'

We are at the Pirie Street playground, around the corner from our new house. I spend a lot of time here, pushing the swing for Chelsie and occasionally catching the eye of another single mother doing the same. For some reason none of the women likes to talk.

'Yes,' Chelsie says. 'He'll be in the adult adventure playground in heaven and he's going to play chess with God.'

I hug her close and think, I wonder who will win.

Ed left a message for us to receive after he died.

In Les's little wooden church in Tītahi Bay, my father lay to rest in his coffin wearing his bowls uniform, while Les, wearing what Ed called his 'God frock', stood in the pulpit and read a message that Ed had meant to comfort Chelsie. It's from John 14:2: 'In my Father's house are many mansions: if it were not so, I would have told you. I go to prepare a place for you.'

My father walks beside me right to this minute.

# 22

# My Mother Told Me

Row after row of young men in uniform march by on the wet streets of Wellington. The band plays as the soldiers turn into the docks to be loaded onto the ship that will take them away for years. The women and children wave little flags and cheer. Occasionally you see an elderly man in a crumpled overcoat, looking circumspect.

There's something odd about this period on film. Everyone looks older. The eighteen-year-olds look thirty. They are not the boys that the later Americans appeared to be. They are country lads, schooled in practical skills. Most of them, like my father, have been working since they were fourteen. They wear their new uniforms with pride and hold their guns with recently acquired correctness. Their chests are out. They are going to fight Hitler. Personally. Some will never return. But for now, everyone is joyful.

'They'll do what it takes, whatever it takes,' says the well-written, carefully low-key voice-over. Impeccable filmmaking from the new National Film Unit.

I am sitting with Clive Sowry, the new Archives New Zealand film curator, who is wearing a white coat and white gloves as the pristine print rolls through a Steinbeck.

It has taken me considerable effort to be sitting here. These images are tightly held and carefully preserved, and there is only one way to see them, as none of them are available in any other format. I feel like

I've cracked Fort Knox. I pay attention to every frame.

It isn't until I have persuaded Clive to show me offcuts that I find a woman crying. She blows her nose just as the camera abruptly stops. Crying women were not going to make the cut in the official version for screening in cinemas before the main feature.

I am beginning to think there is a great film to be made. A feature documentary, using the oral histories kept on the little cassette tapes gathered by Judith's sturdy band, intercut with this archival treasure trove.

The idea will not leave me alone. Though I try to make it go away, it keeps grabbing me. I am going to have to serve.

But: 'Seven elderly women talk about the war'? It's an impossible pitch, but I submit my feature documentary about women's war stories twice to the Film Commission. Each time they turn it down, they tell us it is 'tee vee' rather than 'cinema'. What constitutes TV and what constitutes cinema are entrenched ideas. Big wide crane shots outside – cinema. Sitting around, talking about stuff, particularly real people doing it – TV. It's like the criteria are carved in stone, brought down from the mountaintop by a man with a long beard and flowing robes. The subtext is: No one wants to watch a long educational documentary about what grannies did during World War Two, unless it's on TV after peak time and interspersed with commercials.

I ring the CEO of the Film Commission to organise a first meeting, after *Bread & Roses* has screened to some acclaim. I am asked, 'What's the meeting about?' *Ruby and Rata* had been enthusiastically championed, but when I pitch my new idea she makes an appointment three weeks hence.

I know better than to attend.


A few years later, at the 1994 conference dinner of the Screen Producers' and Directors' Association, the film industry is not entirely sober. We've just eaten dinner. The wine was good. The food, not so much. We are attentive, though. Phil Pryke, the newly appointed chair of the New Zealand Film Commission, is about to take to the podium.

Our futures depend on the speech he is about to give. We are used to hearing vaguely pleasant, slightly oblique missives from the throne on these occasions, when one or two 'successful' films get mentioned and we read between the lines about everything else. We are expecting more of the same tonight.

Not this time. Phil Pryke is clear and direct. In future, he says, the Film Commission will not be considering projects more than once. If your project has been turned down, don't even think about submitting it again. The commission intends to consider film ideas with clear international prospects only. They want movies for the multiplexes, not the art houses.

This broadside against almost everything the New Zealand film industry has achieved up till now is greeted by a stunned silence, followed by subdued applause.

Pryke is a neoliberal man of influence. Like many businessmen before him he has been appointed to the Film Commission by the government of the day to sort out the 'business side'. Code for: 'Get those pesky filmmakers to return money to the commission, so that the government can stop funding films out of the public purse.'

The new policy signals hard times ahead for most of us. But I'm used to it.

There wasn't much point in proceeding with anything if Phil Pryke's missive was really serious. Wasting time developing wonderful projects that are unlikely to attract finance is a filmmaker's lot, but best avoided.

The Film Commission is the only national funding body for film in New Zealand. Their investment is considered 'soft money', which means funding that is not ruthlessly commercial. That money is often required to get a film off the ground. Films go round the houses as they are developed, and without approaching the Film Commission on more than one occasion, life was going to be almost untenable for most local producers. During this time, several really good filmmakers moved fast and departed for far-off shores. If they came back at all, it was years later. I lost more than one generation of peers.

There was also no tradition of distributing feature documentaries in New Zealand cinemas. I could see them at the Film Festival, but they didn't come to a cinema near me at any other time of the year. Thanks again to Bill Gosden for screening *Half Life*, a documentary by the Australian filmmaker Dennis O'Rourke, about the Greenpeace rescue of the people of Rongelap after their island was terminally contaminated by French nuclear testing in the Pacific. Films like this brought us the world.

We were not without feature docs of our own, like Merata Mita's *Patu!*, but it was never an easy road.

By 1994, our oral history project was beautifully recorded and safely stashed at the Turnbull Library. In some quarters there was real interest in the personal stories of elderly women talking about what they did during the war. Geoff Walker at Penguin Books offered me a book deal, and I even had some interviews used in a history exhibition, curated by Graeme Tetley, playing at the Dominion Museum alongside beautiful large portraits by Gil Hanly.

What we didn't have was any interest whatsoever in a film. After Phil Pryke's famous speech from the throne, I now had a project that was not viable. Since it had been turned down twice, and was unlikely on the face of it to have any international appeal nor to play at a multiplex near you, it was virtually banned.

I decided to test the waters. What did we have to lose? If we wanted to know how serious he was, this was one way to find out. This was to be the Gaylene Preston Productions NZFC litmus test. Robin would executive-produce. I would produce and direct for Gaylene Preston Productions. In it was going to go, with a production proposal.

My paper edit of the transcriptions provided the spine of the script interspersed with descriptions of those weekly reviews I had pored over. I used some of the old commentary because it was so funny. Over a shot of women postal-truck drivers freshening up their lippy and taking a morning tea break, an entitled male voice-over says: 'But

301

they're women still when it comes to knocking back a cup of chatter-water, then they're back on the road again.'

Frisky music.

I could make this submission look like a feature film with a script that told the whole story. It began when war was declared and ended with the ecstasy of 'Victory', when drunken street parties erupted on Cuba Street, while Nagasaki and Hiroshima radiated death. (That second part is never included in the official version, and I wasn't going to include it in my film either, but I have always had a short film in my head that juxtaposes the archives of those events. If I am ever asked to make a short film, that is the one I would make.)

I put the script together during a hot summer in Golden Bay. Years after Andy and I divorced, with our friend Steve Brazier we bought a magical, rundown place in East Tākaka. With its springs and tōtara fences, the little cottage and its falling-down woolshed became our second home in the holidays. Friends of all ages would come and stay. Glorious summers, bracing winters around the coal range. Every year, a group of young people would take over the woolshed. Over the years, they arrived in better and better vehicles as the bands they were in got more and more famous. One year they produced an album, *The Woolshed Sessions*. When it was launched at Bat's Theatre in Wellington, Chelsie and I sat there crying, because by that time we knew we had to sell the place. My home in Mt Victoria was falling down. Golden Bay is a beautiful place, but it's the stimulating conversations I had there that I remember most.

At our local watering hole, the Mussel Inn, I worked on my script. Accompanied by a friendly bellbird, I sat on the veranda sipping cold manuka beer and cutting the transcripts for the friendly local typist down the road. Robin alerted me that, unsurprisingly, there were no other project submissions for the Film Commission's January deadline. This was the only one. Not likely to light any fires, and virtually unpitchable, but so far everyone who had read the script reported laughing and crying. If you can't make 'em laugh, you will never make 'em cry. And if you can't do both you are unlikely to get the money.

302

I pushed on. I had to.

During the *Bread & Roses* shoot, I acquired thirty rolls of double-sprocket 16mm that was going to be returned to Kodak in Singapore. By the time freight and penalty fees were added, it made more sense for me to buy it. Cheap. But the tins of unexposed negative had now been sitting on a wooden pallet on the concrete floor of my garage for more than two years. The film stock wasn't getting any younger, and neither were my cast. I had not been particularly rigorous in my selection of interview subjects; I had simply asked the interviewers who had made the oral histories. Every woman had their favourites. Four stood out.

When I rang them to invite them to be filmed, they were all keen but a bit puzzled.

'But I wasn't in the war, dear.'

'Yes, you were.'

'I didn't go.'

'I know, but you were a young woman at that time. That's all we want to know about. We don't want to know about the war, we want to know about you.'

'All right, dear – if you think it will be of any interest.'

Of course, I asked my mother too.

She was not at all keen.

'You've just asked me because I am your mother.'

'No better reason, Tui.'

I increased the mortgage, paid the crew a pittance (thank you all), and had four interviews in the can before the Film Commission board meeting. Presenting projects to the board was always possible in those days. Producers could pitch their film eye to eye, tooth to tooth.

Using your own money to make a film – especially if you are a diligent daughter supporting a small family, 'putting the meat and potatoes on the table', as my father would say – is nuts.

The day of the meeting dawns, and I tell Robin to stand clear. I am ready for battle, and I won't be smiling and waving diplomatically.

303

I am encouraged to have in my back pocket some marvellous stories already processed and printed at the laboratory. Thanks to Sue Thompson, the Film Unit CEO who put the invoices into her 'middle drawer', I am feeling brave.

The room is hot and stuffy. They've had a big day, discussing big things, though obviously not project submissions. We remain the only production application. I take a deep breath, and we begin.

There is usually one filmmaker on the board. I know, having sometimes been that person, that this can be a difficult position. Without meaning to, you can become 'the one who knows'. This makes your opinions rather more powerful than everyone else's and is not always a comfortable spot.

On this occasion, the filmmaker is one with whom I am not aligned. He is more commercially inclined and is not known for his feminist views. We eye one another up. His first comment puts a match to my barely concealed rage.

'You say in this proposal that you don't expect your film to appeal internationally, apart from festivals. Very smart.'

Everyone exchanges what I interpret to be knowing looks.

'I'm not being "smart", that's my honest assessment,' I say. 'Only one feature documentary ever cuts through in the global market every year. We would be pulling the wool over your eyes to suggest that this will be the one.'

'And it won't get picked up by the multiplexes.'

'Very unlikely.'

'We are here to fund cinema releases.'

'Yes, but I have a history of getting my films into theatres across the country one way or another. You and I have both four-walled when necessary.'

'You don't understand what I'm saying.'

'You always say I don't understand when I just don't agree.'

At this point, a most surprising thing happens. Phil Pryke, the very person to whom I am sailing in opposition, intervenes. 'I will mediate,' he says.

And he does. My colleague gets so annoyed he throws down his pencil and notepad, pushes his chair away from the table, and sits fuming with his arms folded as the rest of the board ask mildly polite questions and I calm down.

Afterwards, in the ladies' loos, as Robin and I get ready for the cocktail party, we are pretty sure we have not prevailed. We are already wondering how to get the funding from elsewhere. Not a happy prospect. I have already stretched the overdraft, and there is Sue Thompson's pesky middle drawer. How long will she last before she has to hand over those invoices to the accounts department?

Filmmakers straggle into the after-match function. Free drinks on a Friday with the film commissioners always attracts a small but thirsty crowd. Robin and I stand about with chilled chardonnay, trying to look unbothered. As the party progresses, to my amazement every single person on the board approaches me.

'Great pitch,' they whisper.

On the third application, after five years, seven elderly women talking about the war has become a 'great pitch'.

I guess a bit of drama towards the end of a long meeting in a stifling room in February is no bad thing. We got the money. All of it. I had pointed out that *War Stories* would be the lowest-budget feature film they had made for a long time. Kiwis love to do things cheap, and the Film Commission is no exception.

This film would commemorate the end of World War Two and it was something just for us. If we didn't talk about this hidden history, then who else would?

A word in favour of the producer I argued with in the meeting. We both mellowed, and twenty-five years later he was instrumental in pushing *My Year with Helen* through for investment funding. He also instigated several initiatives to encourage women directors when he was CEO of the Film Commission. He gave me carte blanche to establish a valuable scholarship for mid-career women directors. When I pushed it to three, he laughed and agreed. Great fun, and of long-standing value to everyone who applied. All made possible by a man who, in the end, embraced his feminist side. You have to live long enough.

That was true of the women in *War Stories*. They had lived long enough. By the time they were telling their tales, many had lost their husbands and felt free to talk frankly.

Neva Clark was the only one who had told her story before.

She had lost her first love almost immediately after World War Two was declared. He was killed overseas. Grief-stricken, Neva went down to help with the army medical boards in Gisborne and found herself enlisted in the Women's Army Auxiliary Corps within half an hour. Many adventures later, having sailed to Italy to act as office support to the New Zealand high command, she was raped by an Allied soldier, who was then court-martialled. This forced Neva to tell her tale at the hearing, making the whole thing far from confidential. She learned to live with the infamy.

Neva's interviewer, Jane Tolerton, travelled to Northland to talk to her, and collected a great oral history. But after Jane returned to Wellington, Neva got back in touch. 'I think we both know I left something out, don't we?' she said. So Jane travelled back. At the age of seventy-three, Neva then flew to Wellington and told her story one more time to our camera: of being dragged terrified into a corn field one night in Italy; of being assaulted in the dark by several men. She told her tale bravely.

In the film, Neva's story has space around it, and the audience heals with her. Later, when pitching to a television programme commissioner, I left out Neva's story. I didn't want him to choose to broadcast our film for nefarious reasons. I still need to protect that story. One Anzac Day morning, I heard it suddenly on National Radio. I rang Neva. She was sitting on her bed in her WAAC uniform, crying, wondering how on earth she was going to face marching in the soldiers' parade in Kerikeri. I apologised profusely, but there was nothing either of us could do. Take them to court? Too late. Damage done.

The other women – Pamela Quill, Flo Small, Jean Andrews, Rita

Graham, Mabel Waititi and of course Tui – had kept their stories to themselves. These were not tales told over and over. No one much had asked them.

Though many documentaries are made when people just pick up a camera and start shooting, and in New Zealand it's what I call the traditional approach, I do not for a moment recommend starting without the funding. It's a tortuous path with the finance in place, let alone without. Rule no. 1, use other people's money, if you possibly can. Rule no. 2, ref. rule no. 1. The last thing you need is the bank snapping at your heels while you are trying to do your best creative work. John O'Shea, during his long night of the soul in the Kilbirnie art room, clearly told me not to do it. Until *War Stories*, I had largely obeyed.

Strangely though, all those negative elements worked in our favour. Double-sprocket standard 16mm stock was fast being eclipsed by super 16mm, manufactured exclusively to blow up to 35mm with sprocket holes on only one side of the frame, providing a larger picture area. New gates for cameras were being installed. No one was sorry to see the back of those clackety old 16mm projectors, but finding good-quality standard 16mm cameras was fast becoming difficult. When technology changes, it seems to do so overnight. We had our double-sprocket 16mm negative loaded into one of the last cameras able to expose it. Minutes to spare. However, when we did blow up our standard 16mm interviews, the result was startling. Unlike the super 16mm system, the claw mechanism using double sprockets in the camera gate hold the frame momentarily still as it is exposed to the light. For interviews, with hardly any camera movement, our 35mm blow-up is fresh and sharp.

Of course, to achieve a good result, the cinematography has to be world-class. I was lucky that Alun Bollinger was available. He came up from Reefton for a much-reduced fee for the week. There was no cash for his accommodation, so he stayed in my home, and in his spare time he fixed my hot water cylinder. Water systems are his passion. A 'wen wen', as my Australian nephew likes to say. We were shooting short days, because we weren't able to send our crew all over the country. Shoving the crew in the van and paying travel expenses was out of the question. Instead, our interview subjects were brought to us. As a rule, I believe in travelling to any interview subject wherever they are in the world, understanding that in their own environment they are likely to be more relaxed. Not so for the *War Stories* women.

We purloined an underused sound studio, set up our lights and camera for a week, and brought them to us one at a time. We could save money, look after each woman properly and run a relaxed operation. This studio approach also gave us a creative advantage. I wanted the film to have an aesthetic cohesion. I wanted it to exist exclusively in the time of World War Two, and not be confused by the domestic detritus of 1994 in the background of interviews.

Without money for a painted backdrop, ordinary old garden-variety lighting blacks would have to do. I had seen this once before in Warren Beatty's *Reds* and been struck by the distance it made between the live action and the talking head. A black background turned out to be a most brilliant impecunious discovery. By hanging two strips of black fabric on either side of the subject, the camera frame could capture a full figure and achieve a close eyeline to camera. An unforeseen benefit is that a little lit hut is created, with only the subject and interviewer inside. We added a low table for a cup of tea that sat safely outside the frame.

In the soft light beaming in from the sides, Judith could talk to each woman in this intimate environment. The camera disappeared into the dusk. They were in their own little room, back in the time of their youth. These interviews are golden.

Seventeen-year-old Pamela gains permission from the prime minister to travel to England where, after a perilous journey, she marries a handsome RAF pilot who has fought in the Battle of Britain. They are blissfully happy with their new baby, until he goes missing and she reluctantly returns on the last available ship to New Zealand

308

with her four-year-old daughter. She finds his grave in Belgium many years later.

Flo is a working-class girl whose mother hides her red shoes in the letterbox so her daughter can go out dancing. Flo falls pregnant to an American marine who plans to marry her but is killed. She carries the stigma for the rest of her days, due to bearing the American's baby. The prevailing attitude about the marines was: 'They're overpaid, they're over-sexed and they're over here.'

Aunty Jean Andrews (Ngāti Toa, Te Āti Awa) is a force. The first thing that happened to her whānau after war was declared was that men from the government came and asked them to gift their land for the war effort. They did, believing they would get it back after it was no longer required. During the war, when their land was requisitioned for a military camp and her family was moved to a big Pākehā house in the town, Aunty Jean was camp mother to so many young Americans stationed on leave from the Pacific war. 'They were only babies, most of them,' she says of the Americans. As camp mother, she was fierce and fair. She had wonderful stories to tell of japes with the grunts and drinks with the generals. These relationships lasted all her life.

But she also tells of the racism meted out within the Marine Corps – often among one another – and of the Māori community sorting them out.

The struggle to get all of their land back continues today.

When the huge-rating show *USA Today* came to New Zealand for the millennium, every actor's agent in Christendom was wanting to get their clients on the show, but no – they just wanted to talk to 'Anny Jeen'. When *War Stories* screened in LA, five-star generals turned up looking for her. After a beautiful basket of stories well told and a lavish lunch, I took Aunty Jean up to Buckle Street to see her oral history playing in Graeme's history exhibition. She was impressed.

Weeks after filming her story, I got a message that Aunty Jean wanted to see me. When I found her, she had just come out of hospital and couldn't speak. Her pleurisy had become cancer. The day we had interviewed her was the last day of her life that she could have told those stories. I thought maybe she didn't want me to use them anymore. But no. She sat up in bed, her eyes wide, pointing to her throat. Then she held my hand, and it was clear she wanted to thank me. I felt blessed.

Mabel Waititi, aka Aunty Mabel, also describes the devastating sacrifice paid by the Māori community as the war dragged on. She is a woman of great grace and knowledge of tikanga Māori. In her story, when her husband leaves for war, he tells her that she should know that if she finds another partner in his absence he will understand, but upon his return he will want his son back. She tells how she cracked a rib when working in the family trucking business and had to have a hole cut in her chest plaster so she could continue to breast-feed her young son. 'He was quite happy with that.' When her husband returns – as their son, now four, finds his father at the pōwhiri for the returned soldiers being welcomed back – she brings us all home to the huge wave of grief and joy that welcomed the battered Māori Battalion.

'In one marae there, seven went in the original lot and not one came back.'

The loss of whakapapa was extreme.

By the time the film was funded, I was very specifically seeking certain elements. The pacifist story had been well recorded in the oral history collection, but though the stories and the experiences are well told and deeply illuminating, those women were right. They knew they were right, and history has endorsed their position. No internal conflict. They supported their husbands who were incarcerated for the duration, and though their lives were anything but easy at the time, they told the tale of heroes. They didn't fit among the others. It was after the film had been funded that I received a message from an accountant working at TVNZ. Could I call please?

My relationship with the TVNZ accounts department is to pay up, but as slowly as possible. It was several weeks before I returned his call. Stuart Graham had read about the film in the TVNZ newsletter, and suggested I contact his mother. His father was a Christian pacifist who had been incarcerated, and Stuart thought there was 'some pain there' in his mother's experience, 'something unspoken'. He was right. The highly recommended research tape came down from Auckland damaged, but I had a hunch, and flew Rita Graham down to film her at the studio.

Judith was not available, so I did the interview. I sat in the light of the little black 'room' behind the curtains as the camera rolled. As Rita told the tale of being a young mother loving her husband but feeling harshly judged by friends and neighbours, I leant forward and took her hand in one of the breaks. The ten-minute rolls afforded a moment for us to take a breath, but they could also dissipate tension. This time, we took the moment to cry. When Rita saw AlBol wipe his tears away – his eyepiece was fogging over – she said, 'Oh dear, I'm so sorry, but it gets worse.'

A fresh cup of tea came in, and after the slate was tapped, the camera was rolling again. Rita told of the tragic loss of her toddler daughter and her divided feelings on seeing her much-loved husband home under terrible circumstances with dispensation from the camp to attend the funeral. I sat there silently with tears flowing. The story of the reluctant pacifist who learns to own up is plainly told by a woman of great empathy. Rita's story, which was the last to arrive, anchors the film. Though deeply personal, it illuminates a much larger social history.

And then there was Tui.

Judith had interviewed Tui a full two years earlier, and I had access to the tapes. Every time I saw Judith, she would ask me, 'Have you listened to the Tui tapes?'

'No, not yet, was there anything there?'

'Listen to the tapes.'

Something was holding me back. By this time, Tui was struggling. To my surprise, she was not managing very well without Ed. I had thought she would grab her single womanhood with gusto, but she did not. She became lonely and ill and eventually came to live with Chelsie and me. It felt wrong to listen to her oral history tapes when I could just ask her. But I couldn't. I didn't.

It was only when sitting in the dusky light by the camera, as a ten-minute roll of precious 16mm film clicked over, that my mother's secret was revealed to me.

Tui tells the story of getting pregnant out of wedlock before my father leaves for overseas. After a hasty wedding, although she wants him to stay, he sticks with his mates and leaves with his footy club. She endures a lonely time before she receives the dreaded telegram from the prime minister. Ed is Missing Believed Killed.

In her interview, her vulnerability is visceral. It doesn't seem right to call it an interview, but I can't think of another word. Her grief at being left alone again upon my father's death is evident in her telling. I was forcing her to live through the whole dreadful four years afresh.

Thrown into utter turmoil, and unable to cope with this news, Tui's mind jumps the tracks and she finds it easier to live with the idea that he is dead. She falls for a work colleague. A great dancer. When she receives a telegram telling her Ed is alive, she has a hard decision to make. It is as strangers that she and Ed reunite at the Christchurch railway station.

The camera rolls, and I am hearing for the first time about my mother's love affair with a man not my father, while he was away 'fighting Hitler'. In her emotional telling, her affair of the heart seems like only yesterday.

That is the power of those interviews. Often the teller swings into present tense. That's pure memory, not a memory of how the tale was told last time. Tui thought I already knew her secret, and she had remained in two minds about being in the film at all. I had left her interview for last, so if she pulled out I could send everyone home a day early.

The night before our interview, I had walked into Tui's room and found my mother sitting on the edge of her bed, leaning forward, her head cradled in her hands, listening intently to her oral history tape, as though she was rehearsing it for the next day. It was only then that I knew she would come.

After the interview, we cried and hugged, then went to a late lunch with the crew having shot our quota of film. Everyone had been allocated five ten-minute rolls. Tui got six.

When it came time to the edit, I decided to cut each interview as a whole. I did this not because I was trying to be innovative or clever, but because inter-cutting them like I had done with the paper edit seemed the hard way to approach this complex subject. Besides, there had been twelve interviews to refer to in Graeme Tetley's exhibition transcripts. I felt that seven would be best for the movie. Editor Paul Sutorius raised his eyebrows when, on our first edit day, I gaily suggested cutting each interview one by one. 'Then we can lay them out and see what we have.'

'Bold . . . ?' he said, leaving a question mark hanging.

'Andy Warhol says the best way is the easy way,' I countered.

I don't think Andy Warhol was one of Paul's favourites.

But he attacks the task with his usual good humour. He continues to be one of the most underestimated film storytellers in the country. He has a human eye and an intuitive grasp of story. He can cut anything and make his work invisible. From the moment when Pamela Quill says: 'He came into the room at the tennis club dance, I looked at him, and my heart started thumping, I went weak at the knees, then this marvellous being came and asked me to dance, well, I could scarcely stand up, and we just floated around . . .' the audience knows this film is going to take you to an emotional place. But by the end of her story we know that not all love stories have a happy ending. Once the lights come up at the end, through their experience well told, you feel like you have lived through that time. You know so much more than you do from descriptions of battles. These are battles of the heart – all of them.

Each fifty-minute recorded interview was cut down to around ten minutes. At that point, the film made itself. It was obvious how the order would go. We are taken away with Pamela and returned home with Aunty Mabel and the Māori Battalion. In between, it is not only the female experience we hear about.

As John Donne wrote: 'Love is to a man a thing apart, is a woman's whole dominion.' Women of that generation are not used to talking about themselves. Their telling, like the stories I overheard down among the legs under my mother's kitchen table, is inclusive and personal at the same time. Once the official version told by the great men about themselves floats downstream, truths of a more personal nature can rise to the surface. There is always an official version of anything, but if you ever want to know about what was really going on, ask an elderly woman who was there at the time. She's happy to help.

These seven women speak for so many.

Even the title arrived effortlessly. John Maynard's Footstep Pictures agreed to distribute. John looked at the film and suggested *War Stories Our Mothers Never Told Us*. Perfect. It was only recently, when we were both on the jury for the Sydney Film Festival, that he told me his account of his mother's war story. That title is very personal and universal.

The difficult part was in the technical rendering, particularly with the soundtrack. The film is to be Dolby stereo, but the archive tracks are mono. The thin commentary voice has that rumpty-tumpty music behind it, which dates the stories, makes them retrospective. Once Paul cut that archival material, the music bounced about. With judicious cuts, enhanced by a little band put together by Jonathan Besser, the problem was solved. The musicians played along with the soundtrack, building an audio pad that glued it all together. When it came to the return of the Māori Battalion, the Ngāti Pōneke kapa haka group came into the Radio New Zealand studios, and under the leadership of Uncle Ward sang along with their old people on the soundtrack. Taukiri Thomason came in to record a karanga. With

314

the microphones pointed at the ceiling, in the big dark studio, I stood beside her.

'Shall I do it now, dear?' she whispered.

I nodded.

She took my hand and called. The hairs stood up on the back of my neck as I felt the tūpuna arriving, mine among them.

That day, I went to the piano and played 'I'll Walk Beside You' as I felt my father sitting beside me on the piano stool. He was clearly there. I couldn't play that song. I had given up piano years earlier. But in that moment, it all flowed effortlessly. I didn't just feel him, I saw him. Not with my eyes. With my heart.

We had to have a double-head rough cut to test the pacing. This film had to work theatrically on large screens. Emotional pacing is very specific. How big the frame is affects how fast the eye scans the image. That involved making everything, no matter what format, into a dupe 16mm print. The story rules. The breath is as important as the word.

The National Film Unit, though a shadow of its former self, was still operating as a processing lab and sound studio. They even had an operating double-head 16mm projector. Paul and I would cut on a Steinbeck then screen in the big cinema, adjust the pacing, then screen again.

But I was worried. The film seemed to me to be running fast. 'Impossible!' I was told. In the end, we put a stopwatch on it. Sure enough, it was fast by more than one frame per second. They hauled in the boffins. Guess what? I was right. No apologies, just a mythology about my almost witch-like ability to spot different film speeds. But the women in the system smiled a little. That's what it took for an experienced director who was not in the gang to be believed in those days. Solid proof. I hope that sort of idiocy has disappeared now.

I loved every minute of making that film, but there was one anxiety, and it was a big one. My mother. She had given me a gift. She brings that old but newly found emotional rawness into the studio, and though hers is to some extent a rehearsed performance – she calls my brother 'the little boy' throughout, which after the film came out caused much ribbing from his colleagues in the State Services Commission – her pain and sorrow and loneliness is palpable. She sits at the heart of the film – the middle of the posy, the beating pulse of the collection. Yet almost every week she would tell me, 'For two ticks I'd pull out of that film of yours.' And every time she said it, I would tell her she could.

'Just say the word, Tui, and we'll take you out. No need to discuss it, we'll just do it.'

When I told Paul what was going on, he had a fit. Here we were, slaving over a hot editing bench structuring an emotional arc for the audience to experience, and he was being told that the centre could be pulled out at any time. I was taking a huge gamble. It rested on my guess that Tui would not be able to make a clear decision and tell me to take her out. I gambled on her wanting to discuss the pros and cons, but I gave her no opportunity to do so. I crossed my fingers and forged on. Every artist has a splinter of ice in their heart. Someone said that. The mother stayed in the movie.

Jane Ussher is taking large-format photographs of the six women. They are not living legends yet, but they are about to become so.

They are meeting one another for the first time, but you would never know it. Don't let anyone tell you that New Zealand is a taciturn nation. It is not and it never was. Those women feel great affinity with one another, and show it. Immediate rapport. They hug, they laugh, they kiss one another, and they hold hands. Girls again.

Sadly, Aunty Jean had died shortly after I went to see her.

I travelled with a VHS tape of the rough cut to show each of the others their parts. I sat with them and anyone else they wanted to have with them. I listened to their comments. Pamela wanted an archival shot of a plane crashing on land to be replaced by one crashing into the water. That cost an extra $5000. And it had to be 'Stardust'. Of course it did. That was their song. Another $5000. But these decisions are important. They anchor the film to its whakapapa. My brother watched with Tui and encouraged her to stay staunch.

When I screened to Rita and her husband, he cried and cried, for the little daughter they never got to know, and for the emotional price he had not realised she had paid for his strong pacifist principles. It was a harrowing experience, but one that they embraced bravely with Stuart by their side. By the time I arrived back home, I had support from all the women and those nearest and dearest to them. This was not an unselfish kindness just for their benefit. As the filmmaker, I was emboldened. Confident to sail these stories into the world.

But on this day up at Jane Ussher's studio, though they have all seen their own sections, none of them knows what the others have contributed.

Judith and I know we are lucky to be here. She has worked endless hours with Penguin Books, editing their oral histories for the bookcases of the nation. There's a group photo of them all with me lounging across their laps, and we're goofing for the camera. Once more I feel like I am the naughty eavesdropping girl who got away with it.

In the old Paramount, for a change I'm not worried about the projection. They now have a good 35mm platter and Jim's been sober for years. My cousin Maxine has flown in and has Tui well looked after. Aunty Jean's family has gathered, and we hear the karanga calling them in. Uncle Ward blesses us all with a karakia. They have come from her headstone raising at the coast that very day and are weeping. The Paramount becomes a marae for us all. We are sodden in a river of tears.

As the film plays, I hear them laughing and crying. My work is done. As the credits roll, I scramble down the row to Tui. She grabs my hand with an iron grip and pleads, 'Don't let the lights come up.'

She is awash with fear of other people's recriminations. The credits roll on their unstoppable journey.

'I can't do that, Tui,' I whisper. 'But I will stay with you and get you out of here as soon as I can.'

317

She clings to me, drowning.

When the lights come up, she is hugged out of the cinema. My cousin Maxine wraps her arms around her; Ted, the little boy, stands beside her, and thanks her. She is thanked over and over. They all are. The river of tears from Aunty Jean's whānau has become a waiata and haka of generous thanks. We go over the road to the office that Robin and I share, and out comes the champagne. A Panadol for Tui's headache is dropped into her glass. 'Oh, I'll just have a little splash,' and she is the last to leave the party.

*War Stories Our Mothers Never Told Us* screened at Cannes at the same time as it opened on three prints in three centres at home. I rang Tui from France to tell her of our great success on the Croisette. Lindsay Shelton had promoted our little documentary feature into a must-see buzz. I asked my mother how it was going back home.

'I am walking tall in the city,' was all she said.

And if there was one person who needed to feel free to walk tall in the city, it was Tui. This mother of mine had lived alongside shame for so long, it was ingrained.

At Tui's very heart, if you dug deep enough, you would find shame. Shame at growing up poor; shame at having an alcoholic father – a dangerously unpredictable force, loving and destructive in equal measure, coming and going from the family home. Shame at not being educated. Shame at 'falling' pregnant out of wedlock, shame for loving another man after she couldn't cope with Ed being Missing Believed Killed. And now her filmmaking daughter gaily insisted on committing her story to celluloid. She trusted me, and if I had taken a moment to allow what a huge thing I was asking of her, perhaps I would not have done it. But the art angel was with us, and after that, she seemed to embrace life with, if not gay abandon, then with a measure of genuine pride.

318

# 23

# Pace Yourself, Love

Ed never talked much about what he did in the war. When he did talk, he would drop stories like lollies from a Christmas tree, and I would try to catch them before they disappeared.

'When we were in the desert, Uppy had us lined up. He was our officer in charge of C Company. He was rough as guts. We're having a uniform inspection when the colonel comes over and says, "Officer, do you realise your pipe is in your sock?"'

Much male laughter. The returned soldiers' conspiracy. All his tales were at the expense of the 'marching up and down'.

There was that tin of Sahara Desert sand on the mantelpiece that wasn't even golden sand, just dirt. From under the table, I had found out that he had escaped into Switzerland and that 'Uppy' was Charles Upham, who had won the Victoria Cross twice over there in that big 'overseas'. I wanted to know more. I figured he wouldn't want to talk about the horror and the bloodshed and the starvation, but that year in Switzerland felt like a benign place to start. We were doing the dishes, and he was treading a well-worn path about 'dole bludgers'. It was 1979. I decided to divert him and ask about his time in Switzerland.

It was like trying to get blood out of a stone.

'Where did you stay?'

'The Churchill Hotel.'

'Where was that?'

'Lake Geneva.'

'Gosh, Ed, how was that? One minute you're in a prisoner-of-war camp in Italy, and the next you're lounging about on the shores of Lake Geneva, on the dole. What was it like?'

(I'm the cheeky girl here.)

He washed a cup more evenly than usual, and then, slowly, deliberately, put it on the drying rack.

'Oh . . . the tucker wasn't very good,' he said.

There we have it. A whole year summed up in a complaint about the black bread being too hard. He had my measure. Always.

I persisted, though. It took years. It wasn't until he was suffering from the liver cancer that killed him that he agreed to talk to me on the record. At that time, Tui's mention of the song from *Casablanca* had focused my thoughts on the great mystery that sat across all my childhood. I knew Tui would never tell me her secret, particularly while my father was still alive. Ed, however, was facing his mortality. I would take a cassette recorder and a cup of tea to him as he sat in his chair under the bedroom window by the pōhutukawa tree, and off we would go.

'Okay, love. What do you want to know?'

Finally!

I push record. From that moment, I am transported. Great yarns, straight from the armpit. His story.


It begins with rugby practice. As they are changing their clobber, the boys start talking about the war.

'Jim Smith's going, everyone's going.'

They're ruffians from the West Coast, good blokes. They're all broke and they're sure they'll get an army pension at the end of it. They will all go together.

'We thought it would be over by the time we got there, we'd have a few laughs, come home and get a rehab loan.'

They go straight down and enlist.

Tui was furious. She and Ed had not been married long. She was pregnant, and now, without even discussing it, right at the beginning of their married life, he was buggering off overseas when married men were exempt from having to enrol in active service. That fire was coldly burning when he returned four years later. I was the little blonde chatterbox, born to put things back together again. No wonder I was interested in getting to the bottom of my parents' war.

Ed told his tales with no honour or glory.

After Ed died, I shelved the tapes. For years they sat in a cardboard box in my production office, transcribed but ignored. My mother didn't like the idea that I had recorded Ed's stories at all. Having his memories enshrined after he had left us was a comfort to me, but it made me feel more keenly the importance of collecting Tui's story. She was in such a state of grief that I knew that concentrating on Ed's story was out of the question.

I have never underestimated the challenges of making work that flows from my own close family – particularly on film, that puts private life onto a screen bigger than garage doors. But I have my feet firmly planted in my own experience and I can't turn away. It's a compulsion, but one I had to put aside until Tui had flown this earth.

It was then that I felt those little cassette tapes calling me. It felt like a kind of tripwire in my head had been activated. From experience, I knew that once that happens, there is no off switch.

One afternoon, I am sitting in the late sun on the steps of my house. Nigel Hutchison, a filmmaker friend, lives down the road. He and his wife, Sue, bring down a bottle of wine to share and tell me they are moving to Double Cove in the Marlborough Sounds. To cheer me up, he asks me to stay in their guest house there – an artist's residency, he calls it.

In a little cottage surrounded by water, bush and birds, off the grid and visited once a day by Sue and Nige, I confront the issue of building an authentic script from my father's ten cassettes.

I devised the script as a recreated interview, interspersed with dramatic, rollicking, sometimes terrifying or funny dramatised scenes. I could visualise moments that would translate into pure cinema. The torpedoing of the *Jantzen*, a prison ship Ed was on; his near escape with the White brothers, Māori mates from Invercargill, and their beating and recapture before being thrown into overcrowded medieval stone prison cells in an ancient fortress in Greece.

But the script didn't look like a proper script. Pages of one character talking, followed by noisy dramatised action, looks weird on the page. It is only the devoted who can translate the words into their mind's eye to see how this could work on a big screen.

There was a particular image I kept coming back to.

It is from the time when he escaped from prison camp in Italy over the Alps into Switzerland with two friends, Nutty and Tiger. (No one in the New Zealand Army seemed to answer to their actual birth name.) Ed was in a small working gang bringing in the rice harvest.

When their guards came to tell them that Italy was no longer in the war and that they were free to go, most hesitated and stayed put, waiting for instructions from their officers. Not my father. With Nutty and Tiger, they looked at the mountains, decided that Switzerland was 'just over there', and headed into a haphazard adventure without plans. It should never have worked. They didn't even really know where they were. In this part of the story, the three soldier mates have followed a small group of alpine guards who are leaving the Italian army to go home to their villages. Mussolini has been strung up and northern Italy is in chaos as partisans fight the German advance.

```
INT. AUSTIN STREET FRONT ROOM
The sun is getting lower on the curtains
behind eighty-year-old Ed as he is lost in
his journey, back there in the mountains of
his escape. By now Tiger, Nutty and Ed are
well embedded with the members of the Italian
Alpine Guard.
```

## ED I/V

They didn't want us at first, but
after we'd been on the road with
these chaps for a while, everyone
was getting on well. We became quite
chummy and the Italian officer – he
would tell us all sorts of things
about the areas we were going into,
about the Matterhorn and all that
– it was good. And then we were up
hill and down dale, dropping off
all these chaps as they went home.
And we got to meet their loved
ones on the way – they were just
ordinary chaps like us. They weren't
interested in being under the
command of the Germans, because they
didn't want to fight anymore. They
just wanted out of it. So did we.

## ED I/V CONT.

So the officer said to us, 'Look, the
sergeant will take you where you
need to go,' and he said, 'You'll be
all right with him, he's the best
smuggler in the Italian army.' So
we said goodbye to the officer and
thanked him and he took off and no
sooner was he out of sight than this
. . . sergeant goes 'Money', so I
had about 60 lire I suppose and the
other boys had a few lire – because
we used to sell things in the campo,
you never knew when you'd need a bit

of money – and we were happy to give
him the lot. And our cigarettes, we
gave him all our cigarettes as well,
and he looked at them and he was
going like, 'Not much,' and we went,
'Well, that's all we've got,' and he
said, 'Okay. Well let's go!' And off
we went.

EXT. LAKE NIGHT
Three pairs of hands empty their pockets into
the cupped hands of their Italian guide. He
inspects his haul, counts the cigarettes and
shrugs. Pocketing his loot, he beckons them
to follow him to the lakeshore, but to their
concern there is no boat waiting to row them
across. For a moment they fear that their
guide has tricked them, but silently he finds
a spot on the shore where the remains of
a drowned, half-destroyed concrete weir is
still standing.

He bids them to hold hands, each one with the
other.

Cautiously, they follow him into the dark
water. Step by step with the lake swirling
around their ankles, as the cool sun rises
behind them, slowly on the slippery concrete.
One step – feet together, one step, feet
together.

From the lakeshore, as the dawn rises, they
look like they are walking on the water. In

silhouette, three Kiwi soldiers hold hands
with the best smuggler in the Italian army.

I loved the detail.

Apart from Ruth Harley at the Film Commission and Marilyn Milgrom, the script development person, who understood the script, the funding bodies were not devoted. Without champions in well-placed positions, no film gets made. Then there were the overseas investors to be found. The film was not going to be cheap, and they all had their own wars to make films about.

But *Home by Christmas* would be unique. I decided I had to make a promo reel that would demonstrate how it might work. With a tiny script development grant from the Film Commission, I invited Australian actor Tony Barry to come and play my father to shoot excerpts in the only location I had any control over – my own home. I've known Tony for years. He is an honorary Kiwi, having tooled around in the yellow Mini in *Goodbye Pork Pie*. This son of Queensland has found himself on a postage stamp here in Aotearoa. When I met him in Sydney, he mentioned a small melanoma on his ankle that he'd had removed. Life is short. We agreed to get cracking.

With very little cash, I was on the bludge. Chris Parkin owned a luxury hotel near the waterfront, and offered rooms at no charge. Did Tony want to stay there? No. He came to stay in the room my mother had lived in after my father died. Every night he went to bed as Tony, and every morning he seemed to be a little more Ed. Actors undergo an extraordinary psychological transformation – it's mysterious, almost magical. Internal storytelling turned physical.

AlBol came up from Reefton. He didn't like the hotel either, and went to stay with his family. They just weren't hotel kinda guys, I guess. I would have gladly taken the hotel, as my home was being transformed into a film location with the unit in the garage and my bedroom the green room, but I had to stay home to host Tony, so a true home movie it became.

Nigel, who had come on board to produce, got frustrated and

was promoted to executive producer. Sue Rogers came on board and stuck it out.

I could not pay the crew. Their costs were covered, but they would only be paid on the first day of principal photography, which would happen only if the film managed to attract full financing. I devised a 'phantom invoice' that would give them delayed payment. They would take the risk with me. In Aotearoa, crews are used to working on local films for deferred fees that are traditionally paid from the first returns from sales after the film is completed. Using my phantom invoices, they would get paid much sooner.

Toi Whakaari, the New Zealand drama school, called filming excerpts with their third-year students 'work secondment'. With archival footage edited by Jonno Woodford-Robinson, I had a rough demonstration – showing how the drama and archival footage could be cut together, including stills – that I could wave in front of possible investors. Ruth Harley watched the twenty-five-minute cut, liked what she saw, and dragged a reluctant Film Commission along with her, but it was an uphill struggle.

If this had been an Australian story, there would have been more pathways for funding: they have public service broadcasting and more options for encouraging investment in local stories. With Sue Woodfield at TV3 offering a small licence fee, New Zealand on Air expressed some enthusiasm, but we were still a long way from full funding. Clutching our little three-minute showreel, Nige and I went off to the market at Cannes to see if we could attract an international distribution deal.

We knew it would be hard. In France the general public don't really know that New Zealand fought in World War Two. It's as if the British and the Americans own it, culturally, politically and historically. Our journey was not wasted, though. We returned with real interest from a couple of New Zealand distributors for Australasia – but no promises, and no further investment. Nevertheless, we stayed hopeful.

*

326

In Nice, Sue, Nigel and I hired a Citroën straight from the factory and headed into northern Italy. I sat in the back, hunched over my laptop, reading out descriptive detail contained in Ed's interview transcripts, as Sue sat in the front with maps on her lap, yelling instructions to Nigel behind the wheel, like rally drivers.

I would be staging the escape of the three soldiers through Italy into Switzerland at home. Aotearoa can double as almost anywhere. But I needed to know the reference landscape. So here we were.

We travelled up mountain roads hardly wider than goat tracks. It felt like we could fall off the side any minute and be lost in a ravine.

Why hadn't I just got a map and asked Ed to show me? Why hadn't I made him come over to Italy with my mother to retrace his steps when I was living in England all those years? Maybe all children want their parents' lives to have some remnants of mystery. My mother did try to get him to make the trip, but he was adamant. Who would do the milk run? Why would he go? He'd been there and didn't need to see it again. I have another theory, but it is only a theory. He didn't want to go back, because he was tight with the locals and had a girlfriend or two there. Then there was that year in Switzerland . . .

We went down many wrong roads, but at last we believed we had found the place where the three compatriots had crossed over that lake and found themselves out of World War Two, interned in a fancy hotel where the rye bread was too dry, apparently.

I have guessed that my father's big war secret is that, unlike the boys in his rugby club, he did find a party.

Why do I think this? It could just be my need to be fair to my mother, but four years is a long time to be away from everything and everybody you know. When Italy capitulated in 1943, Ed was with prisoners in a small working crew, toiling in rice fields near Biella. He took great glee in telling a story about how the Kiwis instigated smoko as a daily habit, to the chagrin of their guards. They didn't have cups of tea or cigarettes, but they did have a ten-minute sit-down in the morning. Smoko. They claimed it was their cultural right.

As Nigel, Sue and I travelled, we kept finding roadside memorials to partisans killed, all dated a few days after the three country lads with their retreating Alpine Guards passed through. My father tells this story in a haphazard fashion. It's all 'luckily this' and 'luckily that', all the way to Switzerland. There are three photos of him on skis, and over beers in an inn with his arm around a woman who looks not unlike my mother. One day, I asked Tui who she was.

'Oh, some floozy your father knew in Switzerland.'

When he returned on Christmas Eve 1944, my aunty had had a baby called Georgina, whom Ed always called Trudy. No one knows why. He took that part of the story with him to his grave. The last person he was likely to tell was his nosy parker daughter.

Just after I returned from our Italian adventure, Tony Barry was in touch. His melanoma had got worse, and his prognosis was dire. With Ruth's support, I was able to cobble together a further development loan to finance the interview shoot of *Home by Christmas*.

My home had become location sensitive, mouldering under my nose, with the front falling off and no way to get it fixed, for two reasons: 1. I had no money, and 2. the house had to stay the same, so that if the film was finally made, the house would match any material already shot. Tony flew in business class, courtesy of Baz Luhrmann's production team, after working all day with Nicole Kidman on *Australia*, the biggest feature shooting in the world at the time, to turn into my father in the front room to star in what was surely the smallest. Later he would win awards for his performance as Ed.

Finally, using a new incentive that was not really conceived for local films, Sue Rogers and I got the finance together. But we were still short by $200,000. It is strange how often a film can fail for lack of the last few hundred thousand dollars. Despite Ruth Harley's best efforts, the businessmen on the Film Commission at the time put their foot down. Was there an unconscious bias against a woman-helmed soldier's tale? Who knows? But the whole financial package started unravelling like an old jersey. The international financing held on till the last minute in the middle of a global financial crisis, but I had to ring them to tell them to let go. This ship in a storm was going to have to jettison most of the recreated drama.

I was not about to mortgage the roof over our heads for years into the future and spend the rest of my days trying to shore up the debt. So, right on the brink of going into pre-production, I cut $2 million from a $5 million budget. If I'd had more time, I would have cried, but with a fortnight to go, I restructured the drama script and set out to make the best movie I possibly could. Our distributor Gordon Adams at a Film Commission meeting proclaimed the new script 'less desert but more heart'. With the financial jersey not unravelling any further, we were sailing again.

*Home by Christmas* was pieced together over two years, as Tony got sicker then went into remission.

The movie is weighted on his performance, while the dramatised action is restricted to 'meanwhile in Greymouth, down among the women', with Martin Henderson playing my young father and Chelsie Preston Crayford playing her own grandmother. Many of her scenes are with a fearless toddler, Dimitri Latton, playing my two-year-old brother. We would set up the scene with Chelsie, light it, rehearse it, then throw in a non-compliant unguided missile. He is probably in the circus by now.

My four-year-old brother is played by William Ackroyd. Most of his scenes involved the train journey home. Standing with Chelsie on the Wellington Station platform, as a huge locomotive steams up the tracks towards them, was not to his liking. This is the scene towards the end of the film when Tui is waiting to meet her returning husband, who is a stranger to her. William did not like the belching steaming angry locomotive backing up and down the platform take after take. When I tried to comfort him, he pointed to the electric trains happily coming and going nearby. 'Get a blue one,' he wailed.

Chelsie looked after him in the scene while delivering an emotionally nuanced performance of her own.

We also drew upon a well-researched archive found by Alex Boyd.

We used the old footage as if it were dramatic scenes, with soundtrack and character actor voices added. Sometimes audiences have asked: 'How did you insert Martin Henderson into the archival film?' I have to tell them that they only think they saw him because the sound of his scripted voice suggests he is there. A trick of the ear. Paul Sutorius rendered the editing invisible, and the cinematography is brilliantly realised by Alun Bollinger, David Paul and Simon Raby. The black-and-white footage was treated like hand-tinted postcards by colourist Clare Burlinson, a painter with light who deserves an Oscar if she hasn't got one by now.

Finally, after years of being timid about working together since *Holdup*, my sister Jan was persuaded to compose the original music. We approached the task gingerly at first. The world is full of composers, but I only have one sister. I didn't want a disagreement over a few frames in a sequence to escalate into a row. Sisters we are, and rows we can have. But never on *Home by Christmas*. Jan would call me and say, 'I woke up with this music in my head, I have no idea whether it is of any use, but shall I send it?' Invariably it was beautiful. I could direct Jan using colours: 'How about something yellow for this sequence?' She always knew what I meant. It was like we were sitting in the playhouse in McVay Street again, sewing clothes for our dolls.

Mike Hedges, fresh from his Oscar-winning jaunt on *Lord of the Rings*, brought the soundtrack to life. Out at Park Road Post Production, everyone has Oscars. Sometimes I think I make films just for the pure pleasure of Park Road Post Production – Peter Jackson's swanky finishing house, where, under Vicky Jacques' careful stewardship, I was always treated with high regard.

*Home by Christmas* is a smaller movie than I was hoping to make, and it never reached the screen well-resourced, but thanks to the stellar work by everyone, the audience didn't know that. I'm proud of that film. It is really a cinematic patchwork quilt, intricately sewn. Just as during screenings of *War Stories Our Mothers Never Told Us*, the audience often maintained a parallel conversation as the film unspooled. Some of Ed's mates turned up at the Greymouth screenings and loudly talked their way through it, having a marvellous time. When names came up, they would remember them and add their own anecdotes, so the audience got double their money's worth. I wished my darling dad had had the same experience that Tui did once the film hit the cinema screens of the nation. Maybe both my parents would have gone back to that idyllic part of Italy, but of course it was not to be.

# 24

# Gallivanting

After *War Stories* came out, Tui lived the wonderful life she knew was there but had never been part of. The film premiered in the Sundance Film Festival and was invited to a foreign film season presented by the friends of the American Film Archive. At $200 for a season ticket, it attracted the generous widows of famous men, who looked after us during our Los Angeles screenings. Helene Tobias rang from LA and invited me to come over and bring one of the 'ladies'. I said it had to be all or none, because that's how it was with us. Air New Zealand coughed up the fares, Lindsay found a spare pot for festival travel, and we were hosted in the house of the New Zealand consul-general Terry Baker.

The *War Stories* women were stars the minute they landed in Los Angeles. Even in the usually stony-faced customs hall, the officials stamping their passports wanted their autographs once they found out they were in a film premiering at the American Film Archive.

But travelling with eighty-year-olds is more demanding than you might think. They wore me out. Sleep was not high on their list of priorities, and every morning they were up, dressed, handbags packed, ready to go, having eaten fresh pancakes cooked by Terry himself. No trace of jet lag between them. I would crawl in bleary-eyed, without breakfast, and off we would go for a day of organised adventures.

We went on a VIP tour of Universal Studios, courtesy of the

producer Rob Tapert, of *Xena: Warrior Princess* fame, and a tour of NASA, hosted by Sir William Pickering, the former head of the institution. His car still had a car park there and I got the impression that at over eighty he remained adored and revered by all the staff, years after his little space pod had arrived on Mars. He took a shine to Tui, and, after lunch we were presented with a key to Pasadena. Sir William and my mother shamelessly flirted their way down the highway to Brentwood, with Chelsie and me sitting in the back willing him to take his eyes off her and watch the road.

We spent an afternoon with cocktails at Phyllis Diller's place. She had a whole room for her wigs, and a harpsichord in her bedroom on which she played a Bach fugue for us. The next day, this eighty-year-old was off to play with the Cincinnati Symphony Orchestra. During a tour of the kitchen, Aunty Mabel had her breath taken away by the sight of a rich red fridge. She stood in front of it, not wanting to move on from this vision of wonderfulness.

'Oh Gaylene. What else . . . !'

We were all photographed in Phyllis's 1921 Rolls Royce while Bill Evans blasted from her office. Everyone was getting a bit highly coloured on the mysteriously decorated cocktails.

In her garden-view office, Phyllis demonstrated how she could control the volume of the jazz with her foot while sitting at her desk signing photographs, which she then did for everyone. She asked Pamela Quill her name while signing, and Pamela said to her, 'You're a very lovely lady.'

Without looking up, Phyllis replied, 'Yeah, but you got the cheekbones.'

To which Pamela responded, 'Oh I didn't mean what you look like, but you look lovely.'

'Yeah, well, it took a lot of work.'

A big smile, and the autograph is done.

Phyllis was one of the first women in the world to talk publicly about her facelifts. She was also one of the first women stand-up comedians. Straightforward, fast and funny. She told me that her parents were pilgrims, and that she was glad she had grown up on a farm. Having her feet in the soil made running a long Hollywood career less stressful. I think she was underplaying her own remarkable resilience. She called me 'girl genius'. She knew my name started with a G.

As Phyllis stood on her porch to wave us off, nine-year-old Chelsie was behind the video camera, filming her at waist level. Fingering under her chin, Phyllis said, 'Oh, no dear, not from there, it's pleated!'

We went home to the consular house over the road to rest up, leaving Phyllis preparing for her trip the next day. A few years later, I read that Phyllis had had a heart attack and was in hospital. Her agent put out a press release that was pure Diller. 'Phyllis is fine. She's sitting up cracking jokes. We're thinking of booking her for the cafeteria.'

I basked in the reflected glory of the *War Stories* women. You could take them anywhere and they would be charming and true. The Hollywood widows who hosted us told me they were 'very real'. And I guess they recognised, as Phyllis did, that a face lived in for eighty years is very beautiful. I was constantly told by these very kind, permanently surprised-looking Hollywood widows how great it had been to host the stars of *War Stories*. 'The best thing in my life was my trip to Antarctica,' one told me, 'until today.'

But things didn't always go smoothly. On the third day, after being delivered an egg sandwich that looked more like a hamburger, Flo lost it and yelled at the innocent lad serving her, 'No! I want REAL FOOD!'

This was Flo Small's first trip out of Wellington's Newtown. One day she made a bid for freedom from the Santa Monica Mall, looking for something she couldn't find there: a Croxley airmail notepad. Someone told her they could be found at Woolworths, down the Boulevard. When finally located by her concerned hosts, Flo was on her way back carrying her precious Croxley, being followed by several people waving ten-dollar notes in her direction.

'Say, ma'am – did you mean to give me this?'

Her per diems had been freely dispensed to the homeless people on the street who had asked her for a dime. The Hollywood widows were shocked. But Flo was undaunted.

'No, you keep the money,' she told her followers. 'I know what it's like to be poor.'

Flo Small is the only person I have ever seen being offered change by the beggars on Santa Monica Boulevard. Those women who were born in the shadow of the Great War. They were the ones who sat at our kitchen table above me when I was little, drinking morning tea after washing the sheets. My generation were inclined to think them naive and unworldly, but they had survived much more than they were ever willing to share. True wahine toa, in floral tones.

Chelsie was growing up with two strong-minded women sharing her parenting. This she seemed to thrive on. It is hard to be a family of two. It's just maths. Two can be a couple, a mother and daughter, parent and child, but they can't be a family. Three people is the bare minimum. Add a cat – a very independent one – and there we were. When Tui moved in, I was forty-seven, Tui was seventy-seven, Chelsie was seven, and the cat was a thousand years old. Three generations under one roof living very different lives.

I carried Tui up the front steps into my home to move into the front room for what I thought would be a brief few months. She had become very sick after my father died. I found a doctor who would do house calls. Vitamins and minerals were prescribed. Tui began to take on small daily duties, and picked up Chelsie from school each day, making it possible for me to carry on filmmaking while being in sole charge of one daughter. Tui thrived. That seven-year-old bright boss who lit up my life, and hers as well, saved her. She found her purpose again. Looking after someone else.

If you came up the steps from the street and rang the doorbell, it was Tui who answered the door from the vantage of her large, completely floral front bedroom. Just as her mother, Elsie, had lived with us at Ida Street, so did Tui take the same spot in my home.

Tui had a collection of delicious delicacies. You had to be pretty quick or downright mean to get through the front door without being enticed into her lair for a cup of tea. Across the road lived Isla, who was four years older than Tui and a staunch member of the Mount Vic women's bowls club, until the men's bowls club next door ran out of members and made the women close their club to bulk out theirs. Tui made scones and Isla made muffins. Between them they had a handle on the hood. One day, heads down, they met in the middle of the road, on the way to each other's table, each with a plate with their hot speciality for morning tea.

Down the hall from Tui was Chelsie's bedroom, with me taking the smallest room at the back. The smallest, but the best. I awoke in a room bathed in morning sun, just as I had done in McVay Street when I took over Nan's sun porch. Chelsie and I had the mornings, while Tui stayed put. She left this time to us, only arising once we were out of the house.

We settled into a routine that lasted the next five years. My big old mouldering villa could handle it.

We were always late. The school was just down the road and it was invariably a last-minute dash, no matter how early we woke up. When Chelsie was little, I had trained her to sleep in. Every night after her story and karakia before I switched off the light: 'What do you do when you wake up?'

'Go back to sleep.'

Big kiss and hug from me.

But now we were supposed to be out of the house by eight thirty. Nearly impossible. Tui never interfered. That was the key to our success. By the time I got home after work, Chelsie would have eaten something stodgy at five thirty and I would join her to watch *The Simpsons* while Tui retired to her room to watch *Coronation Street*. So, though we were co-parenting, we retained a certain autonomy. Valiantly, believing that eating together can anchor a family, I would try to cook dinner for all three of us at least twice a week. Not easy. Tui liked to eat early, I liked to eat late, Chelsie liked Coco Pops. But

336

we managed. Chelsie was growing up. She moved into the front room adjacent to Tui's, and with help from her cousin Bonny painted it electric blue, then set up a drumkit in her bay window and filled the place with girl power.

We had a great eightieth birthday for Tui in our home. Cousins and their families arrived from Hawke's Bay and around the motu. When it came to her eighty-first, I suggested something bigger – we could hire the community centre and send out invitations and have a real knees-up. I was hurt when Tui took total exception to this idea. She didn't just not want a party, she strongly objected to it. She thought I was being nasty. I didn't know why. She seemed to be taking against me. But I was too busy to try to get to the bottom of it, as I was completely focused on trying to launch a new feature film, *Perfect Strangers*.

This one I had written out of my own imagination.

When Chelsie was seven, she was the proud owner of new glasses. The first day of school, she put them on and said, 'I can see!' But then she took them off and put them back in the case. On our walk to school, she suddenly stopped to retrieve the case. She must have decided that, despite the unwanted attention she might attract, being able to see properly was worth it. We carried on.

'Now we've got something in common,' she told me cheerfully.

I was a bit taken aback. 'We have other things in common too.'

'No, we don't.'

'Yes, we do.'

'Like what?'

'Well, you like drawing. I like drawing.'

'No, you're better than me,' Chelsie said.

We walked on. I was the anxious mother of one. I tried again. 'What about stories? You like writing stories.'

'You don't write stories,' she said.

'Yes, I do. I'm a filmmaker, I tell stories on film.'

'Yes, but they're not your stories, they are Sonja's story or Tui's story. They're somebody else's story.' With that, she kissed me goodbye and headed into her classroom.

I was left standing outside the dairy with plenty to think about. She was right. Did I mean to spend my entire filmmaking life telling other people's stories? Did I mean to do that? Why?

I went home and cleared my desk and began to write *Perfect Strangers*.

It is a devious fairy-tale full of genre-bending twists in which a woman under threat on a remote island mortally wounds a man, then falls in love with him as she is trying to keep him alive. After he dies, she puts him in the freezer and does her best to live happily ever after with his ghost. Not one for everybody. My imaginative life was now on that lonely, beautiful island and every waking moment was involved with trying to get the film financed, with Robin Laing working hard to seal the deals and Sam Neill attached to play the man. But the little Austin Street whānau were drifting beyond my control.

After Chelsie and her friends had been picked up by the police at an out-of-control party, I stepped in. I moved my office into what had been the middle bedroom to be around more. The kiddie sleepovers had become all-night parties. I thought things were getting dodgy. I decided to set new rules for this clever, spirited girl of mine. I wrote her a letter and included a little heart candle.

Dear Chelsie,
This is not a punishment. This is a new default setting to keep you safe until I am sure you can do that for yourself. I will collect you every Friday and Saturday night at midnight from wherever you are. You will wake up in your own bed with no friends to stay over. I love you, and if you want to know how much, just light this candle and look into the flame.
Lots and lots of love, Mum.

She never lit the candle. But every Friday and Saturday I drove to collect her from parties in hillside suburbs unknown to me. At first there was much resistance – lying on the couch sobbing, gnashing of

338

teeth. I stuck to my guns, and gradually, my little car became full of more and more of her friends, as I dropped them off to their homes after midnight. These girls were glad to say, 'My mother won't let me', and though they were generally pretty intoxicated when I collected them, I could make sure they were all right. Other parents joined in occasionally – not as often as I might have liked – but there was an upside. I got to hear the complete collection of *The Goon Show*, which played on the radio every Friday night, leading to the midnight news. I also became the mother who knew too much, something Chelsie pointed out often from the front seat.

'You are going to be so sorry you said that in front of my mother when you wake up tomorrow.'

On the other hand, the younger set were easy.

Tui was acting irrationally. She had begun to be nasty to Chelsie too. This was out of character in the extreme. One day in a quiet moment, I was sitting with her having a cuppa at the table in her window. We were talking about the future. For Tui, this was her death. She did not want to be a burden. I had always assured her that if she got chronically ill, we would just hire in the help she needed. Her caregiver, Fonda, came every morning to help her bathe and get ready for the day – a wonderful relationship – and I thought I would just add more help as required.

'You can leave here in a box, Tui,' I assured her.

'But I'm not right, Gay,' she told me.

'How not right?'

'I'm getting Alzheimer's.'

I laughed. Tui was prone to dramatic statements and I considered this to be one brought on by her anxiety at me getting close to leaving her with Chelsie for a few months while I went south to shoot *Perfect Strangers*. Tui had a better memory than any of us. I started setting little tests.

'Tui, I need a needle. Where can I find one?'

'There is one threaded with black cotton in the hem of the curtain on the left-hand side of the window in my room.'

339

Sure enough, there it would be.

However, leaving a fifteen-year-old with an eighty-five-year-old is an interesting proposition. Who is looking after whom? My friend Susana Leiataua came to the rescue and moved in, valiantly bridging the vast age and culture gap between my mother and my daughter. I went south to Punakaiki to what was, for me, a blissful shoot. Before I left, I had to make a decision. Film or family? Well, clearly family, but mother or daughter? I decided it had to be one or the other. No contest. Daughter. I told Chelsie that when it came to my filmmaking, she was first, but only just. It was a joke. Chelsie wasn't so sure.

Down on the West Coast, winter delivers wild but predictable weather in pastel shades, and I am making this film with friends. AlBol is the director of photography and the operator. Finally, we get to make the whole thing together. We are shooting the film a few miles from his whānau house in Punakaiki. Helen Bollinger takes her spot in charge of costume, supervising a team of clever local women on sewing machines. Joe Bleakley is the production designer. Robin and Trish Downey set up a production office in the canoe hire base. Sam comes down in his Mini Cooper and goes baching. I go to sleep every night hearing the Tasman Sea rattling the walls, stones rolling in the back wash. Making a film with friends is the best. Whetu Fala is a tremendous director's assistant. Halfway through the shoot, she brings Tui down. Once my mother is in the car at Westport, she becomes the queen of everything. She is taken to Greymouth to visit George Webster, her sister's husband, who is now in a care home but still playing his banjo. She introduces Whetu as her assistant. The minute Tui is out of the room, George corners Whetu.

'You're not Tui's assistant, are you? You're Gaylene's assistant, aren't you?'

He was not having any 'airs and graces' going on around him. The home crowd are like that, but they did treat her like royalty. Everywhere they went in Greymouth, doors opened. Secret doors at brunch time. Tui's cousin, Kevin Brown, long-time mayor of Greymouth, organised amazing clandestine whitebait meals. It was

Whetu's pleasure to be Tui's 'assistant' for those. I kept shooting. Jonathan brought Chelsie down in the school holidays, where she was joined by her Crayford cuzzies – Bindy was back being gaffer. It was *Mr Wrong* thirty years on, in more ways than one. I think of that film as being a bookend to *Mr Wrong*. They are both spooky thrillers with an allegory travelling through. In the case of *Perfect Strangers*, it is about the dangerous deception of desire, that suggests the prey becoming the predator. In the right mood you may find it funny. In a different one, you may just be terrified.

By the time I came home, life at the ranch, despite best efforts by all concerned, had unravelled. To my horror, Tui had booked herself into a care home, one that I considered to be the worst one available, and refused to change her mind. We went up there to this decaying, urine-stenched place for their Christmas party. A sweating, false Santa was giving out soaps. Chelsie sobbed all the way home, with Tui set on moving in.

The day I drove her up there and left her in a little cell-like room with a perfect view of a brick wall, and the bathroom down the hall, I felt like I was committing my mother to prison. But I did not have power of attorney to insist on anything different, and I was by now in the middle of the *Perfect Strangers* edit. Tui had filled in all the forms. I was too overwhelmed to do anything other than visit her every evening, and make a secret plan for later. The day that the picture lock was approved, I got in my car with the Yellow Pages on my knee, and dropped in on every care home within ten minutes' drive of Austin Street. Afternoons on Sundays are the best time to gauge an institution. I knew that if the inmates were sitting in chairs in the day room staring into space with the television blaring, this was no place for my mother.

When I walked into Alexandra Rest Home in Newtown, they were playing a quiz with a lot of laughter in a sun-drenched garden courtyard. And when I approached the nurse on duty, she told me that I was lucky. ('Oh, I shouldn't say that,' she said.) Someone had died the day before and there was a room looking out at the street available.

If I was in the office for the senior manager by nine in the morning, there was a chance that it could be ours. I negotiated a kettle and her own landline. With Joe Bleakley's help we recreated Tui's Austin Street room complete with photographs and floral bedspread. Once that was prepared, I was ready to kidnap her.

I had told them up the hill where she had incarcerated herself that I wanted to move her. They had expressed firm opposition.

'You do realise that your mother is just going to get more and more confused, and moving her is not going to help,' said the doctor.

'Well, she will still be getting more and more confused closer to my home and the rest of her family,' I countered.

The morning I went to collect her, Tui was sitting on the edge of her bed, nursing her pillow, a deep ball of misery.

'I just can't do it, Gay, they'll punish me.'

Who 'they' were I wasn't sure, but I think she meant the welfare department paying her fees. I left her with a cup of tea and went to collect the paperwork. I found the superintendent with the accountant in her office, bent over their budget. This place was on its last legs. They were not about to lose another 'client'. It became clear they were not going to give me Tui's medical notes. They had put the squeezers on my mother, who was now so intimidated she was refusing to leave.

The car is outside the back door and we are going through it. My poor little mother was shuttled out, still nursing her pillow. As we left, a woman we had come to know as Mary, always dressed in a stained tartan skirt and Pringle jersey with pearls, stepped forward.

'And you are?' she said, with well-practised gentility and a vacant smile as she extended a shaking ringed hand in our direction.

She had greeted us this way for weeks. We liked her. If Chelsie had been there, I may have shuttled her out too.

With no backward glance, I sped away. After Tui was settled in at Alexandra Rest Home, I went back to get those precious medical notes. Very calmly, I said I would wait until they were ready. I was in no hurry and could last all day if necessary. Finally, after much huffing and warnings, they were handed over.

On the wall in Tui's sunny room with a view of the buses going by, Joe and I had hung a photo of Ed as a young man. Tui walked into this new room that felt like home. She walked up to his photo and kissed it. 'There you are.'

She had found home.

The former terrible care home was instantly forgotten. A few weeks later it was closed.

Life got much easier for me. Chelsie had moved to the school I always wanted her to go to. Her father and I agreed. This she did not expect. With his help, she was enrolled at Wellington High, where many of her primary school friends were. In this progressive co-ed school with an amazing music, art and drama centre, she thrived. There was a talented drama teacher at Wellington High. Annie Mallard is in the same category as Graeme Tetley. Talented and greatly loved by her students. Chelsie arrived in the school and was no sooner in the drama class than she was cast in the student-directed Shakespeare as Queen Elizabeth in a genre-bent *Richard III*.

Having delivered *Perfect Strangers* to Twentieth Century Fox, and with Jonathan back in town, I was up for anything and accepted a trip to China. I've always wanted to go to China. This was an all-expenses paid film junket. Things were falling into place. Except Chelsie's play was scheduled exactly in the middle of the trip. I did my best to either change the trip or change the season of the play. Impossible. So, no China for me, which turned out to be lucky because on opening night as she was getting ready for me to take her to the show, Tui fell and broke her femur.

I spent that night in an ambulance and at A&E with my poor little mother in a lot of pain, a state she stayed in for almost four days, as we waited for a special piece of equipment to arrive from somewhere or other. Terrible car crashes were pushing her down the queue. We went to visit her often and encouraged her to sing to take her mind off the pain. She was on high doses of tranquillisers and painkillers and by the time she was back in her little room in Alexandra, she had descended into a nasty drug-induced dementia.

I was racing around the world, enjoying film festivals and meeting other filmmakers. I felt relaxed enough now, with Chelsie having moved in with her father, to stay longer when I was away and not just do my usual lightning dashes that had once seen me go to London for lunch and to Venice for three days, and on to Toronto for two days, then home via LA. This time I could take advantage of whatever situation I found myself in. *Perfect Strangers* was a great film to travel with – especially to Créteil where they still remembered *Mr Wrong* and its audacious prize in 1985. Andrea Arnold was there with her first short, *Wasp*. She loved the film and got all her filmmaker friends in Paris to go and see it.

In London for the London Film Festival, I stayed in Piccadilly in a hotel room with the biggest bath with the best view of London straight across the river, where I had lounged in that other bath, the one that started all this, so many years before. I flung open the window and wallowed in the winter sun. For all the struggles, there's satisfaction to be had every so often. My dear heart Stockwellian friend, Vicky Meadows, turned up from Bristol. She has lived an activist life as part of the Fallout Marching Band, a political street band. We headed off to the best theatre in Leicester Square, where *Perfect Strangers* found a warm reception from a packed auditorium.

But when I got home, all was not good news. *Perfect Strangers* had opened well in Australia, but not in Auckland. The further south you looked, the better the box office. They loved it in Gore. But my little wild allegory was not clicking up north, where most of the people live. I had known for a while that trouble was coming. There had been a campaign against the film by powerful film industry forces who were well connected to the *National Business Review*. Before a frame was shot there were nasty articles about how *Perfect Strangers* was funded by a 'tax rort'. (False.) This was one of many anti-Film Commission campaigns that have raged over the years. (They are always worse when there is a woman CEO, I have noticed.) Once there is a relentless media-fuelled industry assault from some quarters, it's pretty hard to correct. The film got a damning review in the *New Zealand Herald*, and limped into cinemas. The audience was not ready for a feminist fairy-tale about a woman with a lover in the freezer.

But I had larger things to deal with. My poor little mother was in a demented rage. She had not been a happy camper either when I left town to support the film internationally, and her dementia had got worse. When she was dark, her rage would be meted out to me. I knew this was not my mother, but unfortunately, relentless meanness undermines, and with the less than stellar reception of *Perfect Strangers* at home, my self-confidence was low. Rapturous reception from screenings at the London Film Festival restored my pride, but I was not looking forward to coming home.

I flew into Auckland on the plane from LA that arrives at five in the morning. The connection to Wellington gets me home by 8am. I had flown this schedule often when Tui and Chels were living with me. This meant that in my completely jetlag-addled state I would walk Chels to school and fall into bed for a broken sleep. Now I was able to walk in the door, dump my bags, go to bed and sleep off the jet lag.

It was not until the next day that I was driving to Alexandra Rest Home to see my mother. As I drove through the Mount Vic tunnel, I realised my knuckles were white on the steering wheel. I was bracing myself for abuse. Tui had reverted to a very Edwardian version of herself. Punitive, and angry. I didn't blame her – her situation was terrible, sunny room or not – but while I was away I had been thinking about my situation. I wondered what I could do to stop the tantrums. Would Tui respond to therapy? I was advised not. But I was becoming desperate. I remembered a little book called *Toddler Taming* that had helped me deal with the terrible twos. Could I apply those techniques to a person with senile dementia? Probably not. I got out of the car and braced myself. I walked into Tui's room all smiles. These days, she was in bed most of the time. She didn't draw breath.

'You're a mean little bugger not coming to see me earlier.'

No hello, just bitter distress aimed at me. Without thinking too much, I swung into toddler-taming mode. I was like a robot. Firm. Clear. I leant down and kissed her on the forehead.

'I love you Tui, but I don't love your behaviour. I'm leaving now and will see you tomorrow.'

I left the little present from London on her bedside table and walked out, steadying myself to not look back. As I went down the corridor, I could hear her.

'No sense of humour. You always were the nasty one. When I die, I'm going to come back and sit from on high and laugh.'

I sat in the car outside shaking. I had just been mean to a poor demented soul who used to be my mother. I couldn't go home. With a couple of hours to kill I went to find Terry Crayford, Chelsie's grandfather. Terry knows and loves Tui. He makes me a coffee and I sit at his table and cry on his shoulder. He is philosophical and has heard my cries of woe before. I calm down before I go to collect Chelsie from school. She bounces into the car. All is joy. But she sees I'm not happy.

'What's wrong, Mumma?'

'I've just been mean to Tui.'

I tell her what happened. To my surprise, she clenches her fists and raises them, staunch in celebration.

'Yuss!' she exclaims.

This is unexpected support, but she won't have to deal with the fall-out.

'But now I am going to have to go over there and apologise, and everything will be hard again.'

'No, it won't. Just carry on as though it didn't happen when you see her tomorrow.'

How did she get so wise? I did what she told me, and she was right. Miraculously, Tui was never nasty to me ever again.

But she did bite a nurse. Who knows what happened, but I got a call from the Alexandra superintendent to tell me that they were going to reassess Tui for dementia care. They had built a new unit across the road and clearly my mother was top of the list to be one of the first residents. Reassessment. I called it being expelled. I did my own due diligence. When I walked into the new 'facility' the next Sunday, though there were only a handful of patients in the brand-new building, I heard people being yelled at. I didn't wait around. I headed over to a place that had a hospital and a hair salon. Rita Angus Retirement Village was the perfect place for Tui, whose dementia was not solid state. She never really walked again after breaking her femur, but with good healthcare, a foot massage every week, her hair done, and plenty of singing, I'm happy to report that she improved and it was here that she died, a year later, surrounded by kind caregivers with me holding her hand.

I think about my mother a lot. I realise that this book and many of my films have her lurking around them. We are daughters of the revolution who have been part of the biggest changes for women for millennia. I am writing this for our daughters, and their daughters, so that they know how valuable our gains have been and how we have to stay vigilant. Our gains need to be safeguarded. Fortunately, at the time of writing, the country I live in feels secure for women's rights. Not perfect. There is always much to be done.

At the moment a staunch group of wahine toa are taking a claim to the Waitangi Tribunal to address the devastating effect of European colonisation on Māori women in Aotearoa. The importance of this claim cannot be overestimated. It is not about land or property but about the very heart and soul of humanity. Resource the women, who, from the moment they are born, hold the future of humankind already in their bodies. Whakapapa is all.

# 25

# Why I Make Films

I grew up with the big black mountains at my back and the Tasman Sea hurling itself to the shore. The land between is one of the most beautiful places on earth. But I never saw it at the movies.

And it was the movies we loved more than anything else. I would go there with my brother on Saturday afternoons. He was made to take me, so he'd give me a double on the bar of his bike. I was a bit of an embarrassment. I thought I was Christmas, hanging out with the big boys – all seven years older than me. I'd listen to them doing funny voices from *The Goon Show*, which I never fully understood, but they laughed so much they nearly fell off their bikes. I hung on tight and tried to keep up.

At the kids' sessions, free of parental control, the old Opera House in Greymouth rocked with our stamping feet. We threw Jaffas just to hear them roll on the wooden floor down to the front of the theatre. We cheered the goodies and booed the baddies in the American serials.

One afternoon, right in the middle of a Western, amid the chaos, the lights went up – suddenly revealing the old fleapit in all its terrible rundown glory. Kids were standing on seats and running up and down the aisles, caught like possums in the light, mid-throw. The manager came down, waving his big torch, and threatened to chuck us all out if we didn't sit down and shut up. In stunned silence we

348

complied, and watched quietly after that. No fun at all. The flicks were for laughing, screaming and cheering together. One big tribe in the dark.

One wet day, we were a few minutes late. I always had threepence to get an ice cream and was licking the melted bits running down the side of the cone. The lady on the dark side of the door asked my brother how old I was. 'Four,' he told her. I pulled at his jacket and protested: 'No, I'm not, I'm six!'

The lady shone her torch down into my face. That was the end of me getting in for free.

I realise now how formative those kids' sessions at the Greymouth Opera House were. Every serial had a woman in distress. All the baddies wore black clothes and were dirty. The goodies were clean and wore tight pants, rode white horses and rescued women all over the place. The baddies had foreign accents and took the women as hostages. The 'Injuns' were the enemy. Our deep imagination gets set at the movies.

Thirty years later, when the time came for me to make my own films, I felt like once more I was the girl getting a double on the big boys' bike, holding tight to keep up.

It was at school that I first saw a locally made film. In the wet, gumboot-strewn corridor of Grey Main School, where we were crammed in like little baby boomer whitebait, the crackly voice of our headmaster boomed through the tannoy above us. After lunch, we were to watch a movie on road safety together.

Blackout curtains had been haphazardly strung across our big classroom windows. A little screen was set up and a projector rattled the film through the flickering light. My first New Zealand movie. Black and white. A car drove up a deserted road in the rain, and the man inside didn't obey the lights at the crossing. A train came. Terrifying. At ten years old, I recognised everything about the place. The road, the houses, the hills, the car, the man. Unforgettable. This was my world, all right. Searingly so.

Many years would pass before I saw another New Zealand film.

349

I didn't grow up watching anything on the screen that I could identify as 'my world'. That went for music and books too. I am part of the *Janet and John* generation, who learned to read stories where 'creeks' were 'brooks', and where Daddy went to work on the train wearing a suit and carrying a briefcase. We really were on the edge of the world, and felt it acutely. In 1995, when the world celebrated one hundred years of film, New Zealand still had very few feature films to 'celebrate'. For the *Century of Cinema* series curated by the BFI, Judy Rymer and Sam Neill made an excellent documentary, *Cinema of Unease*. The title refers to the dark, brooding nature of many of New Zealand's films, which certainly was the case when I saw the train going for that car in the rain, sitting on the floor of our dusky classroom at Grey Main School.

Watching a movie that speaks your own accent, that wears the same clothes, that sits in the same hills – that's a joy. I love it when a film rolls off the screen straight back to the community that it comes from. I don't mean the actors – they are usually suffering everything from despair to relief, and it is personal. It's their mugs up there, when all is said and done. No. I mean the community that come to see the film because it makes them visible. People watch every beat of the story, wanting it to be great, and if it is, they take it into their hearts forever. I don't believe that the movies are all about 'bums on seats'. They are about memory. How long can a story be held in the mind's eye? It's unquantifiable, and funding bodies can't measure it.

Film is the art form closest to actual experience. That's why we need to make our own movies. To render ourselves visible, to gather the tribes, to camp in the dark, to be enthralled and disturbed and delighted and enlightened. Strangers. Together.

And it is why, even now, when I could watch any film I like on my phone, filmmakers like me still make their movies for the big gathering in the dark cinema. Words can't describe the terrifying thrill of standing in front of an expectant crowd to present a new film and finally experience it with them. It is a struggle and it always takes years, but it is always worth it.

*Home by Christmas* was almost exactly twenty-one years old when I sat in the Embassy Theatre on opening night. *War Stories Our Mothers Never Told Us* was a ten-year odyssey. But when it got to the screen, it mattered. Strangers approached me in the street to hug me, and cry. Really cry. I realised we had shared not only battles and army yarns, but lasting sorrow. The family secrets that had lurked unspoken for so many of us could now come out of the shadows. The dark became light. The audience was ready.

When a curtain is pulled back and the world shines and speaks to us, we are never the same again. To be the guardian bringing the waka to the shore is a terrific feeling. When the women from Ngāti Porou sang us out of the cinema on the opening night of Barry Barclay's *Ngāti*, the music from the soundtrack by Dalvanius Prime flowed straight off the screen and into the party.

A few years ago, I presented *My Year with Helen,* my feature documentary that follows former prime minister Helen Clark during 2016 as she makes a bid to become secretary-general of the United Nations. She knows what is needed and will forge through. But no way was the United Nations Secretariat going to be having that. I was able to shape a film that revealed Helen's sheer dogged resilience and the frustration of women's groups whose hopes were dashed as they were left frustrated, once more, in their campaign for the first female secretary-general. *My Year with Helen* premiered at the State Theatre during the Sydney Film Festival.

I stood there in this Australian temple to film, remembering the same moment after the first Australian screening of *Ruby and Rata*. When a full house spontaneously leaps to its feet, it is unforgettable.

I want to gulp it up, make it last. It is one of those moments when you know you are in the right place at the right time. As I stand there with Helen, I feel the strong presence of my parents. They stand with me. I think of my grandmothers and great-grandmothers – what hard lives they lived, and what a gift is mine. No matter how hard the struggle to make a film, their struggle was harder. I have the luxury of serving my imagination, not cleaning up other people's messes and emptying piss pots. I have dined with world leaders and broken bread with beggars. Helen Clark could say the same, probably. We have been part of a revolution that has only just begun.

But you never know how a film is going to play until you hand it over to its own constituency, and it was without Helen alongside me that, a few weeks later, the mighty Civic in Auckland was packed for the first screening of *My Year with Helen* on home turf. Two thousand people watched as I stood on the stage guarded by those golden plaster panthers, now restored to their resplendent former glory, blue eyes lit and glaring. The crowd included the young deputy leader of the Labour Party, Jacinda Ardern. I had met her a few times and put her on the comp list. She and I had a photo together in the foyer.

The crowd are expectant, excited even, but never adoring. They care much more than any other audience. This is our world. It matters to us in a way nothing else does. That's why the home crowd is the hardest crowd. They can eat you alive if they get offside.

*My Year with Helen* is enraging. Inspiring, too. It begs the women in the audience to call out the patriarchal system for what it is, to take up the challenge. In her final interview she is worn out and reflective, having hit her head hard on what she refers to now as a 'steel ceiling'. She says it will be up to the next generation of women to take up the fight.

'Don't get mad, get organised,' was something she said in Sydney at the Town Hall post-screening Q&A. That was to an adoring bunch of Australians, who dream of a leader such as her.

The appreciative home crowd left the cinema mad all right. If a woman like Helen Clark can't conquer, then how is anyone else going to succeed?

A week later, as the credits rolled after a screening of *My Year with Helen* to a packed Embassy Theatre in Wellington, a block of Labour MPs stood up as one and galloped out before the lights came up. I was standing by the screen, ready for my Q&A, and was a bit taken aback. Later, I realised they were hurrying to the meeting during which they voted Jacinda their new leader. Andrew Little, the incumbent, had asked her every day that week to step up and finally, at thirty-seven years old, she agreed. I will never know whether *My Year with Helen* was influential in that decision, but if there was one film that might have encouraged the parliamentary Labour caucus to be brave and back a talented young woman, *My Year with Helen* was the one.

*

I have often been asked if I have ever suffered discrimination as a woman filmmaker, and I have to think about it. Undoubtedly, the tone of reviews and interviews can appear in retrospect condescending. But this was also linked to the general disregard for and ignorance of New Zealand storytelling. All the filmmakers I grew up with were discriminated against. Our accents puzzled most North American festival selectors. The road to international recognition, along with our films, has been long and hard. When it comes to my peers, I consider myself one of the lucky ones. I have been able to stay home, make my films my way, and get them to the audience they have been made for. If I have been discriminated against, at least I have been able to get a few made.

The filmmakers I know who have been most discriminated against are my Māori contemporaries, and in particular my wahine toa friends. Not that many of them made their feature film at all. Some died trying. Tungia Baker, Tama Poata, Wi Kuki Kaa. To spend years developing a film, getting close to financing it and then to have it fall over again and again, is psychologically tough. When the rejections build up, it really wears you down.

The filmmakers who did get films made are an endangered species, in a way. Those art activists of the 80s, who forged an inclusive screen culture in Aotearoa, are heroes.

I used to think that everyone made films for the same reasons as me. Not so. Some people make films just for the sheer pleasure of telling an entertaining story, to take people out of their lives for a couple of hours. The film doesn't need to be about much. Some people make films because they adore the medium and want to experiment. The audience is not their focus. The glorious potential of aesthetics is their exploration. I am not uninterested in that, but I am driven by the cultural, communal power of the medium.

I make films to get the conversation going. To shine a light into something that's bothering me, to illuminate the kinds of lives you don't see in the movies much. The invisible ones. I try to make my films gentle and strong, leavened with humour and a wry eye.

My kaupapa is to show how social inequity shapes ordinary people's lives. To change the world for the better as I see it.

And as my world is the one I live in, it is the audience here in Aotearoa I address first and foremost.

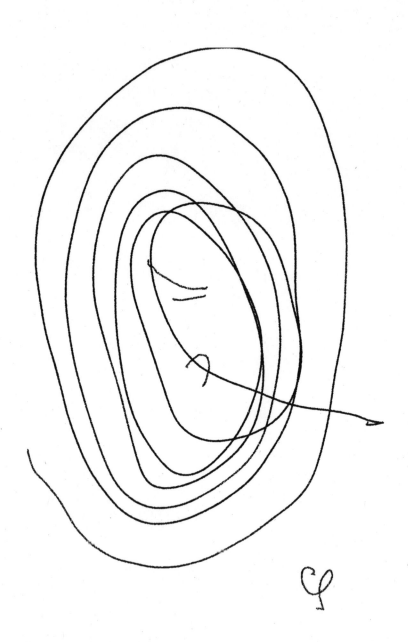

# *Epilogue*

# The Big Boof

Every now and then, I get a strong feeling that I am more than I think I am – that I could do more than I am doing; that there is a disconnect between the power of my own thinking and what I actually do about it.

It's just a flash. As I try to grasp it, it's gone. There are so many lives we could live, so many choices we could make, that we float in a sea of possibilities. Too many. Too many ideas jostling with one another and blurring in and out of focus.

As I perch here typing this, I am in my bed, trying to keep my spine and skull aligned. My cranial osteopath has told me that the correct computer position for me is to stand at a desktop, because I have suffered a head injury and the connection between my skull and the very top of my spine has received a 'complex force'. I refer to it as the big boof.

He came out of the blue, literally. I hear a screech of brakes behind me on the basketball court, followed by a big boof. I fly through the air and land on my head. I'm on the ground. I open my eyes. The sky is blue and people stand way above, looking concerned, but the world is spinning. I'm trapped in the middle of a zip pan. I close my eyes again. A brave young woman driving the ambulance alone instructs everybody, and I am lifted into the belly of the beast. Five days in hospital in a dimmed room.

At home, I am watched over by Kate Jason Smith, who has had two head injuries over her lifetime, and understands. I have cranial osteopathy to relieve the concussion I have suffered. I also chipped my hip and am only just out of the Zimmer frame.

Do I follow my osteopath's advice to stand at a desktop? No, even though I paid for that advice. Why don't I follow it? I *like* writing in bed using my little laptop. My island. I stay in my PJs and don't open the door. I stare out the window from the best room in the house. I try not to hunch. The sun arrives.

My osteo is not the only one to be offering treatment and advice since the accident. Courtesy of ACC, I have a small army of professionals and carers who arrive offering assistance. They are all underpaid and trying to make ends meet. For example, in the beginning, once I came home from hospital, I had the Kerrys. As I gingerly approached my daily bath, Kerry Anne would arrive to watch over me.

She would ride in for miles on her motorbike after dropping off all her kids – 'his and hers' – to kindergarten, school and college in the car. Why doesn't she carry on to me in the car?

'Oh, the bike drives out the cobwebs,' she'd tell me.

She arrives, peels off her leathers and prepares my bath. She is the most comfortable person to be naked in front of. Her strong hands get me under the armpits and gently lower me into the water. Kerry Anne's first marriage was disastrous and she's very happy to be out of that situation with a new partner. They have twin boys who at three years old have their own mini motorbikes and they all go to petrolhead gatherings in unlikely spots on the weekends.

Helping me out of the house to drive me to doctor's appointments are more Kerrys. They are all in their fifties and are recovering from something. They arrive wearing blue T-shirts with DMD ('Driving Miss Daisy') stretched over their ample bosoms and help me walk out to the car and drive me very carefully and early to my destination. One Kerry has a voice like gravel and escaped an abusive new owner of the firm she ran for years. She got sold along with the business.

Does she like driving for Miss Daisy?

'Do I what! It won't pay off the mortgage, but I'm happy. It's very rewarding helping people. In my proper job, I got sick of cleaning up after all the lazy office boys who got promoted over me. Every single one. I like helping people. I'm going to China to a wedding of one of the kids I met driving these cars. I'm living the dream.'

Another Keri (spelt with an i) points to the drooping daisy shoved into the air conditioning vent.

'That's from Johnny. He brings me one every day in summer. I take him to his workshop. They call these people impaired . . .' She shakes her head, incredulous.

Keri talks about not needing to have children because she is a great aunty. She tried to get pregnant for years, lost her partner over it, and suffered from bad anxiety attacks at the advertising agency she production-managed. She's another happy corporate refugee behind the wheel of a little blue 'Driving Miss Daisy' car.

My daughter and her friends have suggested we call it 'Driving Dame Gazie', as the big boof wasn't the only sudden shock I received. Around the same time, I was offered a royal honour from the Queen. It arrived in the letterbox with a crown on the envelope. It was like the Queen had teleported herself into the kitchen and crowned me.

I figured it was recognition of the independent filmmakers of Aotearoa. I accepted it on behalf of that community.

That was the little boof. I'm still recovering from both.

Early on, I was dizzy most of the time. Sophie arrived courtesy of the concussion clinic. I had stopped throwing up, which I tended to do upon just glimpsing a physio when I was in hospital. Now this one fixes me with a serious look, lies me down and does the Epley manoeuvre. This scary move is designed to dislodge tiny crystals in the inner ear that got stuck there by the big boof. Terrifying. Not the boof, because I didn't see it coming, but the look this very young woman gives me as she takes my poor constricted head into her hands. Does she know what she's doing? She is a child. But I surrender to her expertise. I feel like my head could actually separate from my shoulders. One deft firm downward push and twist, and the dizziness subsides.

'Praise the goddess,' I say.

Sophie is here on her OE. She shows me impossible swivels to do with my eyes to help the vertigo. I have never really thought about vertigo other than the Alfred Hitchcock film. She hasn't seen it. I take over her film education and send her to go and see *Vai*. *Vai* is nine short films shot in the Pacific by Pasifika women, and it will be showing at the tiny cinema down the road for roughly two weeks. Sophie loves *Vai* so much she books herself a trip to Tonga for a break.

I wish I could get a break. I wish I could take my head off for half an hour, unscrew it and put it on a shelf to rest.

Then there is Claire, who offers me advice on how to get back to work. This last exercise involves breaking down the tasks I need to be able to do in order to accomplish a full working day. Claire is Irish. She was in the same class at school as Sally Rooney, whose second novel I am reading. *Normal People* is top of the *New York Times* bestseller list. It is brilliant in a sly understated way.

'What was she like?' I ask her. Claire pauses for a moment.

'Oh I didn't really know her. She read in the library a lot.'

With every task we list, Claire's professional demeanour slips.

'I need to be able to go to noisy spaces to meet people,' I tell her.

'Like where?'

'Like to the cocktail party coming up at the British High Commission.'

'That's part of your work?'

'Yes. I need to meet people there – to network for my next project.'

'What is that?'

'I can't say. It's confidential.'

She looks thoughtful.

'When is it?'

'Impossible to say. I have to raise the money – could take one year, could take two.'

'No, the cocktail party at the British High Commission.'

'A couple of weeks.'

'Well, we'll make that a goal in your back-to-work plan.' She writes it on the list. 'What else?'

'I want to travel to a marae for a weekend immersion language class.'

'Is that work or a hobby, Gaylene?'

'It's work. I haven't got any hobbies.'

'No hobbies?'

'No. My hobbies usually become films one way or another – or my films are hobbies until I manage to raise finance for them. I can't separate the two.'

The noho marae goes on the list.

'What were you going to be doing before your accident?'

'I was about to write the last chapter of my book before I got boofed.'

She laughs. 'I like that you call it "the boof".'

'The big boof. I was about to finish the book, I had a clever idea of how to complete it, but I never wrote it down, and now I can't remember what it was.'

'What do you need to accomplish to finish that writing?'

'I need to write.'

'You can write now for how long?'

'Maybe an hour or so.'

'So you can write now already.'

'True. But I can "engineering write" – applications, script editing, that kind of writing.'

'I'll put creative writing on the list. How many hours a week do you need to do?'

'Untold.'

'Well, you have to break it up. Do fifteen minutes, then break.'

'That won't work for me. With personal writing, you never know how long you need to write before you hit that spot where you don't seem to own the ideas, they just flow through you and onto the page. You are the portal, and your imagination is unleashed. You just let the words flow through you, and you are as amazed as anyone to read them as they arrive. That's what writers write for – the pleasure of that moment. Good writers have it every day, I imagine. For me, I often have to write for quite a while before that river flows.'

'How long?'

'Varies.'

She's wanting to write something down for her form.

'I'll put "four hours of creative writing" as a goal. Is that once a week or every day?'

'Every day until I have finished that goddamn book.'

'Along with the engineering writing and the emails and the lunches in restaurants and the cocktail party?'

'Yes.'

'I want your job, Gaylene,' she tells me as she puts down her pencil.

'Work implies wages,' I tell her.

# Tui's Sausage Roll Recipe

1   Go down to the dairy and get frozen puff pastry, taking care to have a yarn with the shopkeeper about more than just the weather.

2   Thaw the puff pastry.

3   Preheat the oven to 180°C / 350°F.

4   To one cup of sausage meat from your favourite sausages, add one third of a cup of finely diced onion and one third of a cup of finely diced potato.

5   Add one egg and mix in a bowl with a fork.

6   The mixture should be the consistency of thick porridge. If it is too firm, add a little milk.

7   Add pepper and salt and a dab of Worcester sauce to taste. Mix together with a fork.

8   Lightly roll the puff pastry on a floured surface. Spoon the sausage roll mixture in a long mound from one end of the pastry to the other. Cut the pastry, leaving plenty of room on one side to roll over.

9   Fold the pastry over, wrapping the filling inside.

10   With clean fingers, seal the two sides of the pastry together using a mix of equal parts milk and water.

11   Make fork holes along the roll and cut into sausage-roll-sized slices.

12   Lay on a floured tray and cook for 25 minutes in a hot oven or until puffed, golden, and cooked through.

13   While leaving to cool slightly, get the neighbours over for a cuppa.

14   Best served hot with Wattie's tomato sauce, and gumboot black Indian tea in thick cups.

# Acknowledgements

In over fifty years of filmmaking, I've accumulated so many people to thank they would fill another book. To everyone who has worked with me over those years, my gratitude is boundless. Filmmaking is a creative business and I have been blessed to work with some of the most talented people of my generation here in Aotearoa. Special thanks must go to Robin Laing, who did the first twenty years' hard slog shoulder to shoulder.

I love filmmaking, so writing a book is an entirely new experience. It began in Cambridge at Jesus College Intellectual Forum. Had Dr Julian Huppert not invited me to the college 'in order to think and reflect', I would surely never have thought of doing such a thing. Fortunately my compatriot, Vanessa Alexander, was living round the road, full of energy and good advice. Like the little red hen, I am inclined to move forward and leave the droppings for others to find. Therefore it has been a most salutary experience. I am blessed to have an assiduous publisher in Fergus Barrowman, of Te Herenga Waka University Press, who from very early days sailed alongside. He gifted me Ashleigh Young to edit this lengthy tome. Ashleigh is a writer whose work I greatly admire, and every moment spent with her has been a masterclass in gentle firm creative stewardship.

There are so many people I love who are not mentioned in these pages. I hold you close. The film industry is a bruising world and the big lesson in life, as in art, is to find ways to stay positive and keep moving forward – the little red hen again. That has been made much easier by my supportive whānau of friends, neighbours and family who give me strength every day in every way. Without a supportive community, every artist is going to have a difficult path.

My brother and sister have over many years coped with my sudden excursions into making corners of their lives public. To them I can only say, your generosity is overwhelming. Working with my sister and my daughter to make big bold beautiful work has been a lifetime's pleasure.

All this work needs funding, for which I must thank champions within institutions, who have put their jobs on the line to travel to the outer reaches of their responsibilities to push my projects over the line. Ruth Harley, Mladen Ivanovic, Jane Wrightson, Dave Gibson – thanks. You know what you did.

Writing a book, unlike making a film, needs only a pen and paper and a room of one's own. I have been lucky to have had all three, with the added bonus of support from Mike McCombie of Balanced Investments, who asked me that essential question: 'What do you need?' His ongoing sponsorship has allowed me to pay calm attention to my writing as well as to a legacy project in partnership with Ngā Taonga Sound & Vision, which has gathered my work for preservation and easy reference. To my trusty cleaner, Margaret Dawod, thank you for your prayers. Your life and humility are inspiring.

When I broke my arm, Danny Bultitude walked in to help me with a few emails. That was a lucky day indeed. He has taken the reins to archive the collection, with tutoring from Ngā Taonga, as well as provide first corrections and suggestions for this book.

To Helen McDonald in Melbourne, thanks for the title.

To the daring Dames Fiona and Jane, who read this book at short notice and provided glowing comments for the cover, thank you for your sisterhood.

To my real sister, Jan – your love and understanding are central to how I travel in the world.

I am grateful to the country I live in. It has given this accidental filmmaker a fine and free education, and free healthcare that has saved my life on more than one occasion. In godzone we are an argumentative lot. Trolling is an American habit that I hope we get over shortly. Keep up the kōrero, Aotearoa.

To my parents, Tui and Ed Preston, thank you for giving me the time I live in. Your smarts and your astonishing goodwill in loving a daughter who was often challenging speaks of great humility and tolerance.

And most importantly, to those bright lights in my life – my darling brave talented Chelsie and her whānau, I love you truly, madly, deeply. And I know that is returned double strength. Thanks for the joy germ who sprinkles shines wherever she goes – Olive. This book is for you.

Power to your elbow and breath to your heart.